# THE DYNAMIC DANCE

October 2004

To Christy,
With my thanks for skilled
work on the gorilla project,
and for continuing superb
discussions about primate
behavior.
Yours,
Barbara
P.S. You're in the index
as well as the acknowledgments!

# The Dynamic Dance

## NONVOCAL COMMUNICATION
## IN AFRICAN GREAT APES

Barbara J. King

HARVARD UNIVERSITY PRESS

Cambridge, Massachusetts, and London, England · 2004

Library of Congress Cataloging-in-Publication Data

King, Barbara J., 1956–
    The dynamic dance : nonvocal communication in African great apes /
Barbara J. King.
        p.   cm.
    Includes bibliographical references (p. ).
    ISBN 0-674-01515-0 (hardcover)
    1. Apes—Behavior—Africa.   2. Animal communication—Africa.   I. Title.

QL737.P96K56   2004
599.88′159′096–dc22                                                                 2004047478

Readers should check the HUP website for web-based features related to this book

For my daughter, Sarah Elizabeth Hogg

# Contents

# Illustrations

Asking different questions will create a different animal.

—*George Schaller, foreword to Shirley Strum's Almost Human, 1987*

I liked being there, and I liked sitting down at the long wooden table next to Alma and feeling her touch my arm in the same spot where Hector had touched me only a moment before. Two different gestures, two different memories—one on top of the other. My skin had become a palimpsest of fleeting sensations, and each layer bore the imprint of who I was.

—*Paul Auster, The Book of Illusions, 2002*

# 1

## Social Communication as Dance

Imagine a first-rate dance performance unfolding before your eyes. You sit in a darkened theater, watching pairs of dancers execute intricate movements on the stage, accompanied by lively music. Perfect coordination marks the movements within each pair; every turn, dip, and lift reflects full attentiveness by one partner to where the other is in space, what movements the other has just made and might be about to make, and so on.

This coordination appears to be automatic and effortless, seemingly reflective of a flawless synchrony achieved only after countless hours of practice. Yet dancers say that the coordination results not from mere practiced matching of movements from dancer to dancer. Rather, each partner must participate, moment by moment, in creating the coordination.

Writing about ballroom dancing, the instructor Jennifer Mizenko captures this quality of attentive participation:

Sight is used by the follower to look for subtle differences or changes in the leader's dance. These differences may include a tilt of the head, a change of the level of hand hold, a general weight shift as reflected by the torso of the body, or even a change of expression in the face of the leader. However, a good follower is not zeroing on [sic] one particular visual signal, but is seeing with a broad vision and trying to "take it all in," as it were; seeing the leader and these changes as a whole. . . .

Touch is extremely important in the lead/follow relationship
. . . The actual physical contact between the dancers gives off so
much information that it is possible for the follower to dance
with eyes closed. . . .

All of these elements of good partnering combine to create a
Gestalt effect, the whole is greater than the sum of the parts.[1]

The unfolding dance can be described by using a term coined by
the psychologist Alan Fogel.[2] It is co-regulated, the result of *unpredictable* and *contingent* mutual adjustments between the partners. So
many variables interact as the dance unfolds that the result will never
be precisely the same twice, even when the dancers follow a well-re-
hearsed choreography.

Contingency and unpredictability characterize other types of human interactions as well. Certain musicians are known for their tendency toward unpredictability on stage; they rarely play a song twice
in exactly the same way. The drummer Max Weinberg describes the
rock musician and songwriter Bruce Springsteen in these terms. On
any given performance night, Springsteen might spontaneously vary
the structure, pacing, or length of certain songs, so that Weinberg
is required to play differently on successive nights, without prior
warning.

Weinberg, together with Springsteen's other supporting musicians, must be able to "read" Springsteen as he makes these spontaneous decisions, and he must in turn be able to "read" them and
their readiness to proceed with a shift in plan. The band collectively
orchestrates a well-coordinated performance. Note the terms used
by Springsteen when he describes his working relationship with
Weinberg, citing the drummer's "long-time knowledge" of how he,
Springsteen, works on stage: "It's sign language, it's the way I look
at him, it's the slightest flick of the hand, it's the slightest move of
the elbow, and he's all *over* me, you know."[3] In acknowledging how
well Weinberg deciphers his slight movements and expressions,

Springsteen is describing a co-regulated dance between the two musicians.

Springsteen seems remarkably aware of the notion that a musical performance, like a dance performance, is more than the sum of its parts. He even extends the idea of collective coordination to include his audience, noting that the word "concert" doesn't mean that the band performs for you, the audience member. Instead, "it means that you are in concert with the band that evening, you know, and you have a part and a position to play, you know, and if we're going to take this thing as high as we can get it, which is my serious intent when I come out at night, you know, not to be deterred from, then I need to be in concert with you. And I need to kind of get you on my wavelength, it means a lot to me."[4] Here Springsteen broadens the idea of coordinated action to include a matching of moods; he cannot achieve the high-intensity, transformative type of concert he desires without the audience members' active participation reflected back to him by their voices and movements.

It's all well and good to note that artists are attuned to the nuanced movements, gestures, and moods of their performance partners and audiences. But is routine human social communication marked by unpredictability and contingency? Do we humans really engage in such attentive, co-regulated communication around the dinner table and at play? And how do these issues concerning our own species relate to social communication in the African great apes, the subject of this book? Answering these questions is my goal in this chapter. I will soon bring African great apes into the picture, but let's continue first with humans.

## Interacting with Babies

Over the last three decades or so, psychologists have spent much time and effort observing human infants together with their mothers, fathers, and other caretakers, aiming to chart the ontogeny of

fundamental skills, including language. Most such research has occurred within the so-called *interactionist* program, in which processes
of social reciprocity between baby and caregiver are seen to play a
central role in the emergence of infants' skills. Interactionist research has provided a major alternative to earlier work that tended to
see child development as proceeding outside any genuinely social
context.[5] Piaget, for instance, portrayed children as developing in interaction with physical objects, thus virtually stripping them of a social world.[6]

The interactionists, following the lead of Vygotsky,[7] restore this social world to human babies, emphasizing back-and-forth reciprocity
between child and adults in their early communication. They point
out that babies, well before they can speak, participate with their social partners in sophisticated communicational sequences. Much of
this work has been detailed and insightful. Yet it stops short of investigating fully what goes on between social partners beyond reciprocity and finely tuned turn-taking. A newer approach, fueled by dy-
namic-systems theory (DST), reveals what can be learned by viewing
the baby and caregiver not as two separate individuals who exchange
words and gestures, but as a single unit creating meaning together—
a unit that sums to more than its parts. A well-known saying often
deployed by infancy researchers reflects this understanding: "There
is no such thing as a baby; there is a baby and someone."[8] In studying this "baby and someone" as one inextricable being, DST sets itself apart from interactionism's tendency to see individuals as wholly
separate beings who are sometimes able to synchronize with each
other.[9] People are seen as inherently relational, meaning that they
are "inherently incomplete and indeterminate."[10] Through this emphasis on relating, and on co-regulating, DST embraces the very creativity and transformation that are underdeveloped in interactionism's focus on matching and harmonizing.

In examining detailed moment-by-moment accounts, it is possible
to identify co-regulated social communication between caregivers

and even the youngest babies. Here is an exchange between a mother and her 2-month-old infant:

M: What are you doing?:
I: /a/ followed by sequence of articulatory movements without
   phonation
M: Yeah?
Yeah, that's great what you are telling me!
   (. . .and apparently. . . .)
I: (interrupts): /a/
M: Oh yes?
I: /a a a/
M: Is that true?
Ah, this is what you mean!
   Yeah, and what else?
I: (vocalizes simultaneously with previous maternal utterances)
/a/
/a/
/a/
M: Is that really true?
I: /a/
M: That's what you have experienced?
I: /a/
M: That's great![11]

In analyzing this bout, the interactionist would note that the baby participates in a lively conversation, and is treated by his mother as a fully active partner. Turn-taking in this conversation is not perfect, because the baby does sometimes vocalize along with the mother, but it characterizes the majority of the exchange. DST theorists would prefer to say that the baby and the mother shape their utterances and movements according to moment-by-moment shifts between them. Because the trajectory of the conversation is not fixed or predictable at the outset, the conversation is not so much an exchange of information as an act of creating meaning.

Of course, my last statement begs for a definition: To what does "creating meaning," or meaning-making, refer? Entire literatures and whole college courses take up this question, with input from anthropologists, philosophers, linguists, cognitive scientists, and others who approach it from wildly different theoretical perspectives. Wishing not to become caught up in this maelstrom of competing definitions, I emphasize here one key point, and amplify it in Chapter 2. Meaning is constructed through action between social partners rather than through transmission of ideas from one mind to another. Thus my understanding of "meaning" comes close to that of G. H. Mead when he writes, "The act or adjustive response of the second organism gives to the gesture of the first organism the meaning which it has,"[12] though I would emphasize mutual rather than unilateral adjustment. Griffin captures the central idea when he writes: "Persons-in-conversation co-construct their own social realities by achieving coherence, coordinating actions, and experiencing mystery."[13] Social partners—whether persons-in-conversation or African-apes-in-interaction—converge on ways to treat a certain movement or vocalization as a request for sharing, or an act of reassurance after a frightening event, or an invitation to reconcile. Results of this process of convergence, or negotiation-through-action, are often creative, but also imperfect; false steps and failures occur routinely, as we will see.

Returning now to the transcribed conversation, we may note a point critical to the subject of this book. Until quite recently, the emphasis in adult-child communicational research tended to be put on the *verbal* aspects of joint participation. Notice the degree to which the transcription reflects the pair's vocal contributions. Good reasons exist for focus on the details of this pair's speech patterns. Thirty years ago, Fernald[14] showed that mothers, when conversing with their babies, engage in a specialized type of speech then called motherese. Because caregivers other than the mother use this speech too, a more inclusive term is "infant-directed speech." Cross-culturally, adults utter speech to infants at a slower rate, with a raised pitch, and with greater variation in prosody and intonation than they do to noninfants. Because at some point in our lives, most of us have probably uttered infant-directed speech and observed the response, it should come as no surprise to learn that babies are very attentive and responsive when they hear it.

In the transcription, no mention is made of the participants' body movements or gestures. Yet I suspect that mother and baby were in motion during all or part of their conversation. Perhaps they leaned in toward each other, or moved their limbs and made facial expressions.[15] Though not every event presented within each study can be analyzed holistically, much is lost when body movement and gestures are not transcribed.

Some exceptions to this verbal focus did occur in relatively early interactionist research. In an article published in *Science* around the time that analysis of infant-directed speech was making its initial splash in the developmental literature, Condon and Sanders[16] reported that babies synchronize their movements with the rhythms of adult speech. Their method was microanalytic and the results were striking. A 2-day-old infant, upon hearing an adult utter the "K" sound in "come," moved its head, extended its left elbow, rotated its right shoulder and the right hip, extended the other hip, and abducted the big toe of one foot. These movements by the baby showed consistent direction and speed during the 0.07-second interval it took for the adult to utter the sound. More significantly, this type of fine-grained synchrony continued across an 89-word sequence uttered by the adult.

The gap between research in infant vocalizing versus infant body movement is now closing, with interest in nonvocal gesture spanning interactionist and dynamic systems research. Trevarthen recently analyzed a videotaped event in which a Swedish mother sang two narrative songs to her 5-month-old daughter. As the mother sang, the baby, who had been born totally blind, lay on her back, in the process of being bottle-fed. Among Trevarthen's comments are:

> The [infant's] left hand is more active, and at several points in both songs, she makes with it intricate and delicate gestures that match variations of both the pulse and the melodic line with appropriate forms of arm waving and extensions and turns of the fingers . . . she "conducted" her mother's singing with an astonishing subtlety and precision . . . She accentuates the flow of feeling in the "story," pointing up high notes, spreading to the side to follow the surges of energy, closing her fingers and/ or dropping her hand eloquently at the close of a phrase.[17]

Trevarthen notes that the infant attended to her mother's rhythm and melody, a finding that at least in hindsight seems predictable enough, given our knowledge of infant-directed speech. Perhaps babies are primed by infant-directed speech to attend and respond to both rhythm and melody. The degree of this Swedish baby's "subtlety and precision" of movement is remarkable, especially given that she had never seen her own, or anyone's, hands in motion in time to music. By "remarkable," however, I do not mean to imply that her ability is likely to be unique or explicable by her blindness. In describing other films representing human behavior in different cultures, Trevarthen mentions "frequent cases where subtle gestures are made in spontaneous synchrony with rhythmic elements of the vocal or instrumental sounds the babies are hearing."[18]

As Trevarthen's observations imply, although infants' movements become, over time, more directed, more precise, and more in tune with those made by social partners, infants participate jointly with social partners from a very early age in the realm of body movement and gesture as well as speech. Other research has shown that strictly defined referential pointing, such as indicating a desired object with an extended index finger, occurs only at age 9 months or after. Babies of 4 months, however, briefly extend their index fingers in arousing social situations, as when the mother indicates excitement by her speech pattern.[19] Co-regulation can be glimpsed just beneath the surface of examples like these and of interactionist accounts like Trevarthen's.

Fogel[20] describes an event in which a mother and her 3-month-old daughter together achieve a shift in the baby's position. At the start, the mother holds the infant in a semi-upright position, so that the two are face to face. Next, the mother tips the baby to one side and, while supporting her head, leans her back so that she is half supine. During this shift, the baby opens her mouth wide and smiles while looking at her mother, and the result is "a smooth shift in infant posture toward a more supine position in which both mother and infant are moving together." Anyone who doubts a significant role for the infant in this maneuver might borrow an uncooperative infant and try it out, or might consider Fogel's report of a second attempt by this same mother to shift her daughter's position. This time, the mother attempts to turn her daughter's head in order to get the infant's attention. At first this seems to work, because the baby does gaze at the mother. Just as the mother relaxes her grip on the baby's neck, however, the baby looks down, then puts her hand to her mouth and turns away again. As Fogel notes, "Getting the infant's attention seems to work best if the mother's attempt to turn the infant's head or move her body is timed to when the infant is already turning toward her and relatively relaxed."[21]

Contrasting the first, successful shift with this second, unsuccessful shift nicely illustrates the point that co-regulated social communication occurs well before coordinated reaching and referential pointing are achieved by the infant. Older infants, interacting with their caregivers, make use of an expanded repertoire of body movements and gestures. Mothers may use what has been called, in order to draw a parallel with infant-directed speech, gestural motherese. In a

study by Iverson and colleagues, Italian mothers were observed gesturing to toddlers of 16 and 20 months of age. Maternal gestures
were "characterized by fewer and more concrete gestures redundant
with and reinforcing the message conveyed in speech . . . [Mothers'
gestures] appear to be used with the goal of underscoring, highlighting, and attracting attention to particular words and/or objects. Gestures that cannot be used for this purpose such as the emphatic gestures widely used by Italian adults when speaking to other adults are
virtually eliminated from the communicative repertoire when mothers speak to their children."[22]

Noteworthy in Iverson and colleagues' study is the finding that
maternal gestures were used to attract infants' attention—a likely un-
derpinning for enhanced co-regulation. The researchers focused on
maternal gestures rather than joint gestural conversations, but a few
other analyses point up clearly the joint nature of the social communication at this age. Following her research in an Australian daycare
setting, Nyland reports what transpired when a child of 15 months
requested a drink from his caregiver:

Child: (Gets a grip on his cup with one hand. Puts the cup in his
    mouth, tilts his head back and drains the cup). Eh (Sounds
    pleased. Puts his empty cup down on the table. Realises his cup is
    empty and looks at the caregiver. He pats his cup with a worried
    look on his face).
Caregiver: (Turning to the child). Where's your drink?
Child: (Turns and points at another child's cup of milk).
Caregiver: (Picks up the child's empty cup without realizing it
    is his).
Child: (Turns and sees the caregiver with his empty cup). Oo gaggi
    (holds out his hand towards the cup. Keeps reaching for his cup
    as it is taken away. Looks around for another. Looks on the
    ground.) Oo ga. (Watches the caregiver walk away with the cup.
    Turns and thumps his hands on the table in front of him. Opens
    his mouth as if to vocalize and coughs twice.) Dae dae (points at

the raisin toast in the middle of the table, there are clean face flannels just behind the toast).

Caregiver: You want some more toast or you want to wash your hands? (Takes tongs to give the child more toast, sees he has a full slice so hands him a clean flannel).

Child: (Has been waiting and now he points to the middle of the table again) Oh baba, dar dar (in a loud voice)

Caretaker: (Removes child's bib) Oh T (wiping child's face).

Child: (Puts his tongue against the flannel while his face is washed).

Caretaker: There you go (picks up the child, off the chair, and sets him on the ground facing the playground).[23]

In this event, the child participates in a conversation via a mix of not-yet-mature speech and gestures that include points, reaches, pats, thumps, and gaze shifts. Interestingly, despite this barrage of vocal and gestural production, the child fails to effect change—he fails to get more milk from the caregiver. This event illustrates a key point, one at which the second infant-repositioning event of Fogel's hints also. It would be folly to use the fact that children and their caregivers are in tune vocally and gesturally to suggest that their interactions always result in perfect coordination. No one who has cared for a tired, hungry child in "tantrum mode" would make or accept such a statement. The study of miscommunication (and repair of miscommunication, often) is a significant facet of DST research. As Fivaz-Depeursinge and Corboz-Warnery note,[24] the terms "miscommunication" and "repair" carry no negative connotations, for in fact they refer to frequent events in human social communication. They are simply part of the dance.

## A First Look at Co-Regulation in Gorillas and Chimpanzees

That social partners may create meaning together through an unpredictable and contingent dance is an insight vital to understanding not only the social communication of our own species, but also that of the African great apes, our closest living relatives. The variability and creativity inherent in much of the social communication of the gorillas, chimpanzees, and bonobos have been underestimated, I believe, by the typical practice of setting out to study the signals that a sender transmits to a receiver. As the foregoing discussion has already made clear, the emphasis on transmitting of signals misses a chance to see how truly relational the African great apes are when engaged in co-regulated social communication. Pursuing questions or testing hypotheses about such co-regulation may bring new insights into the social communication and, indeed, the overall social lives of the African great apes.

When I am observing the western gorillas *(Gorilla gorilla gorilla)* housed at the National Zoological Park in Washington, D.C., the notion of the dynamic dance that resides at the heart of co-regulation often enters my mind. Examining an interaction that's typical for this group, rather than one that is exceptionally complex or gesture-rich, is the best way to convey what I mean.

Six gorillas constitute my study group: silverback Kuja; adult female Mandara; subadult male Baraka, who was adopted as an infant and raised by Mandara; and three of Mandara's male offspring. These offspring are the juvenile Ktembe, sired by a male now living in Florida, and the infants Kwame and Kojo, both sired by Kuja.[25] On the morning in question, August 10, 2002, Mandara rested on an indoor shelf with Kojo. Subadult Baraka sat nearby in an artificial tree:

Baraka moves from the tree to the shelf, and as he nears the shelf, begins chestbeating.

As he approaches his adoptive mother, Mandara opens her mouth.

Baraka hits out with his arm at Mandara, and turns to flee as Mandara gets up to run after him.

Mandara barks with her mouth open and chases Baraka a short way over the limbs of the tree.

Mandara carries her youngest infant, Kojo, in an awkward grasp using one arm, and his body flails as his mother runs.

Mandara stops on the tree. As Kojo settles into a secure ventral cling against his mother's belly, an action achieved by his own movements together with Mandara's repositioning of him, Mandara pats him with her hand four or five times.

Mandara now follows behind Baraka as Baraka descends to the ground. Kwame, the middle of Mandara's three young offspring, observes and begins to follow the pair.

Mandara and Baraka are briefly out of sight as they walk behind the tree; when they emerge, Mandara is co-walking with Baraka, embracing his hindquarters as they go.

Kwame runs toward the pair.

As Baraka turns to face Mandara, Kwame touches Baraka, who lifts one leg partly up onto Mandara's body and puts an arm up onto her back. Mandara backs tightly against Baraka's body.

Throughout this sequence, Kwame contacts both Baraka and Mandara, and infant Kojo still clings ventrally to his mother.

Next, Baraka backs up, and Mandara turns to face him and hold his arm. Baraka turns again, sweeping one arm across Mandara, and walks forward, with Mandara briefly holding him under the waist.

Baraka and Mandara break apart but walk a short way in parallel. Mandara stops at, then steps over Kwame, who rolled into her path; when she continues forward, Baraka moves forward ahead of her.

Mandara and Baraka proceed to where Kuja, the silverback, is reclining, and stop. My view is partly obscured by the artificial tree.

As Kuja first stands, Baraka walks forward, away from Kuja, and eats an item from the ground.

As Kuja walks forward, Baraka turns his head to watch him.

Mandara, with infant Kojo sitting astride her back now, moves forward as Baraka retreats somewhat.

Mandara comes to stand stiffly between the two males, Kuja and Baraka. Kwame approaches his mother and holds her hindquarters briefly, then moves off, bumping her arm. He keeps Kuja in sight by moving backward at the start of his retreat.

Kuja moves quite near Mandara and infant Kojo, and as he does, Mandara leans slightly away from Kuja with her body but does not otherwise alter her position.

Kuja sits near Mandara in a relaxed manner.

As Baraka runs in a mild display across part of the cage (I cannot see this clearly), Mandara flinches and shifts the front part of her body backward, but, again, does not alter her overall body position.

Mandara turns, and departs for the shelf, via the tree.

This event involves five of the six gorillas living in this group; only juvenile Ktembe does not participate. It starts when Baraka hits Mandara without visible provocation. She reacts aggressively, then appears to seek a reconciliation with her adopted son.[26] As these two move close to the silverback, Kuja shifts his position and moves closer to them. Mandara intervenes by placing herself directly between Kuja and Baraka. The event ends when Kuja sits down and ignores Baraka's mild display, and Mandara departs. Infant Kojo is in constant contact with his mother and thus present throughout this event; Kwame runs in and out, often involving himself directly in the action.

Evaluation of this social event as co-regulated social communication must take into account two factors. First, communicative body movements and gestures mark this event among the gorillas. Gestures are particularly evident at the interaction's beginning; these include Baraka's chestbeating, Mandara's open-mouth threat at

Baraka, and Mandara's reassuring patting of Kojo, her youngest infant. Critical, too, are body movements, as when Mandara leans away from first Kuja and then Baraka, but otherwise stands her ground.

Second, the various behaviors that constitute this social event do not occur without some overlap. Often, as one gorilla is moving or gesturing, another begins to shift, move, or gesture. Unsurprisingly, given Kuja's large size and dominant status, his movements are often closely monitored by the other gorillas, who indicate, by their gaze and posture, heightened awareness of his whereabouts. Mandara, Baraka, and Kwame all do this clearly, and Kojo shifts his position vis-à-vis Kuja by virtue of Mandara's shifting her own. Simultaneity of movement renders this interaction, and others like it, somewhat difficult to transcribe using narrative language, which is by its nature sequential. Use of "as," for example "As Kuja first stands, Baraka walks forward," indicates this aspect of co-regulation.

An alternative transcription method involves quantitative microanalysis of these gorillas' movements in a way akin to what Condon and Sanders did to show the synchrony of babies' body movements with adult speech, but with emphasis on overlapping movements rather than strict sequentiality. This method may be quite useful for certain research questions, but in order to underscore my interest in the social creation of meaning rather than mere synchrony of action, I will use the narrative form throughout the book.

Precisely *why* this social event qualifies as co-regulated still needs some explanation, and a larger context for analysis. If, for example, behaviors in this event occur routinely whenever Mandara and Baraka interact, any claim for unpredictability and contingency in *this* event would be weakened. After all, if Mandara had typically responded for years to an annoyance by Baraka with a barking open-mouth run, followed by an attempt at reconciliation, then Baraka could have come to learn by mere association how Mandara would probably act. He could then ready himself to respond in a certain way even before her actions fully unfolded.

The data show no such predictability, however, as can be illustrated by another interaction on a previous morning that same summer. On June 1, 2002, Mandara rests on the same shelf with her two
youngest offspring, Kwame and Kojo:

> Suddenly Kwame, the older of the two offspring, departs.
> Two seconds later, Baraka rushes onto the shelf and flails at
> Mandara, who opens her mouth and moves backward as he
> comes toward her.
> Baraka stands on the shelf, then moves away to sit nearby on
> the tree.
> Thirteen seconds later, Baraka stands, chestbeats, hits the
> wall with one extended leg, and lunges at and hits Mandara.
> Unlike her response in the August interaction, Mandara's re-
> sponse this time is mild. As Baraka starts his lunge, she rises
> up briefly and opens her mouth, and as he gets closer to hitting
> her she leans backward.
> Mandara does nothing further, except to depart calmly with
> Kojo on her ventrum; she passes by Baraka, on the tree, without
> a glance or motion.

Comparing the two social events to each other (and, indeed, to
other observed instances over three years involving these same two
gorillas) indicates that Baraka's and Mandara's interactions are co-
regulated. When Baraka hits Mandara, the outcome depends on the
sum of the choices each social partner makes moment by moment.
The outcome is neither invariant nor hard-wired, any more than it
would be if one member of a human family shoved another one, on
two summer mornings, in the same location in their house. In this
hypothetical human case, the final outcome on each day would depend on the nature of the interaction in ways that cannot be easily
quantified. These include the strength of the push; what had happened between the participants in the hours and days before the

shove; how much sleep the participants had had the previous night; and what words, spoken in what tone, had accompanied the shove. Similar, though obviously not identical, factors probably affect the interactions between Baraka and Mandara too.

For most biological anthropologists, the value of research on captive apes increases when the behaviors studied occur spontaneously—without human intervention—and reflect patterns that may occur in the wild. That wild African great apes, too, engage in co-regulated social communication is key to my interest in the phenomenon. Long-term research projects that yield qualitative as well as quantitative behavioral accounts are rich sources for identifying such co-regulation, although the scientists themselves rarely use the term "co-regulation" or the DST framework.

Together with his wife, Hedwige Boesch-Achermann, and their colleagues, the Swiss biologist Christophe Boesch has observed the chimpanzees of Tai National Forest, Ivory Coast, West Africa, since 1979. In a recent book,[27] the richness of chimpanzee social communication at Tai comes across most vividly in the descriptive data. Here is an example, taken from a day in March 1983 when the presence of two estrous female chimpanzees in the community caused a great deal of tension among the males. Tension was particularly high between one pair of two older males, the highest-ranking Brutus and his ally Falstaff, and a second pair of two younger males, Schubert and Macho:

> Falstaff, the senior male, approached Brutus in what looked like an attempt to quieten him. Brutus stretched his hand towards Falstaff, and Schubert had now to face both. Falstaff barked at him and Brutus chased Schubert and Macho up the big aerial roots of a Uapaca tree. Macho, farther away from Brutus, displayed above him. Schubert waited for Brutus to return to the females that had not moved and looked indifferent.
>
> Schubert and Macho were back on the spot, hoohing loudly

. . . Schubert and Macho threatened Brutus again, who then approached Falstaff sitting nearby. As the ill-tempered team approached, Falstaff wanted to leave, but Brutus, upright, stretched his hand towards him, looking alternately at Falstaff and Schubert. Schubert, undecided, hoohed for a while. Nothing happened. Then Schubert threatened Brutus with a big arm wave. Falstaff made a reassuring move toward Brutus. And once more, the two oldest chased the younger team away. Schubert in a wild display rushed through the forest and chased all the chimpanzees up the trees, while Brutus quickly returned to the two oestrus females.

Just as was evident with the captive gorillas, body movements and gestures are paramount in the social communication of these wild Ivory Coast chimpanzees. Twice, Brutus uses an arm movement as part of a request for help from Falstaff; the requests succeed and the two senior males work together against their two rivals. An arm wave is used as a threat toward Brutus as well. Multiple vocalizations and body movements enter into this social event.

The presence of co-regulation is difficult to assess directly in this example, because Boesch and Boesch-Achermann are not concerned with explaining unpredictability and contingency, and thus do not transcribe the event in the detail needed. Yet elsewhere in the book, the authors hint at co-regulation in chimpanzee interactions. Just after recounting the tense behaviors surrounding Brutus and the estrous females, they remark that dominance relations at Tai have to be evaluated by the chimpanzees for each so-called party— for each constantly shifting subunit of the larger chimpanzee community. Long-term data show that during the study period in question, the five adult males of the community included two males that together can best be described as middle-ranking. These two, Brutus and Macho, behaved in ways that clearly separated them from higher-

and lower-ranking males, but not from each other. In other words, Brutus's and Macho's interactions with each other were not stable over time; the two did not interact in fixed, predictable ways. Further, little predictability can be expected in situations where Brutus and Macho are surrounded by estrous females and rival males, each of whom plays a role in quickly shifting events. Indeed, relationships among adult male chimpanzees generally may be described as unstable, unreliable, or even fickle. As Newton-Fisher writes, "Male chimpanzees appear to show little long-term loyalty to one another and can be extremely fickle in their allegiances . . . Each relationship that a male has with the other males of his community may at any one time be affiliative, neutral, or antagonistic, and this may change repeatedly."[28]

Add to this the knowledge that male chimpanzees form coalitions to disrupt dominance rank; females involve themselves in dominance-related male disputes; and individual chimpanzees' personalities differ dramatically. Brutus is considered, for instance, a "very gifted social manipulator"[29] by the Boesches. Considering these factors together, it becomes exceedingly difficult to argue that a dominance-related event on the order of complexity recounted here could be fixed, predictable, and noncontingent in nature.

As this one example from Taï clearly points up, the use of gesture and body movement among chimpanzees and the other African great apes must be informed by an understanding of the lifeways of the animals in question. Just as the meaning of an arm wave or threat expression cannot be understood apart from the co-regulated social event, none of the events themselves can be grasped without knowledge of wider social patterns in the populations under study. In the remainder of this chapter I thus present needed background information on the African great apes, with an eye toward providing a good context for analyzing the body movements and gestures that mark the social events of these primates.

## Who Are the African Great Apes?

Of the more than 200 species of living nonhuman primates, 6 are great apes[30] (as Parker[31] points out, this number has only recently been revised upward from four). The species living in Africa are the subjects of this volume: chimpanzees *(Pan troglodytes)*, bonobos *(Pan paniscus)*, western gorillas *(Gorilla gorilla)*, and eastern gorillas *(Gorilla beringei)*. Two species from Asia, the Bornean *(Pongo pygmaeus)* and Sumatran *(Pongo abelii)* orangutans, are excluded for one reason. Most populations of orangutans are far less socially inclined than are the African great apes, so that comparatively fewer instances of social communication occur. Orangutans do appear to be relatively gregarious in some locations, for instance at Suaq Balimbing in Sumatra, but too little is yet known about their nonvocal social communication to assess it accurately. Orangutans probably engage in co-regulated social communication with each other when they meet; my exclusion of them should not be read as an expectation that they are less inclined *when they do meet socially* to behave this way.

After brief discussion of the anatomy and socioemotionality of the African great apes, I devote the remainder of this chapter to a comparative review of the social system of these species. The adjective "great" refers to these apes' comparatively larger body size when contrasted with the "lesser" apes, the gibbons (genus *Hylobates*) and siamangs (genus *Symphalangus*) of Asia. Set apart anatomically from all other nonhuman primates by a body designed for brachiation, the apes (lesser and great) lack a tail; have longer arms than legs; and possess flexible joints at the shoulder, elbow, and wrist. This last fact likely has implications for understanding body movement and gesture. As Tanner and Byrne recognize, only the apes among nonhuman primates can produce movement in all directions from shoulder, elbow, and wrist joints: "With these fine rotational movements, a single gesture type can vary in configuration, direction, size, and forcefulness on a continuous scale according to the circumstances of its use."[32] As we will see, this rotational ability underwrites the great apes' skill at producing fine-grained and subtly varied gestures rather than only broad, sweeping ones.

Great ape brains are larger than those of other nonhuman primates. As noted by the biological anthropologist Kathleen Gibson,[33] great ape brains are, on average, about twice the size of baboon brains. Baboon brains are themselves about twice as large as the brains of any other monkey. Prolonged debate has occurred about the validity of absolute brain size as a measure of intelligence, especially when compared to other measures such as the ratio of neocortex size to the size of the rest of the brain.[34] Gibson and Jessee conclude, based on their comparative neurological research and a literature review, that overall brain size in primates appears to have "the greatest predictive value" in assessing neural parameters related to cognition, learning, or sensorimotor skills.[35] For example, from brain size alone, one can predict the sizes of major neural processing areas and neuronal density of various primates.

Research by Reader and Laland[36] confirms that brain size and cognitive ability are correlated in primates. In their analyses, two measures of brain size are of primary importance. Unlike Gibson and Jessee's, their measures depart from absolute brain volume: absolute volume of the neocortex and striatum, or the so-called executive brain, and the ratio of executive brain volume to volume of the brainstem. As measures of cognitive ability, Reader and Laland use innovation, the tendency to discover novel solutions to environmental or social problems; social learning; and tool use. They conclude that "members of large-brained nonhuman primate species innovate, learn from others, and use tools more frequently than members of small-brained primate species."[37]

These data on primate brain size are welcome additions to the fierce debate in primatology about whether the great apes, compared to monkeys, can be said to possess superior intelligence and learning abilities. Probably it is fair to say that more primatologists embrace than reject a "great ape watershed" when it comes to intelligence. These scientists claim heightened abilities in great apes not only in the areas measured by Reader and Laland but also in others: coalitions, alliances, and other multiparty social interactions; "theory of mind," the ability to take another's perspective on the world in order to recognize what a social partner knows or does not know; and facility with human-introduced symbols, whether of math or language.[38] I count myself as an adherent of the notion of a great ape cognitive watershed, yet acknowledge the great interspecific and intraspecific variability that marks the expression of primate intelligence. Some monkeys use tools, for instance, in ways that prove no generalizations should precede extensive research on wild and captive populations.[39]

Problem-solving and cognitive skills of great apes have received far more explicit attention in the literature than have their emotions. Nonetheless, long-term data show that the African great apes frequently act in a way that might be better described as *socioemotional* rather than as merely social. Primatologists have provided good evidence that these apes, both in the wild and in captivity, not only plan strategically for the future (about, say, status and resources), but also become deeply attached to their social partners, including kin, and sometimes empathize with them. African great apes experience a range of emotions when interacting with close associates, acquaintances, and sometimes even strangers, including grief, annoyance, and possibly vengeance and anger.[40] The existence of these emotions will become clear when I present data in Chapters 3 and 4; for now, as I review the variety of African great ape social systems, it's useful to keep in mind that the meaning created when gorillas, chimpanzees, and bonobos communicate has its basis in their socioemotional life.

Turning now to African great ape social systems, I identify three components that should be kept distinct: social organization, social structure, and mating system.[41] Concerned with the first two only, I do not discuss mating systems directly. *Social organization* refers to how many animals of which age-sex classes live together, and the degree of spatiotemporal cohesion that results. The all-important events between social partners that form the heart of my analysis may be highly constrained and influenced by the existing social organization. If, for instance, one African great ape species tends to travel during the day in tightly cohesive, relatively small groups, the possibility of frequent, up-close, face-to-face co-regulated social interactions among group members is likely to be high. Conversely, if a second species tends to travel in more scattered fashion, perhaps in small dispersed parties with occasional solitary individuals, the potential for up-close, face-to-face interactions is likely to be more limited, but accompanied by an enhanced potential for social communication across greater distances (whether between parties or between individuals).

Over time, the patterns that emerge from social interactions between individuals give rise to particular social relationships, and analyzing these moves us into the realm of *social structure*. In short, then, I am interested in describing social organization in order to better understand social structure.

## Chimpanzee Social Systems

Six bright pins mark, whether materially or metaphorically, maps of Africa belonging to primatologists who are passionate about chimpanzees. Each pin corresponds to one of the long-term chimpanzee research sites on the continent.[42] Four are in East Africa, two each in Tanzania and Uganda. The Tanzanian sites include the most famous of all, Gombe, where Jane Goodall pioneered long-term great ape research in 1960.

Before venturing into the realm of long-term research, it's worth noting that the history of chimpanzee research in the wild, pre-

Goodall, is fascinating in its own right. Consider the work of R. L. Garner, whom Reynolds and Reynolds[43] consider to be the first person to attempt a field study of chimpanzees and gorillas. In 1868, Garner ensconced himself in a cage placed in a West African forest. Thus protected, he observed the great apes that walked by. Later, outside a cage, he observed groups of chimpanzees crossing an open area between forest patches. As with all early field workers, some of his observations turned out to be inaccurate. Still, before Goodall's day, the world had been informed about a variety of chimpanzee behaviors, including the use of nests for sleeping and the tendency to aggregate in larger numbers when mature fruits are abundant.[44]

At Gombe, present-day researchers follow the third generation of chimpanzees, a major accomplishment given the longevity of the great apes (who not atypically live into their late thirties and sometimes their forties). "Goodall" and "Gombe" are household names in much of the Western world; fewer people outside of primate studies know that Mahale, another chimpanzee site in Tanzania, has been as influential in primatology as Gombe. Research in Mahale, initiated by Toshisada Nishida, began only five years after Goodall's. Nishida was the first to discern that chimpanzees live in clear-cut, stable communities. Other scientists, Goodall included, had asumed more fluid relationships across social units.[45]

The two Ugandan sites offer crucial points of comparison within East Africa, particularly because they are forested, whereas the Tanzanian sites are found in more open woodland. At Budongo in the 1960s, Vernon Reynolds and others conducted chimpanzee research at erratic intervals. This research was reestablished in 1994 and has since been continuous. At nearby Kibale, full-time chimpanzee studies have been ongoing since 1987 under the direction of Richard Wrangham.

Especially informative data have come from one of the two West African forest sites, Tai in the Ivory Coast, already mentioned in the account of complex social communication among a group of male rivals for estrous females. Chimpanzee behavior at Tai is now quite well described, thanks to two decades' worth of data in articles, books, and films. The second West African site, Bossou in Guinea, was established by Yukimaru Sugiyama in 1976. The Bossou study community of chimpanzees differs in some ways from the others described. Since the onset of observations, it has remained small, holding steady at around 20 chimpanzees. Located near a village of 3,000 people, the chimpanzees' core forest area is both rich (owing to the presence of cultivated fields and secondary forests) and quite limited in size, though occasionally the chimpanzees do travel to adjacent forest areas through a few remaining forest corridors.[46]

Information from all six sites confirms that chimpanzees live in stable communities, as first recognized by Nishida at Mahale. There is, then, a basic species-specific social organization in which multiple males, females, and dependent offspring live together. Community membership is apparently meaningful to the chimpanzees, because boundaries are patrolled. Patrollers, typically males, silently walk the perimeter of their communities, seeking the presence of noncommunity individuals. Although some members may switch communities at certain times in their lives, intercommunity interaction, when it occurs, tends toward the aggressive, and sometimes even the lethal.

Still, a chimpanzee community is not a cohesive social unit. It differs in essential ways from a monkey group. Among the baboons at Gombe, living sympatrically with the chimpanzees, individuals start their day by descending as a group from the tree or trees in which they slept. They set off together to forage, minimally spaced apart and always ready to close ranks should a predator be sighted. They rest, groom, and otherwise socialize together at various points during the day, and when dusk falls, ascend their sleeping trees together.

A chimpanzee community, stable in one sense as a bounded entity set apart from other communities, is quite unstable in another, in the degree to which community members travel together and intimately associate as a group. Ever-shifting subunits, called parties, form the heart of the community. Kano, using the Japanese term "unit-group" in place of "community," nicely summarizes the nature of this fluidity: "If individuals A-B form one party, when that pair joins another party and becomes A-B-C-D-E, the individuals have the flexibility, depending on the opportunities, to divide into two other partylike forms, such as B-D and A-C-E. The constituent members of a unit group do not form parties only in this way. Many become temporarily solitary, but the unit group serves to bring them all together."[47]

In a typical day at Tai, for instance, "Varying parties fuse and disperse as they forage along, maintaining cohesion by loud calls and drumming."[48] Here we can see a critical aspect of social communication in chimpanzees. Just as individuals within parties must monitor each other's behavior and respond contingently, so too must parties keep track of other parties' whereabouts. Two different, if overlapping, contexts for social communication occur, intra- and interparty. (Since some monkeys too live in fission-fusion social groups, I intend no taxonomic differentiation here, but note only that fission-fusion social organization, whenever present, carries implications for social communication).

When looking beyond the basic pattern of fission-fusion community life that typifies all well-studied chimpanzees, and when pooling data from the six sites, one can identify two major areas of variation.[49] The first area concerns dispersal at puberty. In mammals generally, one or both sexes transfers out of the natal group at puberty. This dispersal at reproductive age presumably allows individuals to avoid inbreeding and/or to gain better access to resources. Nonhuman primates are no exception, and a major goal in assessing a population's social organization is to figure out which sex or sexes disperse (and, of course, why).

Nonprimatologists, familiar with Goodall's writings about adult mother-daughter pairs (perhaps Flo and Fifi, or Passion and Pom), are often startled to. learn that female chimpanzees in most populations routinely transfer, alone, out of their natal community at puberty. At Gombe, about 60 percent of adult females transfer from their natal communities to breed elsewhere, which renders long-term social bonds between mother and daughter more an exception than the rule. At other sites, enduring mother-daughter bonds are even rarer. In Taï's main study community, all females but one dispersed over a period of 16 years. At Mahale, all females but a few disperse. Theoretically sound explanations for why females, and not males, disperse in this species involve the idea that female-female feeding competition is too high to permit kin to live in the same community. Relatives should avoid competing for limited resources since such competition may reduce reproductive success.[50]

As Mitani, Watts, and Muller[51] point out, however, this idea fails to explain the noted intraspecific variation, that is, why so many fewer females should transfer at Gombe than at two other long-term sites, Taï and Mahale; these authors note that "direct measures of food availability will be necessary to unlock the key to this puzzle." Similarly, more research is needed to explain the fact that *both* species may transfer at Bossou (though individuals of both sexes also may opt to stay in their natal community).

A second point of variation involves chimpanzee social structure rather than social organization. At Gombe, chimpanzee males tend to associate preferentially with other males rather than with females. Together, males hunt and patrol community borders; they form alliances and coalitions to obtain resources, including fertile females, more efficiently.[52] When male-female interactions occur, they tend to be tense, with males clearly dominating females. In addition, interactions *between* females occur at a low rate. As a result, male chimpanzees are typically portrayed as more gregarious than females, as if this were a species-typical trait. In fact, while male chimpanzee do hunt, patrol, and dominate females, the portrayal of increased male gregariousness seems to mirror the East African data more accurately than the West African data.

Heightened female-female affiliation, including grooming, exists at Bossou, an observation that may be explained in part by the low number of males in the community. As Tetsuro Matsuzawa emphasizes, however, the overall community size at Bossou is low, in the first place, and multiple males are always present as at other sites,[53] a situation that makes substantial female-female affiliation of real interest. At Tai, the chimpanzees "appear to have a bi-sexually bonded society. Large mixed parties are frequently observed, and the two sexes are more frequently associated than in other chimpanzee populations."[54] Tai females are part of attack parties in territorial encounters between communities in more than two thirds of cases observed, and slightly over a third of attack-party members are female.[55] Boesch and Boesch-Achermann suggest that the lower the sex ratio in any given chimpanzee community, the more will males tend to seek contact with females.[56] Primatologists should thus expect to find variation in male and female gregariousness across different populations, one apparent trend being greater male-female and female-female sociality in western compared to eastern chimpanzees.[57]

The pattern of social events at Gombe, then, may differ from that at Tai. More adult mother-daughter, and fewer male-female, social events probably occur at Gombe, for instance. Even if this were known reliably to be the case, though, it would not translate to clear predictions about social communication, for example about the co-regulated nature of vocalizations, gestures, and body movements. If at Gombe male-female social bonds are more rare, perhaps when they are expressed they involve more, or more subtle, co-regulated social communication than they would where such bonds are the norm. This sort of hypothesis testing remains to be done. Once again highlighted is the importance of considering *local differences* in social systems rather than assuming a chimpanzee-level type of social structure.

Cross-populational, or as some prefer cross-cultural, variation in chimpanzee behavior has been a recent hot topic. Socially learned differences in tool use, grooming, and other behaviors[58] across these six long-term sites have been of extreme interest to biological anthropologists who wish to understand the evolution of human culture. Bringing to bear this same scrutiny on ways in which patterns of co-regulated social communication differ across populations would make a fascinating research program.

## Bonobo Social Systems

Bonobos, only discovered in the last century, were first studied scientifically in the 1970s. They are found in a single country, the Democratic Republic of Congo, or DRC, the former Zaire. The DRC is a challenging place to conduct field research. Lanting comments that it is "one of the few countries in the world where travel has actually gotten more difficult over the past fifty years."[59] At times the DRC is so politically unstable as to prevent any primate research at all.

Two long-term sites for bonobo research can be marked on our primatological map of Africa, complementing the six for chimpanzees. Both, of course, are in the DRC: Wamba and Lomako. Wamba was established by the Japanese scientist Takayoshi Kano in 1973, after an extensive survey in the Congo Basin. An adherent of the influential Kyoto School of primatology, which has long aimed to better understand human evolution by study of nonhuman primates, Kano focuses on bonobo social systems and social bonds.[60] Lomako, founded a year later by Noel and Alison Badrian, has tended to host research oriented more toward ecology.

Despite belonging to the same genus, *Pan*, bonobos and chimpanzees differ markedly in some ways. Anatomically, bonobos are lighter and more slender, with relatively shorter upper limbs and longer lower limbs, and faces and hands that are black rather than pink. De Waal remarks that when he first looked a bonobo in the eyes, he "immediately noticed how their curious and sensuous temperament differed from that of the emotionally volatile chimpanzee."[61] When we turn to comparative social organization and social structure, we find, surprisingly, somewhat divergent types of social structure within a basically similar social organization.

Bonobos, like chimpanzees, live in mixed-sex communities marked by fission-fusion fluidity. Party size and composition shift, and females are the ones who usually transfer. In social organization the two *Pan* species are superficially quite comparable; any capsule description would place the two species in the same column or award them the same label. Yet analysis beneath the surface is revealing.

Bonobos tend to travel in larger parties than do chimpanzees.[62] When fruiting trees are abundant, "bonobos seem to be more cohesive, remaining together to visit the same large trees, whereas chimpanzees disperse among many neighboring trees. A similar differences has been seen with a single tree."[63] Further, bonobo parties tend to be bisexual, as chimpanzees are at Tai but not at Gombe.[64] Boesch notes that the sex ratio in bonobos, as among chimpanzees at Tai, but again not at Gombe, tends to be low. He concludes that when within-party social bonds differ across bonobos and chimpanzees, this should be understood "not as a species difference but part of the flexibility of the fission-fusion system."[65]

Yet differences in social structure at the level of the species clearly do exist. Even though bonobo females routinely transfer, females, including nonkin, bond with each other. This bonding is expressed, and indeed probably maintained, via sexual behavior called genito-genital, or GG, rubbing, vividly described by de Waal: "One female clings with arms and legs to another—almost the way an infant clings to its mother—while the other female, standing on both hands and feet, lifts her off the ground. The two females then rapidly rub their genital swellings laterally together. Completely absent in the chimpanzee, this behavior has been observed in every bonobo group, captive or wild, with more than one female."[66] (Since de Waal wrote these words, GG rubbing has been observed in a group of captive chimpanzees.)[67]

GG rubbing has been discussed in the context of prolific sexual behavior in bonobos, summed up by de Waal: "Bonobos have sex in all
imaginable positions and in virtually all partner combinations."[68]
The newest research, though, suggests that drawing a pronounced
interspecies contrast based on sexuality may be unwarranted. As
it turns out, copulation rates of estrous females are *lower* in wild
bonobos than in wild chimpanzees.[69] Nevertheless, the period of
estrus is longer in bonobos and they do engage in nonreproductive
sex more than do chimpanzees. Whether as a result or merely a cor-
relate, bonobos enjoy a more relaxed, peaceful life than do chimpanzees; the striking male-female aggression and intercommunity violence seen in chimpanzees are absent in bonobos. Females often
dominate males; the Lomako researcher Barbara Fruth goes so far as
to say that "adult females are dominant in every possible way. Even
younger females sometimes dominate adult males. I once saw a
grown male try to steal an *Autranella* fruit from an adolescent female, but she chased him furiously."[70]

As Fruth's description implies, by no means are bonobos indifferent to rivalry and competition, or free of tension and aggression. The
media may delight in oversimplified summaries such as "chimpanzees make war, bonobos make love," but primatologists know better.
Kano writes, "The aggressive behavior pattern of [bonobos] abounds
with variety, from violence, including physical contacts such as biting, hitting, kicking, slapping, grabbing, dragging, brushing aside,
pinning down, and shoving aside, to glaring, bluff charging (the
appearance of charging), charging, and chasing."[71] Still, given the
differences in social organization and social structure profiled here,
it is reasonable to conclude that the nature of social events in a
bonobo community tends to differ from that in a chimpanzee community. It remains an open question whether and how patterns of
co-regulated social communication differ in nature between the two
species as well.

What happens to this picture of bonobo social life when variation
across sites is taken into account? Differences in methodology ap-

pear to be rather pronounced between the two long-term sites, which renders difficult any comparisons. At Wamba, but not at Lomako, the bonobos have been provisioned periodically with sugar cane. At Wamba, researchers were keen to observe close details of social life right from the start, whereas at Lomako, a hands-off approach in terms of provisioning dovetailed with the ecological nature of the initial research. Provisioning varies among the six long-term chimpanzee sites, too, but with more than one site in each category ("provisioned" or "not provisioned"); with bonobos, a single site represents each condition. Further, as White[72] notes, Wamba researchers define what constitutes a "bonobo party" differently than do Lomako scientists. At Wamba, bonobos who travel separately but maintain vocal contact with a certain party are counted as members of that party; at Lomako, these separate individuals are considered to be distinct parties.

Adding to these differences is variation in predator pressure between the two sites. Nonhuman predation on bonobos exists at Lomako but not at Wamba, though human population pressure is greater at Wamba. All these factors together mean that any purported intersite variation must be approached with caution. Nonetheless, two especially intriguing differences in bonobo sociality can be identified when one compares Wamba and Lomako: in social organization, the degree of fission and fusion, and in social structure, the nature of social bonds important to adult males.

Wamba communities seem less prone to fragmenting into parties; in one well-studied community, some fragmentation did occur during the day but parties rejoined and slept together at night.[73] Ingmanson[74] emphasizes that the degree of fission-fusion at Wamba is seasonal; as would be expected, more fissioning occurs in the dry season, when fewer preferred foods are available to support large bonobo groupings. By contrast, "all members of one community at Lomako have yet to be seen in one place at the same time."[75] Some larger parties have been sighted at Lomako, however, particularly at nesting times.[76]

Further, the bonds expressed by (and toward) adult males differ across the two sites. At Wamba, "the mother is the core of [bonobo] society, and the males lead a life following their mothers."[77] Kano notes that the composition of the maternal family differs across the two *Pan* species; among bonobos, mature sons join in, whereas among chimpanzees, only the mother and her infants and juveniles are included.

Adult male-male bonds are not as pronounced in any known bonobo population as they are among chimpanzees. Kano explains that at Wamba, males are preoccupied with following their mothers and not with other males.[78] Nevertheless, male-male association is apparently greater at Wamba than at Lomako.[79] Even within Wamba, variation exists in this feature of social structure; males of one community (E2) have been more cohesive, during at least some study periods, than males of another.[80]

Review of the social organization and social structure of chimpanzees and bonobos underscores just how little is conveyed by the flat statement that these species share a fission-fusion community way of life. An insight that emerges from the comparative data, and is emphasized by Boesch, involves the great flexibility of fission-fusion social organization according to local conditions. The social systems of bonobos and chimpanzees are highly responsive to various environmental conditions in ways imperfectly understood to date. Yet these various expressions of fission-fusion life provide excellent opportunities for studying co-regulated social communication: social partners come together, split apart, and rejoin frequently throughout the day. Often, they reunite not just mechanically or efficiently but with emotion. When bonobo mothers and their adult sons, or two chimpanzee males that are close associates, rejoin each other after a separation, they may do so with excited vocalizations and embraces. These reunions between adults, in addition to mother-infant interactions of many types, are among the most *visible* indicators that the African great apes communicate in ways imbued with emotion.

## Gorilla Social Systems

As we enter the fifth decade of research on wild gorillas, one exciting development overshadows all others. Data on social behavior are finally coming in from observation of western as well as eastern gorillas. Until quite recently, primatology has been plagued by a fundamental discrepancy that undermined our ability to understand gorilla sociality. Virtually all gorillas in zoological parks are western, almost always the lowland variety *(Gorilla gorilla gorilla)*, whereas most field research has been conducted on the eastern species, specifically on the mountain gorilla population *(Gorilla beringei beringei)* in the Virunga Mountains at the borders of Rwanda, Democratic Republic of Congo, and Uganda, at the ecological edge of gorillas' distribution.

To be sure, habituated populations of wild western gorillas are still few, and data on social behavior as opposed to, say, foraging and nesting patterns, are accruing slowly. After ten consecutive years of research on western lowland gorillas at Lope, Gabon, Tutin[81] reported data on ranging and social structure that had by necessity to be derived from tracking and nest-site records as well as from outright observation. Still, a picture of this "second" gorilla species is developing more and more by the year. This emerging picture can be viewed against what we know of the eastern species.

When in 1959, George Schaller undertook his pioneering field study of the mountain gorilla in the Virunga Volcanoes region, gorillas were still thought to be highly aggressive. Certainly by that time, the description published in 1861 by the explorer Paul du Chaillu had been moderated; scientists no longer seriously thought of gorillas as "hellish dream creature(s) . . . half-man half-beast" with a "hideous roar."[82] Still, Schaller would be the first to amass detailed scientific data in the long term on gorillas in their own habitat. His research and that by scientists in later years at the Karisoke field station in Rwanda have given the world an unusually detailed picture of one population of African great apes.[83]

Mountain gorillas live in groups of multiple females and dependent offspring, with either one or two adult males. Originally, their social organization was termed a harem, or one-male unit. When it became clear that a full 40 percent of the Karisoke groups contain two adult males, and that males may also be solitary or live together in unisex groups,[84] these terms were dropped in favor of emphasizing the diversity found in gorilla social units. When two males together do control a group, they are sometimes related, for example as father and son or as brothers. If the former situation is the case, and the son eventually disperses from his natal group, the male partnership may be relatively short-lived, but in other cases two males may coexist for many years.

Recent analysis of thirty years of demographic records from the Virungas shows that females in two-male groups reproduce earlier and have higher birth rates than do females in one-male groups.[85] Further, when males do not disperse from the group in which they reach maturity, their success rate in gaining reproductive opportunities goes up. Apparently these benefits associated with multiple-male groups, coupled with the increased protection afforded by two males from infanticide by other gorilla males,[86] are significant, enough so for the resulting reproductive success to outweigh any costs of increased feeding competition. Why fewer than half of the Karisoke groups contain two adult males, then, is not yet clear.

Females typically transfer from their natal groups in this gorilla population. A female may leave her natal group to join up with a solitary male, or may leave one unit to join another during an intergroup encounter. Rarely, an existing gorilla group may fission, which results in a sort of female transfer. Many males disperse as well. Some form their own groups; others become solitary, and still others join all-male groups. These options for males are not mutually exclusive; each one may be experienced, at a different point during the life cycle, by a single male.

As might be predicted, given this social organization, in mountain gorillas the strongest bonds are between males and females. Females are only weakly bonded to each other, and the same statement can be made of males. Within a group as well as between groups, male-male competition for females is high, and relationships between males tend toward the aggressive. Females expend a great deal of energy in maintaining social bonds with males, but not with each other. Females attempt to reconcile with males who have aggressed against them (but not with other females after conflicts),[87] and otherwise follow and groom males. These actions probably increase the females' chances of protection by resident males against infanticide by stranger males, a leading cause of infant mortality at Karisoke.

The other eastern gorilla, *Gorilla beringei graueri*, is known primarily through the work of Juichi Yamagiwa at Kahuzi-Biega National Park in the DRC, where gorillas live sympatrically with chimpanzees. This population's social organization conforms to the profile from mountain gorillas in many respects. Both types of eastern gorillas live in groups that are more cohesive than the communities of bonobos and chimpanzees; no subunit exists in these gorillas comparable to the party that is found in the *Pan* genus. Eastern gorillas travel, rest, and socialize as a unit with relatively little distance between individuals. This difference in cohesion is nicely illustrated by Yamagiwa, who was able to observe the contrast in eastern gorillas' and chimpanzees' foraging strategies in the same forest: "Gorillas usually formed cohesive groups, occasionally visiting fruiting trees for a brief time and revisiting them only after long intervals. Chimpanzees moved individually, often visited the same fruiting trees, and stayed for a long time while feeding . . . Each species of ape tolerated the other's foraging within the same area and seemed to respect the temporary ownership of fruiting trees by other species."[88]

Some intriguing points of difference, however, can be identified between the Kahuzi and Karisoke gorilla populations, each potentially linked to the absence of infanticide at Kahuzi.[89] First, the *graueri* population has fewer two-male groups than do the mountain gorillas. Second, when Kahuzi females transfer, they tend to do so along with other females and their offspring, whereas solitary transfer is the rule at Karisoke. Third, at Kahuzi, female-female associations tend to be stronger than at Karisoke. And last, unlike Karisoke males, Kahuzi males rarely stay with their fathers but sometimes remove females from their natal group, and thus start a new group. As Yamagiwa and Kahekwa put it, "The absence of infanticide in Kahuzi may enlarge female choice of dispersal, promote female-female association, and influence the way that maturing males participate in new group formation."[90]

Primatologists are keen to extend this sort of intraspecies comparison to the interspecies level. They wish to find out whether western gorillas are as cohesive as eastern gorillas, or to put it another way, whether western gorillas might show a relatively fluid social organization, more closely allied to the fission-fusion arrangement of chimpanzees and bonobos. Studies to date tend to emphasize folivory for mountain gorillas[91] and frugivory for western gorillas.[92] Given the abundance and broad distribution of plant material as compared to fruits, such a divergence would predict—even when one takes into account selectivity of feeding by gorillas on particular plant parts and not others—greater fission-fusion for western gorillas. Some researchers[93] have in fact suggested that western gorillas do demonstrate a fission-fusion social organization. Doran and McNeilage[94] report that at all sites, group spread is larger in western lowland gorillas than in mountain gorillas.

Only in the last decade have substantial numbers of western lowland gorillas been closely observed, owing to a critical discovery in the Republic of Congo: swampy clearings called *bais* that bring the gorillas into the open for long periods of time. A turning point came when Parnell[95] published the most complete description of a western population yet available, the results of 1,681 hours of observation of 14 gorilla groups at Mbeli Bai in the Nouabale-Ndoki National Park. Gorillas congregate in *bais* primarily for feeding, and Parnell's data probably are biased behaviorally because of this, but they nonetheless give great insight into a western gorilla social system.

At Mbeli Bai, Parnell observed 13 groups containing one mature silverback male; the fourteenth group contained a younger silverback male, but the dominant silverback had recently died. No two-male groups were observed. Only one group with two mature males has ever been observed at this site; Parnell's data plus those (collected by F. Magliocca) from Maya Bai 180 kilometers away, show a total of 45 single-male groups and no multimale groups. As Parnell puts it, "Given the proposed benefits of such groups to both adult females and males, and the apparently large number of mountain gorilla groups of this nature, these results are astonishing."[96] Whether descriptions from other sites of multimale groups of western lowland gorillas would hold up to intensive observation, rather than being calculated in part via nesting data, remains to be seen. Parnell's tentative conclusion is that single-male groups are the "basic social and mating system" for western lowland gorillas.[97]

Evidence from Mbeli Bai pertaining to social structure is necessarily more limited at this early stage. In fact, female-female interactions are barely known; male-male interactions are known only to be characterized by mutual avoidance or agonistic display. Further study will result in more detailed data on the social dynamics of gorilla communication. For now, co-regulated communication can be assessed only for eastern gorillas, with a few intriguing hints noted about western gorillas.

## On Interspecies Comparisons

In subsequent chapters, when illustrating how dynamic systems theory can aid the study of social communication, I use examples from our own species, as I did in opening this chapter, as well as those from the African great apes. Yet making comparisons across species is a process fraught with challenges.

An easy starting place is to limit consideration of dynamic social communication to the universe of living organisms. Interactions between two humans, two great apes, an ape and a human, a human and a companion pet,[98] a cat and a cat, and so on, are all likely to be dynamic in nature to some degree. Even if, on a stretch, it was claimed that we humans interact with nonhuman objects (our houses? our computers?), no sense could be made of the idea that such interaction is co-regulated. As much as we might joke that our computers or houses are unpredictable, capable of annoying us with unexpected events, they cannot participate, in a dance-like way, in co-regulated social interaction.[99] Reading in the *New York Times* that an architecturally renowned house in Amagansett, New York, had been praised for its "use of very simple, gestural forms in a dynamic way,"[100] I knew that *this* use of "gestural" and "dynamic," applied to the house itself, referred to a different universe entirely.

Venturing beyond this exclusion of nonliving objects, we hit a number of barriers. Primatologists now appreciate the enormous degree of variation, intraspecific as well as interspecific, in primate behaviors ranging from foraging to socializing to communicating. As I have shown, what we thought we knew about "the chimpanzee" or "the gorilla" in the 1960s and 1970s quickly fell away as researchers amassed more data on different populations living in different conditions.[101] This being the case, we need to replace species-level generalizations with more precise data whenever possible.

Although my premise is that unpredictability, contingency, and joint creation of meaning occur commonly in African great ape social communication,[102] I cannot make confident claims about the comparative degree of elaboration of these qualities in African great apes versus humans, or about precisely how the processes of co-regulated social communication unfold across the various species or populations. Such claims must emerge from the data, both qualitative and quantitative, which are as yet unavailable. The appropriate matched analyses have rarely been done, for either broad compari-

sons (say, analyzing chimpanzee versus human social communication for the qualities discussed here) or finer-grained ones (comparing social communication of chimpanzees in West versus East
Africa).

Further, it is outside the scope of this work to review the nature of
jointly constructed communication between social partners in other
mammals. The most relevant comparison would be between the African great apes and other apes or monkeys, a project that would be
one obvious follow-up to this book. Readers who share a household
with multiple cats, as I do, might conclude we do not even know to
what degree social communication of African great apes differs from
that of domestic felines. Visitors to my house, on most days, could
observe our longest-residing cat locked in an aggressive "dance" with
the newest immigrant cat. The two hiss, posture, and circle each
other using that slow, stylized motion known so well to cat owners.
Certainly, when cat S raises her paw to attempt a slap at the other's
face, cat J adjusts her actions, and S then adjusts *her* actions. On
other days, cats S and J may approach each other without overt indicators of aggression, and may sniff noses without incident. Are these
interactions marked by jointly constructed social communication via
unpredictability and contingency?

Rather than attempting an answer, I wish to bring front and center the hypothesis that material in this book suggests, but that I cannot test directly: The unpredictability and contingency that characterize African great ape and human social communication exceed
what can be observed in social communication by other mammals,
and indeed, other nonhuman primates. Put another way, of all nonhumans, the African great apes are better skilled at attending to
subtle movements and gestures, and at interacting in subtle ways
with their social partners, to create ever-shifting, in-the-moment,
dance-like communication. This hypothesis deserves serious attention from primatologists and other animal behaviorists. My own primary aim in this volume is to suggest a new way of understanding

African great ape social communication, with the hope that other hypotheses, as well as the one just suggested, are tested as a result.

In sum, then, the African great apes are social and highly primed to participate in co-regulated, and at times socioemotional, communication of a subtle and nuanced variety. Their daily lives are full of interactions that are routine in one sense, but quite complex and intricate in another. Before offering a close look at these lived experiences, I devote a chapter to the theory and method of dynamic systems thinking as applied to primate social communication.

# 2

## Gesture and Dynamic Systems Theory

G ESTURES and body movements are at the heart of nonvocal social communication, yet I have produced a lengthy first chapter without fully defining and describing what I mean by those terms. Constructing a separate chapter on this issue reflects a realization that is
simple enough yet, for me, developed only gradually over the last
decade. How one defines and describes gestures and body movements, or indeed any actions related to social communication, depends wholly on one's theoretical orientation. To see this clearly, consider the process of social communication generally.

As Hauser remarks, the concepts of *information* and *signal* form
integral components of most definitions of communication.[1] Two
examples underscore his point. For Hailman, communication is "the
transfer of information via signals sent in a channel between a
sender and a receiver,"[2] whereas for Ellis and Beattie, communication occurs "when one organism (the transmitter) encodes information into a signal which passes to another organism (the receiver)
which decodes the signal and is capable of responding appropri-
ately."[3]

Shanker and I have noted that this view of communication originated with Claude Shannon's work in the 1940s on the transmission
of electronic signals.[4] When Shannon described his method of con-
verting sounds and images into binary strings as *encoding* the *information* in the *message* being sent, a new metaphor was born. Terming

it the conduit metaphor, Michael Reddy has captured more cogently than any other writer its overwhelming influence on the way English speakers (and writers) conceive of human communication. Reddy describes the four components of the conduit metaphor's framework: "(1) language functions like a conduit, transferring thoughts bodily from one person to another; (2) in writing and speaking, people insert their thoughts or feelings in the words; (3) words accomplish the transfer by containing the thoughts or feelings and conveying them to others; and (4) in listening or reading, people extract the thoughts and feelings once again from the words."[5]

This framework was soon imported into the study of animal, including primate, social communication. When in 1965, Marler assessed the meaning of primate calls, he noted the importance of the social context, writing that "the communicative act cannot be isolated from the circumstances in which the signaler and the recipient find themselves at the time they are participating in the exchange. Insofar as the surroundings and concomitant behavior of the signaler are perceptible to the recipient they also may contribute something to the response that it gives to a signal."[6] This view is perfectly Shannon-like in its assumption that two animals exchange signals sequentially. Social context may influence this exchange, but only as a variable outside the process.

My guess is that many primatologists, even today, would find nothing to challenge in this view. Aside from the fact that Marler has for four decades been singularly influential in the study of primate (and bird) communication, his perspective may seem a matter of common sense. In a recent article, Maestripieri and colleagues write, for example, that the recent flurry of interest in primate communication and cognition has stimulated research in "exchange of signals and the transmission of information between mothers and infants through social learning processes."[7] That the authors do not question or explore the nature of the terms embedded in this phrase attests to the strength and durability of the Shannon-Marler perspective, as does Strier's recent textbook on primatology. Strier writes, "Communication is a two-way street. There must be at least one actor and one receiver in each interaction, but in primate groups other members may also play active roles. Communication systems can be divided into four interrelated components: signal, motivation, meaning, and function. The *signal* is the form that the act of communication takes. . . . *Motivation* refers to the internal state of the actor who is sending the signal. . . . *Meaning* refers to the message that is received by the recipients of a signal . . . The *function* of communication describes its evolutionary advantage."[8]

The line of thinking embraced by Marler, Maestripieri and colleagues, Strier, and countless other primatologists gives weight to the signal itself—the monkey scream, the chimpanzee arm wave, or the human word. (Nonvocal gestures clearly are meant to be included here, even though studies focus on vocal signals.) By emitting signals such as these, primates are thought to transfer information from themselves to others; the signals can be envisaged as containing bits of information that move from one animal to another across time and space.

It's easy enough to see, if one works from specific examples, the appeal of this information-processing framework. When rhesus monkeys scream during certain social interactions, for instance, they are said to "encode" information, not just their emotions or their arousal level, in their vocalizations. This conclusion, reached by a research team including Marler, is based on evidence from the population of rhesus monkeys living on Cayo Santiago, an island off Puerto Rico. Tape-recorded screams, originally uttered by juvenile monkeys caught up in agonistic interactions, were "played back" to the monkeys later in the absence of any ongoing aggression. The screamers' mothers responded differentially to the playbacks, depending on the nature of the scream. The juveniles produced one kind of scream when under attack from an unrelated dominant animal, but another when threatened only by dominant kin, a less dangerous situation.[9]

Since maternal response to the screams occurred to a tape recording alone, in the absence of any fighting, shouldn't we conclude that the scream is a signal that, all by itself, transfers information? Similarly, envision two people walking outdoors as a storm approaches. As they pass a tree, one says to the other, "Watch out! That branch is about to fall on your head!"[10] Isn't it obvious that those words encode information delivered to their recipient? As we will see, answering "yes" to these questions, one about rhesus monkeys and the other about humans, fails to reveal the full story of social communication.

That signals containing information, whether uttered by rhesus monkeys or humans, should flow in a back-and-forth way between senders and recipients seemed obvious enough to me ten years ago, when I wrote a book about the social transfer of information across the generations in nonhuman primates.[11] My thesis was that most infant primates, exemplified by the baboons *(Papio cynocephalus)* I had studied in Kenya, are responsible for acquiring knowledge about species-specific diet, predators, social conventions, and the like, on their own. The infants' mothers or other older social companions do not alter their own behavior in order to help them gain such knowledge. Some primates, though, particularly the African great apes and humans, engage in what I called social information donation. In these cases, older social partners directly guide the actions of younger conspecifics in various ways related to everyday "problems" encountered in foraging, survival, and the social world. Through various forms of social communication (including, in the case of humans, language) adults may guide youngsters in how to choose appropriate food items, travel paths, and social companions, and how to use objects as tools.

Within this framework, my "take" on social communication was straightforward. Adult African great apes produce facial expressions, gestures, body movements, or vocalizations that can be thought of as vehicles of social information transfer. They are one path by which younger or naive individuals may acquire information, either through monitoring and observation by the inexperienced animals or through active donation by the adults.

This distinction between social information acquisition and social information donation has, in the years since the book's publication, been used for hypothesis-testing by a number of primatologists.[12] It has been incorporated, as well, into analyses of social learning, intelligence, or language written by theorists in a variety of disciplines.[13] In some cases, my specific predictions or conclusions are accepted, and in others rejected, but my core idea is generally taken as straightforwardly evident. Information may be acquired by young or naive primates, or donated by more experienced elders, through the use of actions that may include communicative signals.

Given how snugly this idea fits with the conventional sender-receiver perspective of social communication so typical since Shannon's day, its adoption as a reasonable foundation for further work should be unsurprising. Yet a wholly different theoretical perspective contravenes the notions underlying both the social information transfer framework and the broader information-processing approach to social communication of which it is a part. Having become steeped in this alternative, dynamic systems theory (DST), I now regard "social information transfer" as a concept that oversimplifies and distorts what goes on in social communication. No longer can I make sense of social communication as an exchange of signals between sender and receiver; of information as either donated or acquired; or of screams or words transmitting information in and of themselves.

This chapter is essentially an account of *why* I believe the information-signaling view is inadequate. In short, I wish to explore DST from the point of view of someone who was initially enamored of the information-processing approach. Though the DST approach is not entirely new in primatology (as I will explain below), primatologists embrace it only rarely. A comparison of the nonlinear thinking of DST with the linear thinking of the information-signaling approach will give readers a firm basis on which to form their own opinions. After this comparison is completed, I consider how nonvocal social communication, specifically, is viewed from the DST perspective, and how it can be studied through the use of methods consistent with DST. The chapter then broadens out again, tracing some historical roots and some present-day connections of DST in anthropology, psychology, and primatology.

## Nonlinear Thinking

Upon the publication of my social information transfer book, a few voices, prominent among them that of my colleague Talbot Taylor, gently expressed a fundamental criticism that I was not to hear from within primatology.[14] Though welcoming my description of what nonhuman primates actually do in their daily lives, in terms of sharing knowledge and communicating, Taylor claimed that what they do cannot be reduced to "social information transfer." In fact, no such thing as social information transfer exists, because information is not an entity that can be sent, via signals, from one organism across time and space to another. I struggled to understand this notion, because it fell so far outside the realm of any ideas I had so far encountered.[15] After all, accepting it would mean I could no longer accept that monkey screams and human words transmit information.

Then I was invited to lecture at the Santa Fe Institute. Discovering that SFI was a think-tank for issues relating to dynamic systems, I quickly attempted to educate myself in Systems Thinking 101—and soon encountered a way to understand what Taylor had been telling me. From an account by the science writer Mitchell Waldrop, I learned that SFI scientists "believe that they are forging the first rigorous alternative to the kind of linear, reductionist thinking that has dominated science since the time of Newton."[16] Linear thinking works well when the phenomena to which it is applied are linear also; that is, when separate elements interact with each other in a sequential manner: when A acts and then B responds. Linear systems do exist, of course, as Waldrop illustrates. "If a system is precisely equal to the sum of its parts," he writes, as are linear systems, "then each component is free to do its own thing regardless of what's happening elsewhere."[17] Sound, says Waldrop, is a linear system; sound waves can intermingle and still retain their individual identities, as when an oboe plays together with strings and the human ear can distinguish one sound from the other.

Much of nature, continues Waldrop, is not linear. When the human brain processes sound, "even though the sound of an oboe and the sound of a string section may be independent when they enter your ear, the emotional impact of both sounds together may be very much greater than either one alone."[18] For this kind of situation, linear thinking won't do. Nonlinear thinking, by contrast, deals with systems comprised of elements that are neither separate nor independent, but, rather, internally related to one another.[19] These are dynamic systems, always changing unpredictably and contingently. The brain, as Waldrop hints, is just such a system, yet to think about a dynamic system we need only take a second look at sound, our original example. Linearity isn't always the rule after all. When the object of study is shifted from the sound emitted by human-powered instruments to the active production by living organisms of sound from the vocal tract, we once again encounter nonlinearity.

Fitch and colleagues describe sudden, irregular transitions in the vocalizations of the Cayo Santiago rhesus monkeys that can only be described as nonlinear.[20] These monkeys produce various vocalizations in social situations, among them screams—as we know from reviewing the experiment done at Cayo on maternal response to juvenile screams. Fitch and colleagues recorded and analyzed Cayo rhesus screams (as well as other vocalizations), producing spectograms that chart the acoustic features of the calls. Because the calls are in some cases marked by frequent abrupt transitions in harmonics and other key characteristics, Fitch and colleagues describe them as characterized by nonlinearities (and title their research report "Calls out of Chaos"). Such nonlinear intrusions were found in nearly one third (30 percent) of the average monkey's sample of recorded vocalizations.

Fitch and colleagues conclude that rhesus monkeys, using simple neural commands to the vocal tract, produce complex and individually variable acoustic output. "A certain call may occupy a wholly stable oscillation regime for one individual, while the same call may traverse a transition point to an unstable or chaotic regime in another individual."[21] This variability probably aids the monkeys in the recognition of specific individuals that is fundamental to nonhuman primate sociality.

One lesson of this analysis is that what gets classed, in studies of primate vocal communication, as the "same" call may in reality be a set of calls with quite variable features. A second lessons goes to the heart of my main point in this section; to say that information is contained in the scream itself leaves out the most interesting part of the story. The screams could be described statistically in such a way as to derive a conclusion about the "typical" scream for this population— about the specific features of screams uttered most often at Cayo. (Even this could be difficult because so many varieties of nonlinearity might exist.) Researchers might even construct a profile of the nature of screams used by one individual monkey versus another. But none of this would get at the deeply social and variant nature of the communication going on. Further, in no sense could we decide that "the scream" of rhesus monkeys categorically can be described by a certain set of features, nor could we conclude that it transmits information via a certain set of features.

Building on Fitch and colleagues' work, then, we can see that it is misguided to focus on the call or its information content, apart from the vocalizer or the vocalizer's ongoing stream of activity. In real, everyday life—not in an experiment with tape recorders—the scream becomes communicative when its utterer enters into some type of interaction with another monkey. This second monkey may hear the scream not as a certain type of call (a scream and not an affiliative coo, let's say) but as a scream uttered with certain acoustic features *this way* at *this time* by *this monkey*, as opposed to a different scream, produced earlier by the same monkey, or produced at nearly the same instant but by another monkey. The hearer may interact with the vocalizer on the basis of not just his vocalization but also his facial expression, body posture, and tail carriage, plus any memory of the outcomes of recent social interactions with that individual.

This analysis gets us part of the way toward a reasoned rejection of social information transfer because it shows that social communication cannot be adequately summed up as the process of sending information from producer to receiver via some discrete signal. There's more to consider, however. Research has yet to be done testing whether monkey A could alter its scream by incorporating different nonlinearities when interacting with monkey B versus monkey C. Fitch and colleagues did find that subadult and female rhesus monkeys incorporated more nonlinearities than did adult males into their calls. In any case, this research offers new insight into what the playback method can and cannot tell us about social communication.

Let's confront now the example I paired, earlier, with the one about rhesus vocalization: what happens when one person warns another that a tree branch is about to fall on his head. Are there complications here, similar to the ones just encountered with rhesus screams, leading us to doubt that the words themselves convey a message? When we first think of the warning sentence, uttered as a storm approaches, we probably conjure up an image of the speaker with a serious, alarmed face, using an excited voice pitch and perhaps waving his arm or pointing with a finger as he indicates the impending danger. As the first words are being uttered, the hearer would no doubt look at the speaker and begin to move rapidly away from the tree, perhaps looking skyward and protecting his head and face as he did so. No one would deny the importance of the nonvocal gestures in this example, yet it's also true that were the speaker to convey the warning by phone, from the vantage point of a window inside a nearby house, the hearer (if he had a cellphone) would probably react just as quickly.

Once again, though, we need to probe more deeply in order to see why the words-as-message view is inadequate. If the speaker uttered, in person, the very same words of warning in a casual tone while adopting a casual stance, with no muscular tension in either body or face, the hearer might not react with such alacrity. He might look up and try to discern if a tree branch was in fact threatening him, or might pause, confused by the disparity between the words he had heard and the nonvocal cues he had seen. In other words, the hearer would adjust his own actions on the basis of the total package of what he perceives, and the nonvocal gestures would probably alter his assessment of the vocal ones.

But it's not just paralinguistic cues that matter here. Let's restore to the speaker his urgent tone, his tense face and body, and all the other signs of intent to warn his companion of a genuine danger. This time, though, we factor in recent social history for this pair. Two times in the last week, the speaker had played practical jokes on the hearer, warning him of what turned out to be nonexistent dangers (once a poisonous snake purportedly nearby, once a speeding bicycle supposedly approaching from behind). The first time, the hearer had been taken in by the speaker's gestures (vocal and nonvocal), and had jumped away in alarm; the second time, despite the same apparent seriousness on the part of the speaker, the hearer was immediately suspicious and only calmly turned his head. By the time of our present example, the hearer refuses to take seriously the warning. Any message in the words is not present for him—whether or not a branch, in reality, threatens his safety.

From the point of view of DST, accepting the idea that signals encode information results in an impoverished understanding. The richness of the co-regulation that characterizes primate social communication is missed on the linear message-sending account. As we will see, unpredictability and contingency mark some communicative actions of the African great apes. If we want to study the nature and extent of such co-regulation, linear thinking won't take us far enough.

Co-regulation implies, by its very definition, internally related, nonindependent elements—nonlinearity. When co-regulation is taken into account, we can see that information is not transferred by facial expressions, body movements, gestures, and vocalizations, nor by bits of information that they supposedly carry. These movements (of the face, body, limbs, or vocal tract) *become communicative* when the social partners enter into an interaction. The social partners are anything but autonomous, because they may transform each other as they act.

Now we've arrived at the crux of the problem with the concept of social information transfer. The relevant process in social communication is not transfer, but emergence. As Shanker and I put it, "Great ape and human communication, according to the dynamic systems paradigm, is not a 'telementational' process: to communicate a desire, intention, thought, wish, or emotion, is not to 'transmit information' about an 'internal state' that must be 'decoded' in order to be understood. Rather, mutual understanding is something that *emerges* as both partners converge on some shared feeling, thought, action, intention, etc. Far from following some predetermined format, such a process is intrinsically creative."[22]

A key conclusion to emerge from this kind of comparison is that adoption of one theoretical perspective versus another immensely influences the production of knowledge about social communication. As is already obvious, the questions asked in the DST approach differ from those asked in the information-processing approach. This difference will become clearer as we proceed to explore the ramifications of the DST approach.

Just as scientists at the Santa Fe Institute hoped, a focus on dynamic systems is changing how social and physical science is carried out. And such thinking can be found in wonderfully diverse places, outside as well as within science. On the day I drafted this chapter's initial description of nonlinear systems, trying to make clear that a system's elements intrinsically affect each other, I happened upon a beautiful passage in the novel I was reading. In *Swann's Way*, Proust describes how Swann's life has been changed by his love for Odette: "Like anyone who possesses something precious, in order to know what would happen if he ceased for a moment to possess it, he had detached the precious object from his mind, leaving, as he thought, everything else in the same state as when it was there. But the absence of one part from a whole is not only that, it is not simply a partial lack, it is a derangement of all the other parts, a new state which it was impossible to foresee in the old."[23] Could a scientist do better in describing the nature of a dynamic system?

## What Counts as Gesture?

The word "gesture" carries myriad meanings, many now distant from the sense of the original Latin, which referred to *action,* as in carrying out an activity. Though scientific analyses of gesture hark back to the original sense of the word, denoting action, even here a variety of understandings exist. For some, gestures are limited to voluntary, symbolic representation, whereas for others, gesture is neuromuscular activity pure and simple, divorced from any intent by the gesturer to communicate. Goodwin remarks that a single set of videotaped human movements may be presented and discussed by one researcher as gesture, but dismissed as nongesture by a second researcher.[24] Though most researchers seem to mean *visible* bodily actions when they talk about human gesture, we will see that there is a growing tendency to discuss the unity of bodily gesture and speech.

In studies of African great apes, definitions of gesture tend to be marked by three features: focus on movement of the limbs, hands, or head in a social context, with reference at times also to gaze; a claim for intentional production of gestures by the apes involved; and careful distinguishing of gesture from nongesture. Tanner and Byrne, in their research on captive western gorillas, include as gesture all discrete, nonlocomotor limb and head movements that occur when gorillas are in proximity and engaged in social interaction before, after, or during the movements. In this social context, gestures are assumed to be communicative; they are produced because one gorilla wishes to influence another's behavior. Gestures differ from "ordinary motions" in lacking enough force to be "mechanically effective."[25] Tanner and Byrne describe gestures observed in their study group by noting precise movements and type of social context, so that the gesture "armswing under," for instance, is said to occur when a gorilla's "arm(s) swing from space in front of body back to body between legs," in the context of male-female play.

Similarly, in Tomasello and colleagues' longitudinal research on captive chimpanzees, gestures are described by reference to movement and social context. A hand-beg gesture is defined as "subject places its hand under the other's mouth and looks to the face of the other," whereas "arm-on" is defined as "subject approaches the other with its arm extended and places its arm on the other's back."[26] To qualify as a gesture, a particular movement must meet specified criteria for intentionality. The chimpanzee gesturer must wait for a response from the social partner after gesturing, and/or must alternate her gaze between that partner and some goal (such as an item of food for which the chimpanzee begs). Criteria such as these disqualify other movements, even though of similar configuration, from being tallied as gestures.

Published lists from these studies, one by Tanner and Byrne and the other by Tomasello's team, include only nonvocal gestures, though some of these are classed as auditory or having auditory components. When gorillas chestbeat or clap their hands, and when chimpanzees slap the ground or stomp their feet, sound is clearly involved. No vocalizations, though, are included as gestures.

Some scholars of human gesture argue for a unified definition of gesture that would include articulatory motions of the vocal tract.[27] When we humans speak, we make precisely controlled movements of the lips, tongue, vocal cords, and so on; movement is key. As Sheets-Johnstone puts it, the primary modality is always kinetic,[28] whether the pathway is primarily optical or primarily acoustic. Fowler and colleagues have shown that phonological units of human speech are discrete, independent products of the vocal tract's actions, even though these units are neither independent nor discrete in actual speech. As Goldstein and Fowler put it, "The central idea is that while the articulatory and acoustic *products* of speech production actions are continuous and context-dependent, the actions themselves that engage the vocal tract and regulate the motions of its articulators are discrete and context-independent."[29] These researchers use the term "gesture" to refer to linguistically significant actions of the vocal tract: "The words *pack* and *tack* contrast with one another in that the former includes a lips gesture and the latter a tongue tip gesture."[30] Gestures are then coordinated to form utterances.

More and more scholars are going beyond a focus on either nonvocal or vocal-tract actions alone to argue for the unity of all gestures. This idea is still challenged, unsurprisingly, in part because of certain preexisting assumptions about the nature of speech versus that of nonvocal gesture.[31] After all, speech is characterized by an invisible kineticism. Neither the speaker nor her social partner is usually aware of the actual movements made while speaking. Further, speech production and comprehension are often described in mentalist rather than kinetic terms.

I will revisit the unified idea in reviewing human-centered research and evolutionary theories about gesture in Chapter 5. For now, I note that the unity of vocalizations with other gestures may be extended to the great apes. Specific articulatory motions made by vocalizing African great apes do differ, of course, from those made by speaking humans; many biological anthropologists think that the main obstacle to the production of speech in great apes involves the configuration of their vocal tracts rather than the physiology of their brains. The only point that is of concern here, though, is that the great apes make articulatory motions when they vocalize.

If African great ape vocalizations may be classed as gestures, what about facial expressions? Tanner and Byrne regard as a gesture a movement called "hide playface," observed in only one adult female gorilla. This female, during interactions with a particular male, sometimes hid her "play face" expression with one or both hands. As Tanner and Byrne note, this hiding action clearly implies both that the play face itself was involuntary, and that the female attempted under certain circumstances to conceal her motivation to play (for example when a larger adult male was nearby, when play might result in a dangerous social encounter). They conclude that this female "fashion[ed] a simple negative" by essentially canceling out the play face expression.

This example gives insight into gorilla cognition, but does it also cast doubt on the inclusion of facial expressions themselves as gestures? Neither Tanner and Byrne nor Tomasello and colleagues include facial expressions in their lists, though aspects of gaze are included. Perhaps this exclusion is based on the expectation that great ape facial expressions might fail to meet criteria for intentionality, as is apparently the case with at least some play face expressions. This complicated situation can be treated only briefly in this chapter, along two specific lines of thought. First, the question of whether facial expressions are produced involuntarily or invariantly across populations in primates, including humans, is not yet settled, because too little research has been done. The oft-made claim that facial expressions are innate whereas other nonvocal gestures are learned is very likely too simple, as we will see. Second, DST does not insist upon seeking evidence for intentionality when assessing gestures, for reasons that will become clear. In short, there is no a priori reason to exclude facial expressions from consideration as gestures.

Facial expressions are typically described in terms borrowed from the linear message-sending model. In writing about the information carried by some stereotyped primate facial expressions, Parr and colleagues use terms that are by now quite familiar: "The accurate transmission of such information requires that the expressions are stereotypical both within and between individuals, otherwise the signal would become attenuated and information may be lost."[32] In parallel with studies that focus on specific vocalizations or nonvocal gestures as a way to understand encoded meaning, then, in research on facial expressions the unit of analysis is the single "type" of facial expression or the action of individual facial muscles coded quantitatively.[33]

The universality in the production and comprehension of certain facial expression "types" in humans is a major area of research. Ekman has found that 43 muscles in the human face work in combinations to produce 3,000 meaningful facial expressions. Six so-called basic emotional expressions are considered by Ekman to be produced and comprehended in the same way by humans across the globe, in stark contrast to other nonvocal gestures, such as hand movements, that differ dramatically across populations.[34] Other work, ably reviewed by Schmidt and Cohn,[35] emphasizes that human facial expression "types" actually vary significantly both within and across individuals. At one level, it is known that certain facial muscles present in most people are absent in a minority of others, and that some muscles typically insert in one location but may insert elsewhere in a small number of people. Admittedly, this kind of variation may be of primarily anatomical significance. As Schmidt and Cohn point out, it isn't known to what degree these muscular variations result in differing expressions, or if they do, whether human observers would notice or categorize them differently.

What Schmidt and Cohn call "empirically measured facial behavior" varies according to sex, cultural background, and social context. Subjects asked to view a videotape smiled more when they knew that a friend was also watching the tape, even when the friend was in a

different room. Smiles—key indicators to one of the so-called six basic emotional expressions, joy or happiness—may well (like rhesus
scream vocalizations) be a set of gestures that researchers reduce
to one category by convention. We put qualifying adjectives before
the term "smile" as a way to recognize observed variation, as when
smiles with upturned lips at the corners and involvement of eye
muscles are termed "Duchenne smiles" to set them apart from
smiles that lack these features.

Smiles and other facial movements are integrated with other gestures and inseparable from them, a fact underscored by innovative
research. In one study, subjects were asked to view photographs of
people wearing Noh masks, borrowed from traditional Japanese Noh
theater. When the depicted position of the head changed but facial
expression did not, viewers nonetheless perceived a change in facial
expression. Though this finding was consistent across most British and Japanese subjects, differences between the two groups did
emerge. Japanese subjects were, for example, more likely to interpret
a mask tilted at a given angle as happy. Overall, the Japanese viewers were judged able to arrive at more nuanced understandings of
the emotional subtleties presented. Intergroup differences dropped,
however, when the Noh-mask photographs were cropped in order to
excise the upper forehead and chin. Without these whole-face cues
available, Japanese viewers' understanding converged with the British viewers' understanding.[36]

Most contemporary research into human facial expressions involves the notion of basic emotions as reflected in expressions, and
uses static photographs for experimental testing. Research on emotions that is grounded in DST takes a different starting point and
uses different methods, as Greenspan and Shanker make clear. Here
the focus is on the development of emotions within caregiver relationships, with the unit of study being the co-regulated interaction
between a child and the caregiver. Greenspan and Shanker account
for the universality of certain emotions and expressions by pointing

to "common early nurturing relationships that have developed over many eons and are typically present in all human cultures." [37] Their notion that universality *and* variation can be accounted for via cultural practice is a welcome shift from the easy equating of universality and innateness. Discussing what he calls "cultural naturals," de Waal makes a similarly cogent point in noting that culture should be considered within the larger context of how it builds upon, rather than replaces, universal human tendencies. [38]

Little has been done in the realm of research into African great ape facial expressions beyond cataloguing types of expressions across species, and testing, in the laboratory, individuals' perception of certain facial expressions. Only the most global statements can yet be made. Hauser reports that great apes and humans have "a far more intricate" set of facial muscles than other nonhuman primates, then goes on to note that compared to chimpanzees, gorillas have a "relatively impoverished repertoire" of facial expressions. [39] Though the facial muscles of the African great apes apparently do not permit great plasticity in facial expression compared to the same muscles of humans, facial expressions are undeniably one key part of co-regulated communication in all four species. When a chimpanzee infant becomes separated from her mother, for instance, she may make a pout face, in which the lips are protruded in the same way they are during nursing. This facial expression may combine with whimpers, hand extensions, and tense body posture, all of which may shift and ease as the mother once again approaches the infant.

In sum, no clear justification exists for separating either vocalizations or facial expressions from other gestures such as arm extensions, head nods, and gaze following. Theoretically significant, this point serves as an important reminder that nonfacial gestures and body movements are emphasized in this book because of my desire to guide discussion in a certain direction, not because of any inherent hierarchy in what "really counts" as gesture.

Let's move on to the second point about facial expressions, one that will lead us into a key feature of the DST view of social communication generally. In DST, no gesture is defined in relation to intentionality. As already noted, in DST, when muscle movements result in an arm extension, that extension itself is not a social gesture; the movement becomes a social gesture when two partners interact and create meaning from it. Rather than assuming intentionality or trying to measure its presence in some signal, DST relies instead on assessing visible outcomes such as social coordination— or attempted social coordination—between partners. No theorist has made the point more clearly than Christine Johnson in her research with captive bonobos.

Johnson's essay comparing two models of primate cognition is valuable reading for any student of DST.[40] After explaining the mental representation model espoused by Tomasello and Call in their book on primate minds,[41] Johnson outlines an alternative. Called "distributed cognition," this alternative is steeped in DST. Here's Johnson on the importance of visible outcomes rather than mentalistic concepts: "Traditional boundaries of cognition can be expanded to include not only invisible mental processes going on inside each participant's head, but also the observable activities and materials involved in the interactions . . . the social practices that nonhuman primates engage in and observe during their interactions can be taken as the content of *their* distributed cognition . . . The distributed model . . . . assumes that cognition is created through interaction and is manifest in the observable dynamics of the group . . . *Coordination* qualifies as a cognitive event because it characterizes a particular pattern of information flow through the system—i.e., one that promotes a more reliable and efficient engagement."[42]

DST's focus on observable dynamics, with a premium on coordination, frees the social communication researcher from trying to judge whether a gesture is made intentionally or not, and allows concentration on the question of what role the gesture plays in social interaction. This view leads directly to a new question, though. Given this focus on visible outcomes, does it make sense to separate gesture and body movement?

In the category "gesture," I have not included shifts in an individual's limb position or overall posture, or shifts in degree of muscle tension in the body, even when the social partner moves along with, or in response to, these shifts. Clearly these aspects of movement are important for social communication. From my observations of the apes and discussions with skilled staff members at the National Zoo, I learned how to recognize the difference between tense and relaxed body postures in western gorillas.[43] Tense muscles and the oft-photographed stiff-legged, pursed-lips posture of male gorillas often precede and/or accompany their displays and aggression—clues no doubt monitored carefully by fellow gorilla group members. Schaller observed (and photographed) dominant male gorillas who stand still, facing in a certain direction with legs spread, indicating their readiness to travel; other group members join males who adopt this posture.[44]

African great ape infants, over periods of years, cling ventrally to their mothers or press against them for nursing or comfort. In these positions they probably experience directly any shifts in their mother's muscular tension when, for example, dominant social partners approach or tension breaks out in the group. In Chapter 1 I presented details of a gorilla interaction at the National Zoo in which mother Mandara, with infant Kojo riding dorsally, placed herself, standing stiffly, between two tense males. When the large silverback male, Kuja, moved near the mother-infant pair, Mandara leaned away slightly. Kojo, the infant, doubtless felt in his own body the social tension that was reflected in his mother's body.

Persuaded of the fundamental unity of vocalizations and nonvocal gestures, I am suspicious of introducing absolute dichotomies into a DST-based perspective that seeks to illuminate visible outcomes. Originally, when first observing bonobo and gorilla interactions for my gesture work, I tried to operationalize a difference between a social request (a gesture) and a social reach (an attempt to physically contact the partner). Gradually, I began to see that distinctions along these lines may not always be meaningful for the apes themselves, a point brought home to me most vividly when collecting data on the National Zoo gorillas.

On July 25, 2002, at the start of one behavioral sampling period, the youngest infant, Kojo, was riding dorsally on his mother, Mandara. Shortly, Kojo moved off to play alone at a fire hose, an enrichment object on which the gorillas may climb, slide, and play. There, the juvenile male, Ktembe, placed Kojo against his ventrum and walked away. As Mandara followed the pair, Kojo flung an arm out to the side, with the palm laterally extended. This movement did not resemble other arm extensions—those made rather slowly and deliberately, with palm up and a pause after extension—that I have interpreted as potential gestural requests (see Chapter 3). Yet it was not an uncoordinated flail either, the kind that babies make when they are trying to grasp an object or the mother's breast, but lack full motor control. The questions "Gesture or reach? Reach or gesture?" immediately entered my mind.

At this point, Mandara positioned herself near Kojo. In a nicely coordinated way, Kojo moved off Ktembe's ventrum and onto his mother's. On the DST view, I soon realized, Kojo's arm movement was part of the co-regulated social interaction and as such contributed to the communication that was created between mother and baby, leading to the mother's retrieval of the infant. What to label the movement, what Kojo might have intended, and whether Mandara would have acted similarly in the absence of the arm movement are not the key factors. Most important is that the mother *did* act. In this way Kojo may learn that making such movements shifts the ongoing social interaction.

My conclusion is anything but novel. No single "right" answer exists to the question of whether gestures and body movements, or gestures and reaches, should be differentiated. For certain research questions in which dynamic systems theorists take an interest, conflating gestures and other movements into a single metric may carry more costs than benefits. For developmentalists who want to compare children's reaching for social companions and children's request gestures to these social companions, the two types of movements cannot be equated. If we want to tackle issues related to the evolution of language, lumping together all movements will be obscuring rather than useful. When African great ape gestures are iconic, for example, they may have special significance for modeling evolution of language. Iconic gestures trace a path in space that indicates what the social partner is meant to do, as we will see (Chapter 3). Even here, though, room exists for disagreement. Privileging iconic gestures over all movements in modeling the evolution of language may not be the only way to proceed, as I will discuss in Chapter 5.

## Qualitative Research

That human behavior can be illuminated via research that is qualitative rather than quantitative is well accepted by anthropologists, at least those who specialize in sociocultural research.[45] In his text on anthropological methods, Bernard[46] urges students of anthropology to resist dichotomizing qualitative and quantitative research; no research program, he writes, should be thought of as aligned with one of these to the exclusion of the other. Whereas certain methods of data-processing (let's say, regression analysis) are quantitative, *all* analysis and interpretation are inherently qualitative in that they involve ideas about meaning.

Yet the degree to which qualitative research is embraced or favored may vary significantly within anthropology. Bernard's claim that descriptive notes are the meat and potatoes of field work probably resonates more with sociocultural anthropologists than with anthropologically trained primatologists, who tend to favor statistical analyses and use descriptive note-taking only in restricted contexts. Ethnographers routinely publish works that describe actions, events, and beliefs in particular regions, towns, or clusters of households, without relying heavily, or in some cases at all, on numerical summations and statistical treatments. Research of this nature may be based not only on observations and interviews, supplemented by archival-historical research, but also on the experience of living among the people in question.

At times the focus in such work may be very fine-grained. As its title implies, Marjorie Shostak's *Nisa: The Life and Words of a !Kung Woman* focused on one middle-aged woman living in a hunter-gatherer group in Botswana's Kalahari Desert. Based on extensive interviews, and written so that Nisa's is the primary voice recounting her own life history, the book became a classic. As Meredith Small wrote in 2001, "I doubt there is a single anthropology or women's study student in the past two decades who hasn't been assigned this book."[47] The scholarly and popular praise for *Nisa* reflects the fact that through focus on a single, articulate woman, Shostak was able to convey larger truths about life in hunter-gatherer societies.

Eighteen years after her first interviews with Nisa in 1971, and eight years after the book's publication, Shostak returned to Botswana and found Nisa once again. Nisa was now old, and Shostak herself was struggling with cancer. After this latter period of field work, Shostak once again wrote a book, this time in her own voice. She mixed memoir with an analysis of the shifts in her renewed friendship with Nisa, and in !Kung life as a whole, as these hunter-gatherers increasingly faced pressures from other cultures and ways of life.[48]

Though the status of *Nisa*, Shostak's first book, is exceptional within anthropology, the basic approach used by Shostak is not. Two works by Jean Briggs, one titled *Never in Anger: Portrait of an Eskimo Family*, and the other *Inuit Morality Play: The Emotional Education of a Three-Year-Old*, are similarly intimate in focus. In them, Briggs explores the emotional patterning between adults and children among groups of Canadian forager peoples.

What Briggs writes about her research is enlightening. In the introduction to *Never in Anger*, published in 1970 after 17 months' field work among the Utkuhikhalingmiut (or "the Utku"), she explains that she focused on a few individuals who "illustrate exceptionally well in their relationships . . . the points to be made concerning the patterning of emotion." Further, "I could never write the same book again, nor could any other observer have written exactly the same book."[49] Briggs thus readily acknowledges what primatologists would call her "small sample size" as well as temporal and spatial limitations on her conclusions about the Utku. She wrote about certain persons living in one place at a specific point in time that cannot be revisited or recaptured.

By looking at Briggs's second book, we can see that her qualitative perspective in *Never in Anger* cannot be explained solely by recourse to conventions of American anthropology in the late 1960s. Indeed, twenty-eight years later, in 1998, the focus in *Inuit Morality Play* has become even more intimate. Now she writes about emotional interactions during a 6-month period in the life of one girl, whom she calls Chubby Maata. And Briggs confronts even more directly her reasons for doing so. "The trouble is that when all the rich detail of individual lives, the essence of individuality, is left out, our ability to understand these lives is greatly reduced . . . the more detailed my analysis of *one* event, enacted on *one* occasion with *one* child, the broader and richer becomes my vision."[50]

Of course, as is true with Shostak's work with Nisa, ethnographers may write in this way with the underlying aim of identifying patterns in the larger societies to which the described individuals, families, and households belong. Fredrik Barth makes the critical point that when sociocultural anthropologists summarize behavioral patterns within groups, *without* individualizing the focus or attending fully to the great variation present, they run the risk of prefiguring the theoretical questions that they may ask. "For if the lives of particular Nuer and Tallensi," Barth asks, "are diverse histories of nonconformity and improvisation, how could a set of norms describe, much less explain, the forms of those lives?"[51]

Of central importance to the study of African great ape as well as human behavior, Barth's concern leads him to conclude that anthropology should no longer accept theoretical frameworks that depict only stereotyped patterns and determined results, and instead must systematize available methodologies for recording variation.[52] This sort of discussion, as well as dialogues sparked by the discipline-rocking impact of post-modernism, seem to pervade sociocultural anthropology with little prolonged debate about a prior question: whether qualitative research, decoupled from quantitative research, may be of value.[53]

Quite different is the situation in other disciplines devoted to the study of human behavior, psychology perhaps chief among them. Fish goes so far as to claim that the use of all qualitative, field, and descriptive methodologies are disparaged within psychology. The acceptability of one's methods in psychological research, he says, is determined not by the research question, but by their similarity to the methods of "hard" sciences such as physics.[54] I am in no position to assess the state of affairs within psychology as it studies human behavior, except to note that Fish underestimates the power of holistic approaches within his field. Scholars like Alan Fogel, Esther Thelen, Stanley Greenspan, and Uri Bronfenbrenner have used antireductionist models to study human behavior from within psychology for many years.[55]

A recent book by the psychologists Rumbaugh and Washburn suggests that holistic methods, including qualitative methods, are now under serious consideration within comparative as well as human psychology. Writing about the cognition of monkeys and apes, Rumbaugh and Washburn give compelling evidence for what they call emergent forms of behavior: "skills, abilities and competencies

[that] have no specific histories of reinforcement or experience, but rather take form in response to generalized classes of experience."[56] Though such new skills may seem to emerge magically, in reality they "entail the syntheses of individually acquired responses and experiences" by the animals, especially great apes, and "frequently reflect rearing conditions or early experience."[57] Much of their analysis is compatible with a DST view, though DST would of course stress co-constructed rather than *individually* acquired responses. The key point is that emergent forms of behavior cannot, as Rumbaugh and Washburn make clear, be studied only quantitatively: "If we blend experiences obtained from interactions with chimpanzees and empirical data obtained by scientific methods, we become able to 'listen to a chimpanzee' even thought it doesn't speak."[58] Rumbaugh and Washburn focus on laboratory situations where humans and great apes may interact, but would, as I read them, agree that long-term qualitative study of spontaneous behaviors between the chimpanzees themselves is a legitimate "scientific method."

Let's move now to the situation regarding research methods in primatology generally. Historical analysis shows that several sea changes have characterized American and European primatology over its short life span.[59] Strum and Fedigan consider "the first clear images of primate society"[60] to have emerged in the 1930s with studies by Solly Zuckerman and C. R. Carpenter. After a period steeped in a natural-history mode, with its heavy reliance on description, primatologists avidly embraced a move toward quantification. A push factor here was the emergence of sociobiological theory in the late 1970s, which ushered in an era of "tightly constructed predictions amenable to quantitative testing using behavioral data."[61] Enthrallment with sociobiological reductionism has diminished in the last fifteen or so years. Primary theoretical perspectives in primatology today are behavioral ecology, in which evolutionary principles are applied to survival and reproductive behavior, and cognitive ethology, in which issues related to intelligence are investigated. The question is whether the concomitant focus on quantification has shifted in any way as the strict genetic determinism of sociobiology has fallen out of favor.

Strum and Fedigan say that behavioral ecology and cognitive ethology, just like sociobiology, require quantitative data.[62] Yet at the beginning of a new century, it seems to me there's a fascinating split in the works: In some specific areas of inquiry within primatology, the trend toward quantification is intensifying, whereas in others the field may be experiencing a shift toward readier acceptance of qualitative research. Once explored a bit, this idea leads directly to the role of DST in studying African great ape social communication.

Historical generalizations can easily prove too sweeping, and certainly prominent examples of qualitative research in American and European primatology from the 1980s or 1990s can be found. Doubtless the best known of these are Jane Goodall's life-history studies that compare individual mothering styles at Gombe. Goodall draws detailed portraits of the maternal behavior shown by various chimpanzees she knew well and followed for years; she is able to note the effect of differing maternal styles on the next generation because her research has been longitudinal.[63] Several lines of analysis, however, suggest that this type of research, on its own, has been valued less by primatologists than has quantitative work on its own, or qualitative research that is used to supplement the primary quantitative data.

First, when primatologists cite Goodall's work, they often select her most quantitative account.[64] Scientific convention demands that scholarly rather than popular sources be cited, an opposition that often reduces to the difference between quantitative and qualitative sources. Goodall freely admits she was pushed to be more "scientific"—quantitative—in her approach to studying chimpanzees; she derived statistical summaries of various chimpanzee behaviors at least in part to satisfy this requirement.[65]

Second, though primatology graduate students in the West, whether from biological anthropology, psychology, zoology, or some other field, are trained to test specific hypotheses and to tailor their methodologies to their research questions, their tutoring has generally unfolded within a quantitative context. Qualitative work may be encouraged as the initial step in research projects, a step that allows students to "get to know" their animals. Qualitative accounts are produced in Western primatology, then, primarily in either the initial stages of research or as part of attempts to motivate people to care about (and fund) scientific research. The sense one gets is that quantification represents the "real" science.

A third factor involves the long history of Western skepticism toward the type of qualitative research traditionally prized by Japanese primatologists. Asquith notes that primatological papers written for Japanese-language journals tend to be far more descriptive than those written in English-language venues, which suggests that the Japanese strategically tailor their output for particular audiences. Even so, Japanese scientists complain that their descriptive passages are too often excised or drastically cut by Western editors. This situation may continue given that Japanese graduate students are now encouraged to publish only in English, though equally the Japanese qualitative traditions may be yielding to a push for quantification.[66]

Qualitative research can be defined by no single approach. It may, of course, be poorly done, and amount to little more than a series of jotted-down impressions and a "great many boxes of unused (and probably unusable. . .) data."[67] When Strum says that she values description *and* wants to move beyond it—beyond the case study of behavior in some nonhuman primate—in order to "to build out from the local," she precisely identifies the key challenges of producing excellent qualitative work.[68] The paths taken to "build out" may be diverse. Depending on the scientist's interests and abilities, qualitative data may generate pattern description; may elucidate variation through detailed and rigorous comparison of the diverse ways that behavior unfolds in broadly similar contexts; and may lead to new questions and hypotheses. Thorny questions are inescapable when one is traveling these paths, including how much variation across specific examples is allowable in the identification of a behavioral pattern; in what ways may the expression of behavior by a few individuals link to the nature of behavior as expressed in the population as a whole; and how the occurrence of unusual or extreme behaviors broadens our understanding of the range of behaviors on which natural selection may work.

Underneath these challenges lies the beauty of the qualitative approach, the opportunity to preserve what can only be called, indeed, the *quality* of interactions: those factors that do not reduce to numbers. The tenderness, intensity, hesitation, or power with which primates act with their social partners is restored to them in the qualitative approach. Atypical behaviors are not classed as outliers or reduced to variation around a numerical mean. Quantitative research is necessary in order to test some hypotheses, a fact that any primatologist must appreciate in order to sort out which methods are appropriate in which circumstances. Equally true is that quantitative research can elide the quality and variation inherent in behavior. It may produce a profile of a decidedly mythic "average animal," informing us not at all about the nonconformity and improvisation of which the social anthropologist Barth has written.

Ultimately, since the choice of qualitative or quantitative methods is so tied to the research question, we find ourselves back at Bernard's original point: opposing the two methods by asking which one is better overall is as fruitless as discussing whether some human behavioral trait is innate or learned. When some of that oppositional flavor is still encountered in primatology, the results are disappointing. Sometimes, those who employ thoughtful qualitative methods face the risk of having their reports dismissed as "only anecdotal." Though the use of anecdotes in primatological research has been thoughtfully explored, most notably in a collection edited by Mitchell, Thompson, and Miles,[69] the distinction between anecdotal and qualitative research has not.

Contributors to Mitchell's volume, to be sure, express different ideas about what constitutes an anecdote and how useful anecdotes might be in attaining scientific understanding of animal behavior. In an introduction, the three editors write that "anecdotes," for comparative psychologists, usually refer to descriptions in narrative form of unique or infrequent behaviors. Writing individually, though, the senior editor, Mitchell, notes that for him, anecdotalism is specifically the *psychological* interpretation of an animal's actions.[70] Byrne distinguishes between the single observation made by an inexperienced observer, or "the anecdote" in common parlance, and the observation by an experienced and trained observer, or what he terms "the record."[71]

Byrne's distinction is useful, but still does not move us fully into the realm of qualitative research. Notice how Byrne sums up his contribution: "The approach of this chapter, using a scheme for sorting evidence, is intended to enable a proper scientific treatment of the rather messy but potentially important data that result from collecting good but unsystematic observations of rare behaviors."[72] What about good and systematic—but qualitative—observations of routine behaviors? Byrne notes that a "record" probably will inspire testing about the observed phenomenon via systematic, controlled observation or experiment. Presumably he includes qualitative sampling methods as part of "systematic, controlled observations," but widespread conversation on this topic doesn't seem to be taking place in primatology.[73]

Occasionally, systematically derived qualitative data are conflated with anecdotes. Some years ago, I was profiled in a scientific magazine, along with three other primatologists, in an article about interdisciplinary research into nonhuman primate behavior. I described to the interviewer my qualitative methods for collecting data on social communication in captive bonobos, only to read later in print: "Data is [sic] something of a sore point with Barbara King."[74] I had, in fact, said (and this was also quoted) that feeling pushed to collect *quantitative data* for my work had been a concern.

Egregious dismissal of qualitative work may be on the decline. Increasingly, it is recognized that some vital areas in primatological research cry out for systematic qualitative data. Primate cognition is a good example. In many situations too few events occur to be subject to statistical analysis: when monkey or ape individuals use or construct tools in an innovative way; show evidence of deceiving others, an ability likely to prove effective only when performed rarely (otherwise leading to a "Cry wolf" syndrome); or react intelligently to rare events such as the death of a close companion at the hand of predators, an unusually aggressive intercommunity encounter, or complex cooperative hunt of a prey species. Quantitative treatment, in any case, would leach the accounts of their most telling details.

Numerous primatologists, in their scholarly work on primate cognition, include rich qualitative descriptions that, to my mind, go beyond anecdotalism. When Frans de Waal writes about power struggles and politics in captive male chimpanzees,[75] and about culture in animals more generally,[76] or when Sue Savage-Rumbaugh and colleagues detail the processes by which the captive bonobo Kanzi came to understand and produce symbolic utterances,[77] they rely on systematic qualitative research (sometimes in addition to quantitative research), not on single observations loosely strung together. Another example is Boesch and Boesch-Achermann, whose book on the Tai chimpanzees (already mentioned in Chapter 1) presents a high-quality mix of quantitative and qualitative data.

Boesch and Boesch-Achermann offer lengthy case studies, and even discuss the personalities of various chimpanzees. They include a report of the community's reaction to the death of a juvenile female chimpanzee, Tina, during a leopard attack.[78] This report is stunning in its implications for chimpanzee emotional life as well as chimpanzee cognition. Chimpanzees attended Tina's body constantly for over 6 hours. They pulled on Tina's limbs, and groomed her body. They did not attempt to groom her wounds, a deviation from their behavior with wounded and bleeding, but living, companions. Most strikingly, the only infant allowed to inspect and groom the body was Tarzan, the dead chimpanzee's 5-year-old brother; as he was doing so, and pulling on Tina's hand gently, the dominant male, Brutus, chased away from Tina an unrelated adult female and her juvenile daughter.

Tina and Tarzan had lost their mother about 4 months earlier. We can only guess at the precise emotions felt by Tarzan as he touched and groomed his sister, who had died so shortly after his mother. What's beyond doubt is that his social companions recognized in some way his association with, and bonds to, his sister, just as they made a distinction between an organism that is totally motionless, and one that is wounded but still breathing. Is this event properly called "an anecdote"? Boesch and Boesch-Achermann label it so. Perhaps they are right, though Byrne would ask them to use "record" instead. They have no other comparable observations from Tai, and other hour-by-hour detailed descriptions of social behavior surrounding death are rare, at best, for chimpanzees and indeed for African great apes generally. In the context of their book, woven as it is into the conclusions derived from case studies and statistics, it is a meaningful product of careful research, whatever it is labeled. It will prod other field researchers to remain with their study groups for hours after a dead body is discovered, to observe the events surrounding the death, and to ask new questions about them.

Boesch and Boesch-Achermann supply, in this same volume, statistics about party composition of chimpanzees, dominance behavior in males, and other topics that would be understood much less thoroughly and accurately without a quantitative approach. Yet we should not conclude that the optimal solution is *inevitably* to marry, in a single study or publication, qualitative and quantitative data, the one reinforcing the other. Though striving for balance in this way may sometimes be the optimal approach, no reason exists to consider it so a priori. With this statement, we can finally return to DST, for my research is predicated on the notion that qualitative methods alone work well for studying the contingency and unpredictability in African great ape nonvocal social communication.

My main goal in pursuing qualitative research on African great apes is to assess whether and when co-regulated social interactions mediated by gesture and body movement result in coordinated social behavior within dyads, families, or social groups. In order to do this, I must be able to record aspects of the contingency and unpredictability that mark the unfolding interactions. What's required is a method sensitive to coordination and miscoordination, as has been discussed. The rigor of the work thus emerges not through tallying instances of contingency and unpredictability but through demonstrating the nature of unfolding, mutually continuous adjustments as they vary from social event to social event.[79] For my research questions, the work required is qualitative at *all* stages, not just the initial one; without it, the very phenomena of interest would be missed.

Various data-collection processes have proven of use to me in going about this qualitative work. Of primary importance is videotaping, since filmed records can be viewed countless times, and repeated viewings allow one to notice and study dance-like contingent movements as the social partners act together. Filming the infants that are my subjects can be thought of as a type of focal-animal sampling,[80] since the camera focuses on each infant in turn for a predetermined amount of time. Any behaviors generated by the infant or social interactions in which he participates are captured. During the sampling period, interactions that exclude the focal infant are ignored, unless an exceptional event occurs, such as a major outbreak of fighting between two other apes. Should the infant sleep, rest quietly, or go out of sight for a prolonged time, I may prematurely end that sample and shift to filming another infant instead.

Similar rules of priority mark a second type of data collection, on-paper event sampling, during which detailed data are taken of any social interactions in which subject infants participate. In this case, the observer does not shift the focus from one to another infant successively, but instead scans the group for relevant social events that include one of the infants, then focuses on these as they unfold. Probably unworkable in larger groups, this method has succeeded in families with only one or two infants. Collecting data from filmed records is still preferable; in dealing with fleeting interactions among multiple animals, it is impossible for the human eye to note all contingencies as they unfold in real time.

These methods show that my research is systematic, but not that it is qualitative. What makes my research qualitative is not the act of filming or of taking event samples on paper; these methods may be used in quantitative work as well. Only with data transcription and analysis does the significant qualitative aspect enter the picture. In describing all the mutual adjustments, coordinations, and miscoordinations between social partners via gestures and body movements, I aim for rich description of multiple social events over years and years of infants' lives. Patterns and variation in those patterns, across infants and within the infants that are studied longitudinally, can then be identified. I can show not only how infants come to participate in creating gesture through social interaction but also how the quality of the co-regulation in which they take part shifts over time and across different social partners.

Many behavioral research projects on nonhuman primates now utilize digital video recording, and an array of exciting options exists for carrying out microanalysis of the data. In research on triadic interactions in a captive group of seven bonobos, Johnson and Oswald analyzed a sample of 16 video segments. They explain, "we recorded all changes, at 1/6 second intervals, in relative trajectory, relative body and head orientation (open, peripheral or closed to another animal), and whenever possible, gaze. We also recorded the source, timing and duration of social interactions (groom, aggress, etc.) that occurred in those segments." Results of the microanalysis were represented along time-lines. Further, "transitional probabilities for a change in any one of Animal A's dimensions being immediately followed by a change in any one of Animal B's dimensions ('triggering'), and for simultaneous changes ('syncs'), were computed for each dyad."[81] Johnson and Oswald thus bring together qualitative and quantitative methods in their microanalysis. In this, they depart from my own approach, but share with me an interest in describing how individual African great apes' movements are part of a system, so that change in one part of the system causes changes in other parts.

Room exists in the study of African great ape social communication for my approach and for Johnson and Oswald's. Cross-fertilization may come from sources as disparate as agent-based modeling[82] or family systems therapy,[83] as well as from the DST-engendered approaches to children's development that are sprinkled throughout this book. If questions about co-regulated social communication become increasingly recognized as important, a shift in the study of primate communication may parallel the change already visible in the study of primate cognition, where qualitative research is increasingly valued. The idea that qualitative research may be fruitful outside the contexts of preliminary research or popular accounts for the public may be relatively radical for primatology, but it is helpful to remember that it is an unremarkable one in some other fields. Having started this section on qualitative research with a foray into sociocultural anthropology, I will conclude it by looking at some of the historical antecedents of DST in that field and others, and by considering once again how DST in its various applications differs from interactionism.

## Theoretical Links, Linear and Otherwise

Within sociocultural anthropology, historical roots of DST are perhaps discernible in the work of theorists, including A. R. Radcliffe-Brown in the 1950s, who wrote about human societies using the concept of networks.[84] For a DST theorist, though, the clearest chords of recognition may be struck by reading the words of Gregory Bateson in his *Steps to an Ecology of Mind*. By referring to the thinking and acting human as a *"system* whose boundaries do not at all coincide with the boundaries either of the body or of what is popularly called 'the self' or 'consciousness,'" Bateson describes the embedding of a person within a larger dynamic system that includes all other organisms, nonliving things, and even pathways of sound and light. [85] His most famous example shows that when a man uses an axe to chop down a tree, the relevant unit of analysis is "the total system, tree-eyes-brain-muscles-axe-stroke-tree."[86]

The British social anthropologist Tim Ingold contrasts the views of Bateson with those of Claude Lévi-Strauss, the famous structural anthropologist, using terms immediately recognizable to readers of this chapter. As contemporaries, Bateson and Levi-Strauss set out to question the accepted division between mind and nature that was so ingrained in social science in the 1960s and 1970s. There, the overlap ends, as Ingold illustrates by detailing two major points of contrast. For Levi-Strauss, the mind equaled the brain, and ecology referred to the external world. For Bateson, understanding the mind and ecology could only be accomplished through study of the relationship between the brain and the environment. Further, for Levi-Strauss, "the perceiver could only have knowledge of the world by virtue of a passage of information across the boundary between outside and inside, involving successive steps of encoding and decoding by the sense organs and the brain."[87] Bateson, of course, recognized no such boundary; he thought of information as created by the perceiver as he or she acted in the world. In the way units of study are conceived, either atomistically or in relation, and in the way information is viewed, either as transmitted-and-decoded or as socially created, the scholarly differences between Levi-Strauss and Bateson map nicely onto the differences between the information-processing and the dynamic systems views of social communication.

Ingold's own work[88] beautifully illustrates how a Batesonian kind of relational thinking can produce new insights into human behavior. Human beings, for Ingold, must not be seen as amalgams of the biological and the cultural, with the psychological as some sort of intervening cement. Referring to humans as biocultural is for Ingold no marker of intellectual progress. Doing so may avoid the suggestion that humans are either primarily biological or primarily cultural, but the term "biocultural" is wholly inadequate still, because it parses individuals in unacceptable ways. Humans are at once organisms and persons, in Ingold's terms, and cannot be divided further.

Where this theoretical position produces maximal dividends is in Ingold's analysis of the role of skills in human life. Ingold refers to the whole person, body and mind together, in defining skills as the capabilities of action and perception of a person situated in his environment. Skills, being what they are, cannot be transmitted from person to person, or even from generation to generation. Rather, skills are *regrown* in each generation. When young Telefol girls in New Guinea learn to make string bags, for instance, their skills develop at a time when their bodies are experiencing rapid growth. "These skills, then, far from being added on to a preformed body, actually grow with it. In that regard they are fully part and parcel of the human organism, of its neurology, musculature, even anatomy, and so are as much biological as cultural."[89] This perspective is a useful one for considering the ontogeny of skills in any slowly developing, highly social species, including the African great apes. The gorilla infants I watch, in other words, do not in Ingold's view acquire gestural skills; their gestural skills grow with their bodies as those bodies increasingly participate in varied forms of co-regulated social events.

Citing among his influences the work of scholars outside anthropology, primarily that of James Gibson on perception, Ingold reminds us that theoretical links flow not only vertically through time but also horizontally across disciplines. I have already noted the enormous influence of psychologists such as Fogel on the study of co-regulation in human-child communication. From the perspective

of linguistics, Goodwin shows that conversation between social partners is mutually constructed, so that a speaker literally reshapes a
sentence as his audience shifts gaze or makes other minute adjustments in response. The speaker may restart an utterance, insert
breaks, and add unplanned segments as the partner acts, so that the
sentence itself should be seen as a collaborative product.[90]

Ever since Vygotsky, a minority of scholars interested in human
learning and problem-solving have looked beyond the individual as
the unit of analysis. The work of Hutchins demonstrates that people
may solve navigation tasks *as a group,* in advance of any of the individual participants coming to recognize the solution. Hutchins considers as part of a system not only the group itself but also the
group's interaction with artifacts (tools, including diagrams and
charts, for example). As Hutchins puts it in his study of navigational
skills in the U.S. Navy, "The cognitive properties of the navigation
team are at least twice removed from those of the individual members: first as a result of the transforming effects of the interactions
with the tools of the trade, and second, as a result of the social organization of distributed cognition."[91] That Hutchins chose the word
"transforming" is particularly telling for recognizing links between
his views and DST. The contingency and unpredictability of social
interaction come across clearly in both Hutchins's work and
Goodwin's.

Reflecting on what is shared among scholars who practice DST, or
a historical antecedent of it, encourages revisiting a fundamental
point: DST differs in its emphases from interactionism. This distinction is especially critical when one is considering work in primatology, where interactionism is identifiable much more frequently
than is DST, but where, at times, the two are mistakenly conflated.[92]
While it is common enough for primatologists to talk about reciprocity, the sender affecting the receiver (and vice versa), or even interactional synchrony, less attention has been given to the ever-chang-
ing and transformative internal relations among parts of a social

system, as in co-regulation. As Fogel reminds us, interactionists, even when studying social relationships, focus on the individual as the unit of analysis; those who embrace co-regulation look at social relating and social engagement as the unit of analysis.[93]

The implications of this difference can be seen even in the work of interactionists who venture outside the strict information-processing model when analyzing animal social communication. Most influential here is Robert Hinde, who has written with brilliant clarity about social relationships in nonhuman primates and other animals. In assessing animal social signals, Hinde ascribes to both actors and receivers (I am using Hinde's terms) a great deal of active adjustment to others' behavior and to the prevailing social context. He urges that we think of signals in terms of negotiation, as in this passage about the threat displays of birds: "Threat displays would be useful only in moments of indecision: if what the signaler A should do depended in part on the subsequent behavior of B, threatening by A might elicit a response from B that would permit a decision by A. Such a view is in harmony with the protracted duels shown in some species . . . It supposes that the displays do not predict *either* attack *or* stay, but that they predict either attack-or-stay or flee-or-stay."[94]

For Hinde, contrary to the tenets of DST, the signaler's internal state is an important consideration, but the reactor's response is integral as well. He envisions a signaling continuum that remains unrecognized by the information-processing model: "At the extremes, expressive signals are broadcast independently of the presence of a receiver, whilst signals used in negotiation appear in intimate interactions and are directed with respect to the recipient, depending in part on his behaviour."[95] Hinde isn't alone in theorizing outside the box of information-processing in animal studies. In what they call an assessment-manager approach, Owings and Morton,[96] too, give greater weight to active behavior on the part of the signal's receiver than does the typical information-processing approach. In their formulation, Owren and Rendall even write about emergence when they describe the "complex interactive process" that is animal social communication: "Information does not literally reside in the energy of a signal, but represents an emergent property of the combined attributes of the individual producing the signal, the individual perceiving the signal, and the circumstances under which the signal is emitted."[97]

Like Hinde's, these two scenarios are welcome because they move the study of primate social communication beyond the transmitting and decoding of signals. Even while I recognize this fact, my intent is to underscore the ways these approaches diverge from DST's focus on constructed meaning-making and co-regulation. Hinde refers to his own position as interactionist,[98] a term I would use to characterize, as well, the formulations of Owings and Morton, and Owren and Rendall. About primate vocal communication, for instance, Owren and Rendall write: "The individual that is dominant in a given encounter inherently has greater control over the outcome of this interaction than does the other. As a result, the dominant animal can routinely pair its calls with other actions that elicit significant unconditioned affective responses in the subordinate. Such pairings produce conditioning, which the caller can thereafter use to elicit learned affective responses in this other animal in both affiliative and agonistic circumstances. The subordinate individual has less opportunity to shape the outcome of an interaction."[99] This passage, together with the other interactionist ideas discussed here, emphasizes how individual B may affect animal A's signaling, and vice versa, and how the relative roles of A and B may shift with social context, but leaves aside (or never recognizes in the first place) the question of how the social unit AB may create meaning.

Emphasis on the individual is as clearly seen in empirical as in theoretical analysis within primatological interactionism. Slavoff microanalyzed the videotaped behaviors of capuchin monkeys, with focus on changes in body positions, muscle movements, nonverbal gestures, and so forth. Rejecting the idea of social communication as information exchange in turn-taking, Slavoff instead considered the flow of information as a continuous variable. Her goal was to assess the degree to which each monkey entrained, or adapted his or her movement, to another. A close look at the language she used when interpreting a representative result is revealing: "Troop members entrain their movements to the most dominant animals in the group. The dominant male and female in this troop were highly coupled in their spontaneous movements about their home cage."[100] This research is interactionist; "synchrony" in this work means that one animal maps its movements onto another as the two interact. Left unconsidered is the full potential for contingency and unpredictability: for co-regulation when social partners act with each other.

Although I think it unlikely to be correct, one reasonable hypothesis is that capuchin monkeys simply do not exhibit much contingency or unpredictability in their social communication. Given this possibility, let's turn briefly to research that will be assessed more completely in Chapter 5, the study of African great ape language, or language-like, skills. This line of inquiry has been singularly effective at conveying the power of nonhuman primate social communication and socioemotionality. African great apes trained in, or enculturated with, human symbol systems such as American Sign Language or lexigrams on computer keyboards have shown beyond doubt that they understand and produce aspects of human language. Integral to this approach is recognition of the importance of social bonds and social context in the development of language, but co-regulation itself has rarely been studied by ape-language researchers.[101]

When Patterson writes about her success in training the gorilla Koko to use aspects of American Sign Language in conversation with humans, she uses the term "interactional synchrony"[102] to emphasize that Koko and her partners participated in coordinated ways as they conversed. Use of this term, as we have seen, reveals a focus on one social partner acquiring signs from another and sequential exchange between partners, hallmarks of the research with Koko.[103]

Ape-language research is fertile ground for going further and assessing the unpredictability and contingency of interspecies social communication. Working with the chimpanzee Washoe and her social companions, Jensvold and Gardner nicely demonstrate the use to which a focus on contingency in ASL conversations can be put.[104]

With this background in DST and the ways in which it differs from interactionism, it's time now to consider in detail the research on African great ape social communication, both qualitative and quantitative, and begin to evaluate the fit between the data and DST's claims about co-regulation. In the following two chapters, I present data in order to assess the presence and nature of co-regulation in African great ape social communication. Because the intricate processes of contingency and unpredictability are more readily identifiable in fine-grained work on captive populations than in most field work, I will start with presentation of the data on captive African apes in Chapter 3 and then move, in Chapter 4, to data on wild African great apes.

# 3

## Gesture in Captive African Great Apes

T HOUGH rarely intersecting with the concept of co-regulation or related ideas from DST, the history of primatological interest in gesture among captive great apes is long and fascinating. Mitchell[1] reminds current primatologists that previous generations of great ape observers provided, as early as 1800, a fountain of information about social gesture, as well as about other aspects of great ape communication and cognition. That some of these accounts deserve serious attention is brought home forcefully by publication of the first English translation of a book that appeared, in Russian, almost seventy years ago.

In 1935, Nadezhda Ladygina-Kohts published a long monograph detailing the communication, intelligence, and emotions of a chimpanzee, comparing them to those of her son.[2] Ladygina-Kohts, well known within the Soviet Union for her work in comparative psychology, had purchased the chimpanzee, Joni, from an animal trader in Moscow. She observed him closely from 1913 to 1916, when he died at the age of 4 from a respiratory illness. Keeping an amazingly detailed diary of the ape's behavior, Ladygina-Kohts noted that Joni had "developed a series of gestures and body movements that cater to the expression of his desires."[3]

Joni made social requests to people by extending one hand forward, or in the case of heightened emotion, by extending both hands and vocalizing; a single extended hand might also form a point toward an object desired by Joni. Offered food that he didn't want, Joni would shake his head. The ape's whole-body posture varied significantly according to his emotional states, ranging from joy to depression. A joyous chimpanzee, wrote Ladygina-Kohts, has arms and legs in endless movement, touching and slapping at various objects as he goes. When initially sad, a chimpanzee extends his arm for help in a pleading gesture, but when he becomes depressed, he may form his body into a kind of hump, sitting "motionlessly and mournfully."[4] Vocalizations, ranging from grunts, hoots, and laughs to groans and screams, may accompany the chimpanzee's actions in different contexts.

Richly emphasized by Ladygina-Kohts are the chimpanzee facial expressions that she thought underlie eight "mental conditions": general excitability, sadness, joy, anger, fear, repulsion, surprise, and attention. What's striking is not only the level of detail Ladygina-Kohts offers in describing the mobility of the chimpanzee face in each particular condition,[5] but also her insistence that any given facial expression is unlikely to reduce to a single emotion. Dual explanations of the meaning of facial expressions are often needed, as offered by Ladygina-Kohts in the following representative example, recorded when Joni was shown a dead hare.

After initially exhibiting fear at the sight of the hare, and upon recognizing that no aggressive response was forthcoming from the dead animal, Joni began to attack. "In the end, his attack was fairly amiable, and the expression of his mouth clearly reflected this. The corners of his mouth were stretched into a smile, as in joy; his mouth was half-open, but characteristically, his lower teeth and canines were exposed, as in the initial phases of the angry mood. Attacking in such a manner, Joni probably was not quite sure of his safety, and these elements of fear [are] the reason why the configuration of his upper lip was reminiscent of a position characteristic of the initial phases of fear, particularly of timidity."[6]

From the high quality of this reporting about gestures and body movements, it is clear why Ladygina-Kohts's "primatological master-piece"[7] was first excerpted in English by Robert Yerkes in his 1929 book *The Great Apes,* and recently made fully available in English. The value of Ladygina-Kohts's observations for understanding great apes is evident, but they raise many questions echoed in more recent research into captive African great ape social communication. How much of Joni's gestures and body movements were influenced by her close association with Ladygina-Kohts, other humans, and the objects in his enriched environment? Does the captive environment distort the natural behavior of the animal, making suspect any conclusions derived from observing animals in captivity? Do we learn anything of value about chimpanzees from close study of one or a few captive chimpanzees at a time?

In this chapter, I first discuss, using the questions posed above as a springboard, the value of including captive great apes in research on social communication. From there, I go on to review data from major studies of spontaneous gesture and body movement by group-living captive African great apes. Data from my own work on captive gorillas and bonobos constitute a sizable chunk of the chapter. Because here I wish to highlight only spontaneous social communication among group-living apes, studies that feature African great apes communicating primarily with humans, whether under enculturated or experimental conditions, are considered later, in Chapter 5. To the degree allowed by each researcher's methodology, I focus on the degree of unpredictability and contingency in gesture and body movement; my goal is to evaluate not only the presence but also the quality of co-regulation in captive African great ape social communication.

## Questions of Captivity

Though it is easy enough to dichotomize "the wild" and "captivity" as the two alternative settings in which African great apes may live, in fact these creatures reside in diverse contexts, some not easily

summed up by a simple label.[8] Free-ranging African great apes may
be fortunate enough to live in relatively undisturbed or protected
habitats, without direct human interference. But such areas are now
rare and increasingly under threat. Others may live in the wild but
under pressure from encroaching humans or human populations.
At one end of a continuum in this category are populations provisioned for research purposes; at the extreme opposite end are those
populations living under severe pressures from logging, poaching,
and the bushmeat trade, in which animals are killed and eaten for
food.

Captive African great apes may be housed in large, lush, relatively
naturalistic habitats in accredited zoos, or in single, small cages in
poorly managed roadside zoos. Enculturated apes typically live not in
zoos but out of the public eye, in uniquely enriched research centers.
Still other African great apes reside in orphanages and sanctuaries,
some focusing on eventual rehabilitation and release to the wild and
some trying to offer permanent safe haven. Finally, some African
great apes are kept in biomedical laboratories, where they are used in
research related to human health and disease.

Given this array of possible living conditions and the stresses
within each, clear pronouncements about what is "more natural" or
"better" for African great apes, and about behavioral research upon
these apes, are difficult to make. Noting that life in a protected area,
or an area remote from people, is the best possible option for chimpanzees, Jane Goodall goes on to say: "Nevertheless, when compared
with the life of chimpanzees living in danger zones of Africa, it
sometimes seems to me that those in the really good zoos—those in
which there are large enclosures, rich social groups, and an enriched
environment—may in fact be better off."[9] Such a view, expressed by
the world's preeminent field researcher of chimpanzees, is surprising only to those unaware of the full array of dangers facing great
apes in the wild today, particularly from the bushmeat trade (see
Chapter 6).[10]

By no means do all primatologists agree with Goodall, however.

Fouts urges the zoo community to work toward the eventual aboli-
tion of zoos. In his vision, zoos would change their mission entirely:
"[Zoos] would turn their exhibits into sanctuaries where the needs of
the individual ape would come first and public education and hu-
mane nonmanipulative, noninvasive scientific study would be secondary."[11]

What does this controversy mean for research on captive apes?
Most behavioral research on African great apes takes place in good,
science-friendly zoos or in noninvasive (nonbiomedical) research
centers. Should the concerns expressed by some primatologists
about these environments lead us to conclude that captive behavior
invariably equates to unnatural behavior? When Goodall says that
some apes may be better off in the good zoos as opposed to dangerous areas of Africa, does this speak only to the question of survival,
or does it suggest also that in some cases the behavior of captive African great apes may approach that of their wild counterparts?

In answering these questions, it is necessary to separate the issue
of *behavioral identity* across captive and field contexts from that of *behavioral validity* of research in captivity. Even western gorillas living
in an arguably optimal enclosure, the Wildlife Conservation Society/
Bronx Zoo's $43 million habitat, do not behave the same way as go-
rillas in the wild. They need not range widely to search for food, so
their daily time budget is altered from that of the wild state. Resident
group males need not fend off challengers for control of females,
nor do females experience the threat of infanticide from such rival
males, so the degree of aggression observed may be quite different
from that in the wild. No primatologist would undertake in that or
any other zoo habitat a study of foraging, time budgets, or male-male
aggression in order to seek species-typical behavior.

Yet in any captive setting that preserves social groups of kin and
close associates, interactions between social partners can inform scientists meaningfully about gorillas. It is not some essential "gorilla
nature" that primatologists seek to understand but rather the range

of diverse behaviors that characterize the species. Furthermore, the *quality* of social interactions may well be durable across habitats where gorilla socioemotional bonds are allowed to develop and flourish. Wherever mother-offspring and other affiliative bonds can be fully expressed, gorillas will be gorillas; their fundamental sociality in turns encourages the expression of gorilla communicative and cognitive problem-solving skills.

Ladygina-Kohts's study of Joni the chimpanzee, then, imparts valuable knowledge to us about a chimpanzee and how that chimpanzee behaves with, and solves problems with, humans. It is a thorough and insightful product of its time. Primatologists know now, though, that primate behavior is better studied through observation of well-constituted social groups in which ape-ape sociality can be expressed and observed.

After decades of studying nonhuman primates, including African great apes, in diverse captive settings, de Waal expressed a view similar to the one just laid out: "In general, I believe that chimpanzees face, in their social lives at least, basically the same sort of problems in the forest as under enlightened captive conditions. They arrive at the same solutions, whether it be with regard to mother-offspring relations, power politics, or the mutual exchange of favors. Also, their communication, such as vocalizations and facial expressions, is essentially the same under both conditions."[12] That vocalizations, facial expressions, and—I would add—gestures and body movements are likely to be similar in captivity and in the wild is a sound conclusion, but requires a qualifier. They are likely to be similar *qualitatively*, not because the gestures and body movements are hard-wired or instinctual but because they emerge in response to the development and expression of social bonds among the apes, wherever those bonds are found.

For those of us seeking co-regulated social communication, then, social groups in captivity hold much promise, and may even offer benefits compared to groups in the wild. Conditions for observation and filming in zoos and research centers are often quite good, though by no means always excellent. For researchers, a welcome irony of working at an enlightened zoo is that one's subjects may disappear into thick trees or bushes, or select to stay hidden within recesses or grottoes. Still, the level of detailed observation of gesture and body movement allowed may lead researchers to uncover subtleties that suggest hypotheses for field testing. Given that the very recognition of co-regulation relies on fine details, research on captive animals is vitally important.

Despite this optimistic picture of research in captive settings, two inescapable truths remain. First, captive African great apes do behave in ways not observed in the wild. Although in the wild gorillas and bonobos do not forage with tools, captive members of these species may rake in or "fish for" food that is out of reach. Documenting such tool use points up previously unsuspected capacities, but also indicates that for any given instance of behavior seen in captivity, no guarantee exists that it will be found in the wild. Hypothesis-testing is, of course, the solution. Moreover, it should be remembered that even when a behavior is observed in the wild, it may turn out to be specific to a single population. As Chapter 1's review of African great ape social systems revealed, cross-population behavioral variation is not confined to the captive versus wild context, but exists too across free-ranging populations.

Second and perhaps more critical, captivity alters the life-history stages of the great apes. In the wild, ape infants nurse from their mothers, and are otherwise highly dependent on their mothers, for at least 3 years, and sometimes longer. In captivity, African great ape infants are typically weaned earlier than their wild counterparts, becoming independent from their mothers at an earlier age. Interbirth intervals of great apes in captivity are thus reduced compared to those in the wild; when infants supplement their milk diet with solid foods provided by humans, interruption in infant suckling causes cessation of natural birth control, and mothers become fertile again earlier than would be the case in the wild.

The National Zoo gorillas introduced in the previous two chapters provide a striking example of this altered life-history profile. The mother gorilla, Mandara, has, at the time of this writing, three male offspring under the age of 7 years. Kwame, born in November 1999, became an older brother shortly before his second birthday in November 2001. When his new brother, Kojo, was born, Kwame spent much time interacting socially with his own older brother, Ktembe. His bond with Ktembe may have buffered Kwame to some degree from the effects of this early weaning. Nevertheless, that Kwame has sucked his thumb intermittently since the birth of his younger brother probably indicates not only that he may wish to suckle still, but also something about his emotional state. His social bond with his mother is intact (as data reported later in this chapter make clear), but at 2 years of age he was already weaned, a situation that would not occur in the wild unless the mother died. An altered life-history profile may have consequences for the timing and nature of social behavior in captivity.

In sum, research on captive animals, like any research, carries with it costs and benefits that shift according to the topics and questions being investigated. For a focus on the quality of gesture and body movement in African great ape social communication, study of captive groups may yield rich insights.

## Iconic Gestures and Mutual Shaping: Key Studies

In the 1970s and early 1980s, the possibility of teaching human symbol systems to captive African great apes, in order to unlock their linguistic capacity and discover what they might have to talk about, generated enormous excitement. American Sign Language and computer-generated or plastic symbols were used to investigate the communicative behavior of chimpanzees Lana, Sarah, Washoe, and Nim, and the gorilla Koko, each of whom interacted with humans.[13] These apes became flashpoints in the scientific community, with linguists and philosophers as well as primatologists drawn into heated evaluation of data on the apes' performance. Comparatively less celebrated were two projects from this same time period, prescient in their focus on the importance of gesture and body movement in socially housed great apes.

In the 1970s, Emil Menzel conducted a series of studies that attracted researchers' attention in a new way to gesture and body movement within social groups of nonhuman primates. His studies explored how captive chimpanzees reacted when food was hidden in particular locations in their outdoor enclosure. In one variant of his experimental procedure, a single chimpanzee was removed from the group, allowed to observe the hiding process, and then returned to the other chimpanzees. In this case, the possibility exists of social communication from the "leader" chimpanzee to the "followers" as they set out toward the location of the hidden food, known only to the leader.

According to Menzel, the leader chimpanzees drew on a broad repertoire of communicative behaviors in trying to lead their social partners to food: "If others did not follow, the leader might stop and wait, glance back and forth at them and the goal, 'present' his back for tandem walking, whimper, 'beg' with his hand extended palm up, tap a follower on the shoulder, hold a follower's thumb lightly in his teeth and start walking him thus, scream and bite the follower on the back of the neck, drag him along by a leg, or throw himself on the ground in a 'temper tantrum'—according to the precise circumstances and the degree of obtuseness shown by the followers." From this description it is clear that the chimpanzees communicate a great deal to social partners while in a state of heightened emotional arousal. But Menzel, writing at a time when emotional and referential communication were often strictly dichotomized, saw no reason to consider emotional communication of this nature as inferior to other forms. Further, he concluded that "the ethological hope of understanding primate group communication systems principally via an identification and analysis of individual classes of signals" is not an approach rich or detailed enough to get at the phenomena in question.[14]

Menzel comes close here to rejecting the sender-receiver framework in favor of a more fluid and dynamic model. He demonstrated beyond doubt that chimpanzees acutely observe aspects of their social companions' behavior when confronted by unusual, stimulating conditions in their environment. Subsequent research on great apes showed that gestures and body movements may be complex and nuanced even when unfolding spontaneously between social partners, without human involvement.

Gestures in a study of three bonobos by Savage-Rumbaugh and colleagues were defined as hand and/or upper forelimb motions only, a fairly restricted use of the term.[15] Analysis was confined to those gestures preceding copulation, resulting in identification of 21 individual gestures by an adult female bonobo and 2 juveniles, one of each sex. These gestures were then clustered into three categories. Bonobos made positioning motions with their hands, to push the partner's limbs or body in such a way as to facilitate the adoption of a certain posture. The limb or body in question was not forcefully moved, but rather was started along a particular trajectory by the gesturer, as when the juvenile male bonobo touched the adult female on the shoulder and pushed her upper torso away from his own body.

Gestures that comprised both touch and iconic hand motions constituted the second category. In this case, one bonobo touched another then indicated the desired direction of movement by tracing a path in space, as when the juvenile male touched the adult female's shoulder and then gestured across his body with his left hand. Savage-Rumbaugh and colleagues interpreted this cross-body gesture as a signal for the female to move forward and assume a dorsal orientation. In the third category iconic hand motions may occur alone, made in the air without an accompanying touch.

Analyzing videotaped data of these gestures, Savage-Rumbaugh and colleagues found a "close correspondence" between gestures and the subsequent body movements of the social partner.[16] Further, the use of gestures increased the likelihood that a copulatory bout would be completed. Beyond these robust conclusions, two aspects of this study are noteworthy for evaluation of gesture from a DST perspective. The body orientation of both social partners, not the exact form of the gesture itself, most affected the semantic interpretation of the gestures. One and the same gesture may apparently be interpreted by the bonobos as a request either to approach or to move past the gesturer, depending on the partner's initial proximity to the gesturer. Savage-Rumbaugh and her colleagues, though they refer to gestures as "signals," do not see gestures as meaningful units of communication (or analysis) in themselves. They see the bonobos as internally related elements in a system, with meaning created by the social partners. The idea of co-regulation, with its inevitable unpredictability and contingency, is embedded in this study, even though dynamic systems terms are not used.

Second, noted almost in passing in one of the article's photo captions, is a point remarkably important for understanding gesture. When one bonobo makes a gesture in a social interaction, the partner often ignores it and adopts a position he or she apparently prefers, or takes actions other than those requested by the gesturer. That a social partner does not comply with a partner's request does not invalidate the request *as* a social gesture. As discussed briefly in the previous chapter, DST defines a social gesture as one created by unfolding interaction. Yet this in no way obliges the social partner to take some specific action.

Turning one's back on, or looking away from, a social partner, or failing to respond despite being able to see the social partner, may all be highly social acts. A moment's reflection allows us to see this fact clearly. Native users of American Sign Language consider it a social act, indeed a rude act, to break off gaze while the social partner is signing. Whether using signed or spoken language, who has not experienced having a partner turn away from the conversation or fail to respond to an utterance, then drawn meaning from that act? As data analysis below confirms, it is not always possible to discriminate among movement that is not social gesture because it is merely routine motion (stabilizing one's balance while moving quickly, let's say) or made by an individual outside a social context; movement that is not social gesture because it was not seen by the social partner, who thus has no opportunity to participate in co-constructing it as social gesture; and movement that can be considered social gesture because two partners engage with each other as the movement is made, but that leads to no joint action, perhaps because one partner ignores the gesture or leaves the scene.

More recent research on western gorillas at the San Francisco Zoo by Tanner and Byrne nicely complements the Savage-Rumbaugh study. As noted in the previous chapter, gestures, for Tanner and Byrne, are nonlocomotor limb and head movements used by gorillas in the course of social interaction. Three categories of gesture were described in an intensive study of videotaped gestures made by the young silverback male, Kubie. Audible gestures included slapping, pounding, or slapping a surface, and chestbeating. Physical contact did not often follow audible gestures, but the receiving social partner often did redirect her attention or otherwise alter her ongoing activity. Audible gestures were often made without first securing the partner's visual attention, contrary to the case with gestures termed "silent visually received gestures." Armshakes, armswings, head nods, taps on the partner, and other silent, visually received gestures invited further attention, elicited activity, or promoted contact. Tactile gestures "trace[d] or mime[d] on the body of the receiver movements that the gesturing gorilla apparently desire[d] the other gorilla to make."[17] In this third category, gestures indicate desired movement, but without enough force actually to move the body.

The San Francisco gorillas, Kubie and others, consistently used iconic gestures as they interacted. Although, unlike Savage-

Rumbaugh and colleagues, Tanner and Byrne don't fold the term "iconic" into their gesture-category labels, iconicity is highlighted in their analyses. Here is a passage about Kubie's frequent gesture *arm-swing under*, generally preceded by the gesture *tap other*, and made in this case to the female Zura: "Kubie would tap Zura without force, presumably gaining her attention as subject of activity (a deictic gesture), then having her visual attention, would swing his arm toward himself (an iconic depiction of the motion desired from Zura), moving his open palm to a final position between his legs."[18]

In their descriptions of gesture use by gorillas, Tanner and Byrne's language implies an understanding of social communication at odds with that in DST. Tanner and Byrne isolate the producer from the recipient of gestures, for instance, and indicate that gestures themselves are responsible for conveying meaning in a social interaction. That they should do so is unsurprising; most studies reviewed in this book reflect the same understanding, for reasons already explored. But Tanner and Byrne's research is so rich in terms of recorded social events, and so detailed in its level of analysis, that it nonetheless serves as an appropriate vehicle for seeking co-regulation in gorilla social communication. This can be accomplished both by building on analysis by Tanner and by viewing, with a dynamic system theorist's eye, filmed instances of the San Francisco zoo gorillas' social interactions.[19]

Tanner stresses the process of active negotiation by the gorillas as they communicate. The gorillas employ both gestural phrases and gestural exchanges in this negotiation. A gestural phrase is formally defined as a continuous sequence of two or more gestures by one gorilla, occurring after a period of at least 2 seconds in which no gestures occurred, and where the gestures follow each other without any pause longer than 1 second. Gestural exchanges, which may include gestural phrases and occur in a conversation-like manner, take place between social partners. Serving to negotiate matters such as the timing, location, initiator, and type of play, gestural exchanges are defined as continuous sequences of two or more gestures performed by more than one gorilla. Usually the gestures occur one after the other, but may on occasion be made simultaneously. As with gestural phrases, in exchanges, the gestures follow without pauses longer than 1 second.

Tanner identified, working from data collected on the gorillas Kubie and Zura, phrases of up to eight gestures. (In the eight-gesture phrase, two gestures were repeated, though not consecutively.) Tanner notes that the gesture *armswing under,* which she previously had transcribed as one continuous movement—as reported in the iconicity example above—may be parsed as three gestures combined into one phrase-like expression. First, Kubie extends his arm to another gorilla or taps that gorilla; next comes the actual motion of the arm as it swings; and third is the ending point, at a location between Kubie's legs. Providing what she terms "rich interpretation" together with notes about the form and timing of the gestures themselves, Tanner transcribes social events that include gestural phrases and gestural exchanges. At the start of one event, Tanner notes, Kubie and Zura sit facing each other on the rocks in their habitat, then Zura stands up and begins armshaking. Her rock perch is above Kubie, so her foot is near his face level. Here is Tanner's interpretation of what ensued, with gestures put into italics:

With her *armshake,* Zura calls Kubie's attention to her motivation to engage in play activity; he responds to her approach with a play face. Zura, standing on the rocks while Kubie watches intently, makes a *down* gesture, ending by *tapping her foot,* thus drawing Kubie's attention to her foot. Kubie takes hold of her foot and begins to pull her down; but she then changes her mind and turns away to struggle from his grasp. When he makes a tactile *around* gesture on her body, she returns her gaze to him. When they have eye contact, he then indicates his own play intention with a *bite* on his finger, *knocks his fists* together, and *extends his hand* to Zura. Zura *bites* her finger in agreement, and contact follows in wrestling and biting play.

Tanner discusses some of the gestures in order to give support for her interpretation; the *knock fists* gesture, for instance, is rare, but in all observed instances was followed by the two gorillas in question coming together. Tanner thus speculates that the gesture is iconic. Notable for my purposes is that the gestures in the reported example are linked with coordination of action between Kubie and Zura, and that they clearly embody both unpredictability and contingency. Only when Zura gestures toward and on her own foot does Kubie pull her foot; only when Kubie makes a tactile *around* gesture on her body does she engage with him visually; and so on. Together, the two gorillas use their body and limb movements to create meaning that results in play.

The contingency that is identifiable in Tanner's interpretations was readily visible upon my independent viewing of the filmed event between Kubie and Zura. The interaction in question lasts 15 seconds. Watching it, I saw all the gestures Tanner notes, though without her transcription for guidance I might well have overlooked the two instances of "bite finger," a motion made very rapidly at the gorilla's own mouth. To Tanner's analysis I would add one further aspect. At certain points, one gorilla begins to move and act *as* the other is moving and acting. Seeing the behavior this way (which is easy to do on a slow-motion viewing) makes it easier to recognize the mutual construction that is going on. For example, *as* Zura first rises up from the rocks and begins to move her arms, Kubie turns his head to her; *as* Zura's leg comes toward the ground in the *down* gesture, Kubie's hand rises up. His hand slows its motion *as* Zura taps her foot. His hand then begins to move back down, rising up again to grab Zura's foot. The unfolding act is dance-like in its degree of mutual adjustment.

In some of her work, Tanner discusses the ontogeny of gesture in captive gorillas, a topic I will explore shortly. It's worth noting here that co-regulation can be seen in the San Francisco gorillas at much younger ages than those represented by Kubie or Zura. In Tanner's compilation of video clips chronicling events in the first 2 years of life of the male Shango, the following social event can be seen between Shango and Kubie (the analysis is mine, not Tanner's):

> Shango, 18 months old, is sitting on the rocks near Kubie, who lies on his back, and Zura, who sits one level above the two males. Kubie and Zura are gesturing to each other with chestbeats, head movements, and arm movements. Shango watches them, then shakes and beats a branch against the rocks. As Shango turns and stands up to begin to move toward the other two gorillas, Zura gets up from her sitting position. At this point Shango's body and Zura's are oriented toward each other. Zura climbs down, reaching the same level as Kubie and Shango. She pushes Shango completely off the rocks.

This event reminds us that social communication can involve asymmetric action, since Zura alone was responsible for Shango's quick departure from the rocks. That co-regulation begins in infancy and that asymmetry is compatible with co-regulation are issues taken up in greater detail in the presentation of my own data, below.

The studies by Savage-Rumbaugh and colleagues and Tanner and Byrne, then, demonstrate co-regulated gestural communication in African great apes, and suggest iconicity in their gestures. The ability to make iconic gestures is cited increasingly as a skill on which natural selection may have acted in producing human language (see Chapter 5), but some theorists contest its very existence. Reviewing these two studies, Tomasello and Call write that the so-called iconic gestures probably developed "as ritualizations of physical manipulations themselves, not as gestures that the signaler thought would be interpreted iconically by the recipient. If this is so, then the 'iconic' relationship of the gestures to the desired action may be from the human point of view only, as for the [apes] they may just signal the desired action in the same way as other ritualized signals, that is, based on the mutual shaping of behavior in previous interactive sequences."[20] Further, looking for gestural iconicity in two groups of captive gorillas, Pika, Liebal, and Tomasello found none.[21] As these researchers note, however, their subjects were all 6 years of age or under, whereas the ability to make iconic gestures may develop only later in life.

We may wonder, too, whether *human* gesturers invariably think, upon producing an iconic gesture, that their social partner will interpret it as iconic. For DST theorists, iconicity is no more "in the head" of the communicator than is the meaning of a social gesture. Tomasello and Call's focus on intention clues us in to their own position, and leads naturally into a discussion of Tomasello's research on gesture in captive chimpanzees.

No other researcher has advanced the study of gestural learning by captive chimpanzees as much as Tomasello. Especially significant is the longitudinal nature of the research; he and his team have published data on gestures observed over a span of 12 years. They offer four main results.[22] Juvenile chimpanzees use many gestures not employed by adults, and vice versa; over time, some juvenile gestures are replaced by adult-like gestures; idiosyncratic gestures occur; and low concordance marks gestures used across generations. Tomasello concludes that chimpanzees learn gestures by a type of dyadic shaping called ontogenetic ritualization (OR).

In OR, some bodily action that is repeated frequently between the same social partners becomes reduced over time to a gesture. The classic example of OR involves infant suckling. An infant chimpanzee may pull on her mother's arm (to remove it from blocking the breast) or her nipple when wishing to nurse. After numerous instances of such pulling, the infant's mother may come to respond *before* the infant contacts the nipple. Eventually she may respond when the infant simply touches her arm or the nipple. As Tomasello puts it, "a communicatory signal is created by two organisms shaping each other's behavior in repeated instances of social interaction."[23]

At first glance, OR may sound a lot like co-regulation, given that Tomasello talks about "creation" of a signal via mutual shaping by two social partners. But as formulated by Tomasello, OR seems to indicate a circumscribed period of mutual adjustment between two partners, during which the form and meaning of the signal become refined. When the creativity is completed, the signal itself transmits meaning, though flexibly: "Chimpanzees use their gestures flexibly—using one signal for several functions and several signals for the same function—from early in development, and they adjust their choice of signal to the attentional state of the recipient from early in development as well."[24] The emphasis is on *individual* creativity, however. The potential for continual, renewed creativity between social partners, inherent in co-regulation, is not part of OR.

That young chimpanzees acquire gestures (in Tomasello's terminology) via OR and not imitation is a second major thread, in addition to assessment of individually flexible signal use, in Tomasello's publications. In the universe of alternative learning mechanisms, OR is seen by Tomasello as an inferior cousin to imitation, which is a form of social (or cultural) transmission. With these two research questions driving the research methodology, Tomasello's analysis is quantitative. Detailed reporting of social events is not included, leaving no way to assess directly the presence of co-regulation in the chimpanzees that Tomasello studies.

Tomasello, then, sees OR where DST theorists would look for co-regulation. What's more, DST-oriented researchers reject the concept, individual creativity, at the heart of OR. For African great apes, born into a deeply social world and shaped by that world at every moment,[25] in what way could creativity (or learning) be individual? With reference to the work of the social anthropologist Tim Ingold (Chapter 2), we may phrase this question another way. If skills are not acquired but grown in life, as an individual matures in his body and lives with his social group, isn't creativity profoundly social even when an individual is alone?

Another way to understand differences between Tomasello's approach and that of DST emerges when gesture is analyzed across great ape groups. Pika and colleagues observed 33 different gestures in 13 gorillas, age 6 and under, housed in two separate groups (in two countries). A major focus of their analysis is on learning: "We found high levels of agreement concerning the performance of gestures between groups, individual variability concerning the performance of 25 gestures, and three idiosyncratic gestures . . . Overall, [the] findings support (based on our defined indicators for individual learning) the hypothesis that ontogenetic ritualization is the main learning process involved. They further imply that the overlap in gestural repertoires among individuals could be accounted for by commonly available individual learning conditions."[26] Pika and colleagues go on to mention that some form of social learning may play a role in the armshake gesture, seen in six of seven individuals within one gorilla group but absent entirely from the other group.

This study, welcome both for its focus on the ontogeny of gesture in gorillas and for its comparative nature, uses the traditional sender-receiver framework. Pika and colleagues preserve the focus on mechanism so apparent in Tomasello's earlier work: OR is described as an *individual* way of learning. Only when group-specific gestures are found is a significant role for social learning allowed. As already noted, this distinction doesn't compute for DST theorists. Does a high level of agreement in cross-group gestural performance, together with variability in gesturing among individual gorillas and a few idiosyncratic gestures, necessarily implicate OR? Might the same outcomes result from the profoundly social process of co-regulation? In other words, does the presence of significant individual variability, plus a few idiosyncratic gestures, *preclude* the presence of social creativity at the heart of co-regulation?

Breaking away from a narrow individual- versus social-learning framework to include observation of the *quality* of social events may open up new vistas on learning. Interestingly, Tanner and Byrne, who as we have seen do not directly discuss co-regulation in their analysis of gorilla gesture, neither fully embrace nor fully reject the idea that OR—which they call "conventionalization"—may account for the development of gesture in the San Francisco gorillas. To see how they do treat OR, let's revisit the gestural phrase "tap other plus armswing under" that may be seen in gestural interactions between Kubie and Zura. Tanner and Byrne use OR to suggest a possible path of development for this gestural phrase: Perhaps when Kubie first wanted Zura to come to him, he physically pulled Zura to him. After that, Zura might at times have moved toward Kubie when his arm merely brushed first down her body, then toward himself. Later still, the motion of his arm swinging toward himself, on its own, might be enough for Zura to move toward Kubie.[27]

But Tanner and Byrne go further. Data from other periods of Kubie's life, before and after the time of intense interaction with Zura, suggest that "if conventionalization was the process by which Kubie's gestures were established, he went through a similar process three different times with three different females and later again with his son. We have no evidence that this happened; on the contrary, there is evidence that it did not."[28] At age 8, for instance, Kubie used with an older female called Pogo many of the same gesture types he would use with Zura 5 years in the future. The authors note that Kubie might have generalized his gestural use to a number of different gorillas, but without the process of OR, the "receptive half" of the communicating partnership would be left in the dark as to meaning. How can we then make sense of Kubie's gesturing? Does the similarity of his gesturing with different gorillas indicate that there isn't much creativity, after all, between social partners?

Finding no completely satisfactory answer by trying to single out one distinct learning mechanism—OR or observational learning—Tanner and Byrne instead turn to a more comprehensive view to explain Kubie's gestural profile. "Something like the process of conventionalization led not simply to a learning of a gradually more finely shaped association of stimulus and response, but to an understanding of the partner in communication as an intentional and responding being . . . The *tactile close* gestures performed by Kubie support this explanation; these gestures varied so greatly in type and size and force (being performed in a three-dimensional space on the body of another gorilla) that an individual conventionalization of each gesture would seem an unwieldy process. The understanding of iconic motions on the body and in space may instead be a normal part of great ape development when conditions make such gestures useful. Even the far more complex symbols of human language are often learned, after all, not by a gradual process of shaping or careful teaching and demonstration, but by active integration into contexts of daily action where the experienced language-user and the child, or student, commonly interact."[29]

By moving into the realm of "active integration into contexts of daily action," Tanner and Byrne leave behind the constraints of a finite, limited OR process. In a way, this idea fits, theoretically, between Tomasello's focus on OR and my own focus on co-regulation. All three views converge in rejecting imitation as an important process in African great ape gesturing. Where they differ is in the degree to which they encourage study of the contingent, unpredictable, and creative nature of social communication.

## Co-Regulation and the Ontogeny of Gesture in Bonobos

In 1997, I first felt the excitement of observing gesturally mediated interactions involving a very young African great ape. My student Erin Selner and I had been observing and filming the bonobo Elikya since the day of her birth at the Language Research Center (LRC) at Georgia State University. Elikya is the sixth biological offspring of the bonobo Matata, herself wild-born in approximately 1970. Matata and Elikya were housed with Matata's two other young daughters, Tamuli (born 1987) and Neema (born 1992). Sometimes these four were visited by Elikya's older sister, Panbanisha (born 1985), or her adoptive brother, Kanzi (born 1980 and adopted by Matata as a young infant).

On this day in 1997, Selner and I noted that Elikya, 9 weeks old, was as yet unable to walk or even properly crawl, though she could creep forward unsteadily. We filmed this social event:

Elikya sits near her mother Matata and 5-year-old sister, Neema. Matata hands Elikya over to Neema.
As she is transferred, Elikya makes a facial pout toward her mother.
While held by Neema, Elikya extends her arm three times in succession back toward Matata. Although Elikya is close enough to her mother to touch her, she instead makes this movement, slowly and deliberately.
As Elikya is making the third arm extension, her mother takes Elikya back.
As Elikya relaxes against her mother's body, Neema pats her gently.

Despite my avowed agnosticism on the question of intentionality, it was tempting to embrace the interpretation that Elikya had expressed a desire to return to her mother. What Elikya intended with her arm movement cannot be known for certain. What's clear is that Matata acted as if her daughter's movement had been a request. Joint action followed, resulting in Elikya's return to Matata; this much can be said without implying intentionality on the part of either bonobo. Even in the potential absence of intentionality, mother and daughter together constructed a social gesture from Elikya's arm extension. If Elikya had not intended to make a social request of Matata, she no doubt learned from this incident that she was capable of helping to effect change in her social situation through her movements.

With students Selner and Heather Bond, I continued to study

Elikya's gestures and body movements through her seventeenth month, a project that helped prepare me in two ways for my longitudinal work with captive western gorillas. First, the four female bonobos, plus their occasional bonobo visitors, gestured with each other as a routine part of their daily lives, which afforded me ample opportunity to recognize the degree of mutual adjustment between social partners.

Whether all captive bonobos gesture as routinely I cannot say. Though primatologists in addition to Savage-Rumbaugh have studied aspects of bonobo gesture,[30] the corpus of material is still quite minimal. I have no reason to suspect that the four bonobos I observed were unusual; unlike the famous Kanzi and Panbanisha, they were neither enculturated nor language- competent. Matata is, in fact, best known as Kanzi's adoptive mother who *failed* to learn the aspects of human symbol usage on which she was being trained (and which Kanzi mastered without direct tutoring).[31] At the time I studied them, these bonobos were not in close contact with humans, beyond routine contact for maintenance. Matata had experienced extensive contact and training earlier in her life, however, and the possibility exists that her experience with humans increased Matata's tendency to gesture with her offspring (which in turn might have increased their own tendency to gesture). Further, zoo populations of gorillas differ in their gestural profiles even in the absence of heightened contact with humans, and the same may be true for bonobos.

In any case, over time, Elikya increasingly participated in social interactions with her family members through gesture and body movement. Social requests played a part in some social interactions, as the data attest:

Eight months old, Elikya moves toward her youngest sister, Neema. Elikya may lightly touch Neema's outstretched leg, but it is hard to be certain.

Neema lowers her leg, then begins to stamp her feet on a

platform as Elikya stands bipedally facing her. Elikya has a play face and raises her arms.

Immediately, Neema moves to Elikya and hugs her, covering her with her whole body, then quickly moves back and resumes her previous position.

Ten months old, Elikya sits with her older sister, Tamuli, but watches Kanzi, her adoptive brother, play with Neema.

Elikya makes an extended-arm movement toward Kanzi as he walks by, but Kanzi's head is turned and he does not see it.

Elikya runs to Kanzi, touches him on the back of his thigh, and returns to Tamuli.

Immediately, play partners Kanzi and Neema approach Elikya.

Kanzi pushes Neema away, then awkwardly pulls Elikya onto his shoulders, where Elikya rides as Kanzi and Neema resume play.

Eleven months old, Elikya climbs up a chain-link fence outdoors and approaches Kanzi, who rests on his back in a hanging tire.

Elikya stops, then extends one leg and foot to Kanzi.

Kanzi spreads his own big toe apart from the other toes; only then does Elikya climb over to Kanzi, and along his body up to his face.

Kanzi wraps his arms around Elikya and pats her.

From these interactions we see that Elikya's body and limb movements help to effect social outcomes. We may call these movements social requests because they were *constructed* as such in the ongoing social event. At times, as when Elikya touched Kanzi as he played with Neema, meaning was constructed from light touches on the body, at other times, as when she made a play face and raised her

arms near Neema, or extended her foot toward Kanzi, from movements made in the air without bodily contact.

Unsurprisingly, given the age differences between the two older
sisters, Elikya's relationship with Tamuli seemed of a different nature than that with Neema. At age 10, Tamuli had no offspring of her
own; because of health problems involving her heart, she had not
been bred. At one point in the past Tamuli found a dead squirrel in
her enclosure and lifted it on her ventrum, "making certain to position its head upright and to pull its little feet around her waist as
though it were clinging to her. She groomed it carefully and pre-
tended to nurse it, just as she saw Matata do with her younger sister
Neema."[32] Whether or not we should conclude from this action, and
from her actions toward Elikya, that Tamuli desired an infant of her
own, her behavior with Elikya can be interpreted as helpful, protec-
tive, and comforting. Tamuli also participated with Elikya in sexual
encounters, including the mouthing of Elikya's genitals (a common
bonobo behavior). The pattern between Elikya and Tamuli is one of
mutual accommodation, but as the data show, such a pattern does
not mean that Tamuli allows Elikya her own way at every moment,
any more than a human child would be so allowed.

At 11 months, Elikya follows Tamuli and, when Tamuli lies
down, climbs on Tamuli's stomach.

Tamuli spreads her arms and legs so that Elikya can position
herself on Tamuli's stomach.

Chewing something that appears to be an orange, Tamuli
pushes a chunk of the fruit out her lips.

Elikya brings her face right to Tamuli's face, puts her mouth
on the fruit, and then observes Tamuli chew.

Tamuli leans her head back; Elikya sits up a little and
touches Tamuli's face with one hand as Tamuli lifts her head toward Elikya again.

Elikya takes a bit of food from Tamuli's lips.

Elikya again "close faces" Tamuli as Tamuli takes more bites of orange, then again touches Tamuli's lips with her mouth.

Tamuli sits up higher and Elikya again "close faces" her, then touches Tamuli's face with her foot.

Elikya watches Tamuli eat, then pulls on Tamuli's hand (the one holding the orange bits).

As Tamuli chews, Elikya attempts to take a bit of orange but Tamuli turns her head away.

Elikya again tries to take a bit of Tamuli's chewed orange but Tamuli pulls her head back; Elikya climbs off Tamuli and goes to her mother, Matata.

Tamuli has been grooming Elikya, age 14 months.

Elikya picks up and manipulates a white object that seems to be a bit of paper.

Tamuli takes it from her, puts it into her own mouth, then takes it out and uses it to wipe or clean the area around Elikya's nose. Tamuli's motions are very focused and deliberate, and Elikya squirms.

Tamuli applies the paper to her own nose and carries out the same actions.

Elikya takes the paper back from Tamuli briefly, then the two touch hands as they both hold the paper.

Elikya comes in closer to Tamuli, against her ventrum, with Tamuli holding her.

Tamuli grooms Elikya once more, then presses the white paper up to Elikya's nose.

Elikya mouths the paper.

At 15 months, as Tamuli walks behind her, Elikya leans her body back slightly and moves her hand toward Tamuli.

Tamuli does not acknowledge Elikya.

When Tamuli comes past again, Elikya follows her. Tamuli

has food now, and Elikya vocalizes and begs at Tamuli's mouth and hands.

Tamuli leaves her own hand (with food in it) very low, near Elikya.

When Tamuli wants to eat, she brings her mouth down to her hand, instead of bringing her hand up to her mouth, thus enabling Elikya to get some scraps.

Elikya continues to beg, with her arm around Tamuli's neck.

When Elikya was about 14 months old, her oldest sister, Panbanisha, stayed in Elikya's enclosure for about 3 weeks; the quality of Elikya's relationship with her differs dramatically from that between Elikya and Tamuli. A scribbled note from this time period captures my initial impression from the filmed data: "Panbanisha perturbs the system. . ." (though of course, she perturbed this "system" of bonobos while simultaneously being part of it). Elikya's closeness with Tamuli, and her apparent uncertainty near Panbanisha, are mirrored in her body movements and gestures during the early part of this visit:

As Panbanisha goes by, Elikya approaches and touches her sister, Tamuli, with an arm-around on Tamuli's back, then moves on and wraps herself around the back of her mother Matata.

Elikya leaves Matata, but soon returns and touches her again.

Panbanisha approaches Matata.

Elikya jumps off her mother's back (and Tamuli leaves Matata's vicinity too as Panbanisha approaches).

As Panbanisha is walking away again with her back turned, Elikya, her mouth open, swings out rapidly with her arm toward Panbanisha.

After Panbanisha passes by, Elikya climbs up her mother's body to a fire hose, then jumps down and moves backward to Matata as Panbanisha approaches once more.

Elikya climbs on Matata again as Panbanisha moves off.

When Panbanisha approaches yet again, Elikya stays put on Matata, and Tamuli returns.

As Tamuli sits down, Elikya jumps up, and goes and leans against Matata with her back to Tamuli.

When Panbanisha goes by this time, her foot hits Elikya right in the head (my interpretation of the filmed action is that Panbanisha deliberately hit Elikya with her foot).

As Elikya clings tightly to Tamuli's arm, Tamuli wraps her arm around Elikya's head.

In another event, Panbanisha comes through a door into a tunnel. Elikya, in the tunnel, steps back and leans away from Panbanisha. As Panbanisha passes by with her back turned, Elikya hangs on wire mesh over Matata and reaches out her arm at Panbanisha.

Now Tamuli walks through the same door into the tunnel; Elikya neither steps back nor leans away as she had with Panbanisha just minutes before.

Elikya follows Tamuli, then climbs up the wire mesh toward Matata.

Interestingly, Elikya, who had, from her earliest months, participated in social events using gesture with her social partners in successful ways, chose to make arm movements to Panbanisha two times when Panbanisha could not possibly have seen them. Certainly, Elikya also at times makes movements that bonobos other than Panbanisha cannot see, as when she first made a movement toward Kanzi when he was playing with Neema, then followed up by touching him on the thigh. That Elikya does not follow up these two arm movements with Panbanisha, that she moves and leans away from Panbanisha, and that she seeks comfort from Tamuli and from her mother when Panbanisha is near all tell us something useful about her relationship with Panbanisha.

Ten days later, Panbanisha is still with the group:

At the chain-link fence, she walks behind her mother, Matata, and her sisters Tamuli and Elikya.

As Panbanisha goes past, Elikya turns from Matata's ventrum and touches Tamuli on the arm.

Elikya breaks contact with both her mother and Tamuli, then turns back and touches Matata on the arm.

Elikya breaks contact once again, moves, and leans away but touches Matata as Panbanisha passes by.

Panbanisha's foot hits Elikya as Panbanisha goes by.

Panbanisha sits down near Matata and Elikya, but Elikya moves away while holding her mother, pivoting around Matata's body to her other side. In between Matata and Tamuli now, Elikya breaks contact with her mother. (This event continues in a similar vein.)

I cannot explain with any confidence the reasons for the difference between Elikya's easy familiarity with Tamuli (which had occasional tense moments) and her more strained relationship with Panbanisha (which wasn't constantly tense; at times, Panbanisha passed near Elikya without the infant moving away or flinching). Accounting for the difference in patterning of the two relationships by invoking Elikya's previous history and intimacy with Tamuli is important, but probably only part of the story. After all, social events between Elikya and Kanzi were marked by fluidity and affinity, though like Panbanisha, Kanzi was not housed with Elikya routinely. Panbanisha's personality, and the group dynamics at work when an adult female bonobo temporarily resides with her mother and younger sisters, also probably played a role; of most interest is how the bonobos' body movements and gestures reflect the differences in quality of socio-emotionality across these relationships.

A second insight from the bonobo study emerges from my opportunity to monitor aspects of Elikya's relationship with her mother, right from the moment of her birth. That the foundation for Elikya's social gesturing occurred in her earliest bodily experience with and of Matata became evident from the data in the first days and weeks. Routinely Selner and I noted that Matata supports Elikya's limbs; shakes Elikya as she holds her; weighs Elikya down with her arm and leg; removes Elikya's hand from the cage fencing; pushes Elikya up with her thighs; pries Elikya's hand from her side; pulls Elikya in toward her chest; holds Elikya's hands; and puts Elikya down on a blanket. Not only did Matata shift Elikya's position in space by manipulating her daughter's body and limbs, but she also used her own body and limbs to apply pressure in ways that affected Elikya's position, orientation, and freedom of movement. Elikya at times participated in these shifts in visible ways, as when she shifted her grip or position on Matata's ventrum and only then did Matata move, pull, or shift her further.

Often in primatological studies of mother-infant behavior, these early, subtle, and routine actions between the mother and infant are absent from discussion; simply implied in a statement that great ape mothers and babies are physically inseparable for a prolonged time period after birth; or mentioned for their part in the process of ontogenetic ritualization in which physical actions are "reduced" to gestures. Yet by examining these routine actions in detail, we see the intimate, dynamic physicality through which infants come to discover that their own bodily movements can affect social interactions, and help bring about social coordination:[33]

One day old, Elikya gazes up at Matata. Elikya moves her head down, then gazes up at Matata, then moves her head down once more. Matata, using her whole hand, moves Elikya's head back up and gazes into her eyes.

Three days old, Elikya roots for the nipple; as she does so, Matata pulls Elikya's arms up.

One week old, Elikya suckles on Matata's right breast. The

nipple comes out of her mouth, either by accident or because
Matata slightly shifts. Elikya roots at the right nipple, but
Matata shifts her to the left nipple.

One week old, Elikya has a pout face and gives a tiny peep
vocalization. She reaches out her left hand. Matata looks down,
then hoists Elikya up on her body and supports Elikya with one
thigh.

Not all of Elikya's social interactions occur dyadically. Her sisters
Tamuli and Neema may participate even at this early point:

A week and a half old, Elikya is held ventrally by Matata; her
head rests on her mother's legs.

Neema moves (swings) nearby; as Neema moves closer to
the pair and brings her arm toward Elikya, Matata covers
Elikya's head with her hand, blocking Neema's touch.

Matata touches Neema's arm with one finger.

Neema withdraws her arm, but after a pause, touches Elikya
lightly.

Elikya squirms and moves her head back and forth.

Matata's legs shift, which serves to shift Elikya.

Matata's hand comes up near Neema's; Neema relaxes her
hand away from Elikya.

Matata rolls onto her back with Elikya still ventral.

Neema sits nearby as Elikya roots on Matata's nipple.

As she shifts position again, Matata covers Elikya's head with
her hand. Moving quickly, after Matata is settled, Neema
reaches in and touches Elikya's head; as she does this, Matata's
hand moves towards her hand, but Neema withdraws her hand
rapidly.

Matata grooms her own leg with her lips and one hand, while
holding 2-week-old Elikya against her body with the other arm.

Elikya roots at Matata's breast.

Matata stops self-grooming, shifts, and puts her hands up on the mesh caging, leaving Elikya's head unsupported. She resumes self-grooming. As Tamuli begins to groom Matata, Elikya is gripping Matata's hair but her head bobs and flails unsteadily beneath Matata's breast.

When her head falls far back, Elikya moves and regrips, and pulls her head upright again.

Elikya's head continues to move unsteadily then crashes against Matata's ventrum.

Matata puts her hand behind Elikya's head, then pushes Elikya up on her body with her hand and a thigh.

Matata keeps her thigh partially raised. Elikya's head bobs a little, but is more supported than it had been.

Tamuli touches Elikya's head as if to groom it, but Matata lowers her elbow, and Tamuli withdraws her hand and resumes grooming Matata.

At the outset, then, the interactions between Elikya and mother can be described as asymmetric. Elikya participates as an active partner, with her own movements affecting the action because they are part of the ongoing web of movements. Matata, though, is capable of more controlled, more powerful action. Elikya's first observed social-request gesture, the one recounted above that happened at 9 weeks of age, follows close on the heels of these earliest asymmetric interactions and is itself followed by development of social requests in a variety of situations. Co-regulated gestural interactions emerge from early, mutually adjusted bodily actions within the mother-daughter pair.

## Co-Regulation and the Ontogeny of Gesture in Captive Gorillas

When my study of Elikya's communication ended in 1998, after 17 months, I cast about for an alternative research setting, in order to institute truly longitudinal research into the ontogeny of gesture in

African great apes. Fortunately, the Great Ape House at the National Zoological Park both welcomed a research proposal and predicted a gorilla pregnancy in the near future. Indeed, the gorilla mother, Mandara, gave birth to Kwame in November 1999, and on Kwame's 4-week birthday my research began.

Kwame was born into a small group of six western gorillas. Like the bonobo Matata, the gorilla Mandara is a very experienced and competent mother. Born in 1982, she had produced three previous biological offspring and adopted a fourth. All but her eldest offspring (a male born in 1991, now living in another zoo) were part of Kwame's group when I began observations: Mandara's daughter, Kigali (born 1994); her son Ktembe (born 1997); and her adoptive son, Baraka (born to female Haloko in 1992). Other gorillas in the group were Kwame's father, Kuja, a silverback male (father also of Ktembe but not of Mandara's older offspring), and Haloko, Baraka's biological mother. Changes in group composition have occurred since Kwame's birth; during 2000, both Kigali and Haloko were transferred to another gorilla enclosure, to be housed with a male whose cagemate had died of old age. In 2001, just short of his third birthday, Kwame became a big brother when the infant Kojo was born to Mandara and Kuja.

With the aid of students Kendra Weber, Christy Hoffman, and Rebecca Simmons, my study of Kwame (and now Kojo's) gestures and body movements is in its fourth year.[34] As discussed in Chapter 2, these gorillas are responsible for turning my attention fully to the seamless continuum of body movements and gestures in great apes—to the idea that gestures shouldn't be privileged a priori over other body movements in coming to understand co-regulated social communication. Though I had, naturally, noted the bonobos' body movements, the social partners in that group produced abundant gestures, and I tended to regard those gestures as the "nonvocal holy grails" of my study. Combined with an awareness of the complex gesturing by the San Francisco gorillas as studied by Tanner, and an interest in filtering gestural data into origins-of-language theories, this fact led me to a state of some disappointment when it became clear that Kwame and his social partners were not gesturing as readily as I had expected.

Today's literature is replete with acknowledgments that science, including primatology, is not free from social influences and expectations.[35] Scientific hypotheses derive from multiple sources; in this case, mine were influenced by an emerging zeitgeist that suggested African great ape gesture should be set apart from other forms of nonvocal communication. The irony here is striking: Many gesture studies had been initiated to counteract an overwhelming focus on vocal behavior, but ended up privileging one type of nonvocal social communication over others. No longer a novice primatologist, I should have better attended to a message I impart to my students: let the data, not current theory, point you in the most promising directions.

Soon enough, with more hours logged in front of the gorilla enclosure (and at the VCR, rewatching the taped data), I began to see that the members of this gorilla group express themselves nonvocally in ways just as nuanced and complex as those produced by the bonobos I had watched and the San Francisco gorillas, though not identical. In the following analysis, my primary goal is to present data on the gradual development of Kwame's social requests.[36] In doing so, I show that Kwame's social gesturing emerges, as Elikya's had emerged, from co-regulated action with the mother and older siblings. Along the way, I hope to convey how much the social communication among these gorillas depends on co-regulated gesture and body movement, and how a reading of this co-regulation can lead to greater understanding of socioemotional patterns in the group.

The star of my gorilla study to date is Kwame, who, as his Swahili name implies, was born on a Saturday, gaining national media attention because Mandara delivered him outdoors in full view of the public. As he has grown, Kwame has come to use his body and limbs in various ways to construct requests with his social partners. As before, the term "request" is not meant to imply intention (though it does not deny intention either), and the emphasis in analysis is put on visible outcomes, or the failure to achieve such outcomes.

Starting from the study's first weeks, we can chart movements and behavioral shifts by Kwame and his mother that are co-regulated. Though not gestures, these earliest movements set the stage for the development of gestures. The data reported derive from analysis of a subset of filmed observations:

One month of age, when Kwame shifts on his mother's ventrum, Mandara shifts her limbs and pats him several times gently with her hand.

Five weeks of age, Kwame is outdoors in Mandara's lap, reclining against her arm.

Kwame reaches for, and moves his head toward, Mandara's breast. He may suckle, but from my angle it is hard to be sure.

Kwame turns his head to the side, definitely not suckling now, and flails his arm, touching Mandara's breast in an uncoordinated way while looking elsewhere.

Mandara withdraws her arm, and lacking support, Kwame's head drops back.

Kwame reaches over Mandara's arm and tries to pull his head up, but Mandara's arm still blocks him; he pulls on her arm and squirms. Kwame kicks out with his feet, continues to squirm, stretches out his body and grips on Mandara's body.

With her other arm, Mandara reaches behind Kwame's head and pulls him closer in to her body, positioning him so that he sits upright. Kwame begins to nurse.

As Mandara eats hay, debris falls onto 6-week-old Kwame, who rests in her lap.

Kwame rubs one hand broadly up and down over his body then partially extends it up toward his mother's hand and the hay stalk. His reach movement is wobbly but still controlled, with the palm out toward Mandara. Mandara stops eating and shifts her body.

A few minutes later, Kwame rests against Mandara, who sits in a relaxed posture with an open ventrum. She is eating hay.

Kwame shifts, reaches up to Mandara's breast area and pulls his body up; Mandara draws in her legs and closes up her ventrum so that Kwame is more tightly enclosed in her lap.

Mandara resumes eating hay. Kwame's head turns markedly to the side and we see Baraka pass nearby.

A few minutes later, Mandara sits, again eating hay with Kwame against her ventrum. Kigali comes to sit near the pair.

The three gorillas sit quietly near each other. Kwame, after squirming and gripping Mandara's arm, pushes up a bit with his legs.

Mandara supports Kwame, stands, and departs; as she moves we see Baraka walking near to where the two others had been sitting. Whether Mandara departed because of Kwame's shifting, or Baraka's imminent approach, cannot be known.

Two months of age, Kwame rests quietly against Mandara's ventrum. When Kwame shifts and moves his head up a bit higher on her ventrum, Mandara cups the back of his neck with her hand, and brings him to her right breast. He suckles.

A short time later, Kwame brings his lips near to Mandara's breast. Mandara brings her arms down, blocking Kwame from her breasts. Kwame's head bobs unsteadily.

Mandara brings one arm back around him in support.

Mandara regurgitates and reingests into her hand (in zoo

lingo, she does an "R&R"), and Kwame reaches and touches her hand near where this "food" ends up.

Mandara puts that hand down against her body.

Kwame stretches out his torso laterally away from Mandara's ventrum and looks out, with his head hanging down (so that he's looking out upside down).

When Kwame pulls himself in again toward the ventrum, Mandara brings her arms down, again separating him from her chest.

Kwame touches his mother's arm and flings out his hand. He is blocked from a close or apparently comfortable position by Mandara's arm position, and he struggles until finally Mandara supports him around his back with one hand.

Less than a minute later, Kwame touches Mandara's breast area. Mandara touches his hand.

Kwame pushes up and suckles.

In these first months of life, Kwame is virtually tethered to Mandara's body. When he moves and acts, he experiences movement and action not as a separate entity in the world, but as part and parcel of his mother; he moves and acts *on* her body and *with* her being. Often, though not always, when he shifts, Mandara too shifts, guiding him in a co-regulated way to her breast or to a more secure position. Kwame does not, however, suckle at will, even at this very early age; some of the contingencies between them involve the movements in Kwame's shifting and Mandara's blocking her breasts. Altmann has emphasized, using her data on wild baboons, that primate weaning is a gradual and lengthy process between mother and infant rather than an event,[37] but the precise nature of the kind of suckling contingency demonstrated early on by Mandara and Kwame is still largely unexplored in studies of African great apes. An important phenomenon, it could tell us much not only about the course of nursing and weaning under different environmental and rearing conditions but also about the infant's first experiences of contingent action.

In these earliest events, Kwame begins to reach toward specific places, such as Mandara's breasts or hands. Though these reaches vary greatly, some characterized by unsteadiness and others by direct, "on-target" connecting, they differ from uncoordinated flinging because they show a clear trajectory of movement. As we have seen, what I interpret as a reach for food in Mandara's hand occurred by 6 weeks, and reaches for Mandara's breasts had occurred even earlier. It is not clear that Mandara treats these reaches as requests; she may just respond to Kwame's movement as to any bodily shift. As Kwame develops, more and more of his reaches begin to look coordinated in terms of motor control, and help bring about social outcomes. As noted in Chapter 2, the distinction between reaches and tactile gestures like those described for gorillas by Tanner and for bonobos by Savage-Rumbaugh may be a fine one, if it exists at all:

Nearly 4 months of age, Kwame rests in Mandara's lap; Kwame's older sister, Kigali, sits next to them.

Kwame stretches an arm out and explores the ground, then orients toward Kigali.

Kigali is looking off to the side, but as Kwame reaches out and touches her hand, she moves her head and gazes toward him, then moves her hand closer so that the two joined hands, one hers and one Kwame's, move back toward Kwame's body.

Kwame and Kigali's hands remain linked. Kwame pushes with his legs and moves himself more towards his sister.

Mandara does an R&R, at which point Kwame's and Kigali's hands break contact.

Kigali moves her hand slightly, and Kwame reaches back to Kigali's hand again; as he does, Mandara gets up and departs, carrying him away.

A bit later that morning, Mandara does an R&R into her hand. Kwame is at her side, supported by one of Mandara's arms.

Mandara eats from her hand.

Kwame stretches out his body, looking away in one direction as the subadult male Baraka approaches and sits on Mandara's other side. Kwame sits back up.

Mandara licks her hand. Kwame reaches repeatedly to her mouth but Mandara repeatedly blocks him with subtle hand movements of her own.

Still later that same morning, Kwame stands unsteadily, holding onto the cage mesh, near Mandara and Baraka.

Mandara takes what seems to be hay from the floor.

Kwame turns his body, still holding onto the mesh with one hand, and reaches for the hay; Mandara holds Kwame's hand—the one he had reached with—as he gradually shifts his body weight from the mesh to his mother's body.

Kwame moves back to the mesh, taking half-steps as he is supported, but moving mostly through this shifting of his weight.

The data from this day illustrate the development of greater motor control in Kwame's locomotion and in his reaching. As Kwame gains some degree of independence in moving away from Mandara's body, he increasingly reaches for other substrates: the floor; Kigali; the mesh; food. When Kigali and Kwame join hands, Kwame's reach to his sister results in an affiliative social outcome. Just as he does not have free access to Mandara's breasts, though, Kwame doesn't always gain access to what he reaches for, as can be seen by his failure to chew or ingest food as Mandara eats.

The varied nature of social events involving Kwame reminds us that the degree and quality of co-regulation between social partners may vary markedly. The events included so far in this account of Kwame's developing social requests are characterized by frequent joint action; Mandara joins in with Kwame's movements, reaches, and gestures. Yet right alongside, and at times embedded within, such visibly coordinated events we find instances in which Kwame is physically moved or guided by his mother in a much more asymmetric way. While Kwame still may respond fluidly to the contingencies of the action unfolding around him, in these cases his participation as an active co-constructor of the action is reduced, which results in a qualitatively different type of co-regulation:

As Mandara eats hay, Kwame, now nearly 5 months old, lies in her lap, moving his limbs and head around.

Mandara rises to a partial stand, with her body over Kwame, then sits in such a way that Kwame is positioned half underneath her body.

Mandara stands again, turns 180 degrees, and as Kwame moves and raises his arms, she bends forward first at her head, then so that her whole body lies flat atop Kwame's. The two gorillas now lie in a ventral-ventral position with Kwame's body covered and the top of his head and face just visible beneath Mandara's genital area.

With one hand, Kwame touches and grips Mandara's lower back. As Mandara scoots her body forward, Kwame's entire head is freed from beneath her genital area. (Though Mandara had apparently positioned her genital area over Kwame's face, she made no visible thrusting motions.)

Mandara shifts, reaches back with one hand, and cups Kwame under the head; she pulls his head forward as she rolls onto her back.

As Mandara lies on her back, Kwame sits against her, and reaches for a nearby wall.

As Mandara shifts her leg, Kwame shifts too and is carried away from the wall.

Kwame climbs around on his mother's body.

Mandara brings one leg over toward Kwame and, with her toes, grasps his arm, supporting his elbow with her other foot.

Mandara raises one leg, releasing Kwame from the grip of her toes.

Kwame's gaze shifts and follows the leg's trajectory, and he pushes up to a partial stand against Mandara's body, then sinks lower again.

At this point, one of Mandara's legs is raised in the air, and Kwame shifts around against the other foot.

Mandara raises this other foot, again gripping Kwame.

Mandara's two legs are now straight up in the air as she continues to lie on her back. Kwame hangs from one raised foot in a kind of modified "dangle" posture (with some of his weight on Mandara's torso). As Mandara shifts and lowers one leg, Kwame is suspended from the other, his limbs somewhat splayed out.

Teeth visible, Kwame makes a facial expression that I interpret as a distress face.

Mandara lowers Kwame against her side.

Kwame shifts and turns against her body, as he is still held by his mother's foot.

In this intriguing event can be noted a series of moves on Matata's part that don't seem to be well described as co-regulation. Matata positions Kwame beneath her genital area in what may be a sexual maneuver, and carries out "dangling," which has been reported by other observers of African great ape mothers.[38] Her actions don't seem to come about as part of co-constructing a request with Kwame. Looking at the earlier social events, we can find other examples of this phenomenon, as when Mandara gets up from sitting near Kigali and departs with Kwame, effectively ending an in-progress interaction between Kwame and his older sister. Not every component of every social event is co-regulated fully, though some degree of mutual adjustment may still occur. As noted in the first chapter, researchers of human adult-infant co-regulation routinely find examples of everything from pronounced asymmetry to missed cues, absence of well-coordinated action, and need for repair between social partners. My focus on social requests tends to highlight interactions in which Kwame takes an active co-constructing role, but he participates in social interactions of all kinds, some asymmetric in action and others not co-regulated at all, characterized instead by a lack of mutual adjustment.

Recognizing this state of affairs, we can return to data on the infant Elikya in order to build upon earlier analysis of co-regulated body movement and gesture in captive bonobos. When Elikya interacted with her sister Panbanisha, her body movements and gestures indicated her unease, in marked contrast to her evident comfort and familiarity in interacting with her sister Tamuli. (Panbanisha even kicked Elikya twice, which suggests that Elikya's unease was not unwarranted.) Certainly, the two sisterly relationships experienced by Elikya are different in quality. Taken together with observations on the gorilla infant Kwame, this fact leads to some new insights about co-regulated social communication.

Co-regulation is not a unitary phenomenon; it may be characterized by greater or lesser degrees of coordination or symmetry between the social partners. Coordination or symmetry may tend to vary when the infant interacts with partner A versus partner B, and may also vary within a single dyad, as the social partners interact on different days in different socioemotional and environmental conditions. More than a theoretical point, this realization carries implications for analysis and interpretation of the data.[39] In working with qualitative data, what becomes vital is not just documenting the presence of co-regulation, but also aiming for rigorous comparison in order to document the various ways in which co-regulation may be present, and when it may be absent. Such analysis requires sensitivity to the quality of mutual adjustment in any given event, and to how it may shift over time as an infant develops or interacts with various social partners. As we resume tracing the ontogeny of Kwame's social requesting, it is helpful to look for instances in which coordination is at a premium, or asymmetry relatively minimal, versus those characterized largely by asymmetry or lack of mutual adjustment.

As Kwame gets older, social events often contain elements of fluid co-regulation mixed with miscoordinations:

Nearly 6 months old, Kwame sits near his mother, Mandara, gripping her on the arm.

Kwame puts his other hand on the mesh, pulls up his body, takes his hand off Mandara and stands supported at the mesh.

Kwame climbs partway up the mesh and puts one foot down onto Mandara's shoulder.

Mandara opens her mouth (a mild threat) but is facing forward so that Kwame cannot see this.

Mandara reaches to Kwame and pulls on his leg, then releases him; Kwame has started to turn his body and now hangs facing out, frontward. Kwame swings his body around toward Mandara but as he contacts her, again at the shoulder, she first leans away then shuffles away from him. As she goes, Kwame makes an arm extension, palm up, toward her (so that Mandara cannot see it).

Still oriented toward Mandara, Kwame moves closer to her on the mesh and touches her back lightly several times.

When Mandara does nothing, Kwame returns to the mesh.

Kwame moves closer to his mother and touches her again. He could easily climb on her body, but does not.

As Kwame hangs on the mesh, Mandara turns her head in his direction, then back again.

Kwame crosses his far arm over to reach toward (but not touch) Mandara, with his palm out, then returns to the mesh.

Again, Kwame reaches to Mandara, this time with his closer hand, and he does touch her.

Again firmly on the mesh, Kwame stretches his body backward a bit; Mandara looks over her shoulder at him, raises one
arm up a ways, and turns.

As she is turning, Kwame makes the same expression (with
teeth showing) that I have interpreted before as a distress face.

Mandara's head angle indicates that she may or may not
have been able to see his expression.

As she completes her turn, Mandara cups Kwame behind the
head and pulls him in toward her ventrum. As she does so,
Kwame makes what may be a quick pout of the lips, and
reaches for Mandara as she brings him in.

This event seems to be a mix of fluid co-regulation and missed opportunities for coordination. Mandara ignores Kwame for quite a
while, as he seems to want to request to be taken down from the
mesh. This even might be read as Kwame *trying* to request to be
taken down, but at times his movements are not even visible, or
probably not visible, to Mandara (though his touches were of course
felt by her). Captive ape infants often become adept at climbing *up*
mesh before they can climb *down,* so it may well be that Kwame
wanted help from his mother, yet he showed no obvious distress until near the end of this event. Eventually, he did get help, at a point
coincident with his showing real distress: co-regulation characterizes
the end of this event, when Mandara turns to him, possibly noting
his distress face. As she brings him toward her, Kwame reaches
for her.

Kwame gradually experiences more off-mother time than he had
in the past, and thus discovers what it is like to communicate with
her at a distance. Around the time he reaches 6 months of age,
Kwame begins toddling around on his own, a few steps at a time.
Though he had interacted before with his siblings, as we have seen,
he now enjoys greater freedom to approach them, and they appear
to enjoy increased opportunities to interact with him away from

Mandara's immediate protection. Three days after Kwame turned 6 months old, the data indicate numerous instances of this sibling interaction:

> The subadult male Baraka, lying on his side, extends his arm along the ground toward nearby Kwame, who touches the arm and crawls along it up toward Baraka. A short time later, older brother Ktembe pulls Kwame off the mesh and embraces and mouths him, then tries to move off with Kwame but is restrained by Mandara. Ktembe takes Kwame again, walking away this time with the infant held against his ventrum. Ktembe holds Kwame for 55 seconds, then older sister Kigali takes him. Keeping him for just over 6 minutes, Kigali walks all over the enclosure, Kwame often riding upon her back.

During these 7 minutes when Kwame is carried by his siblings, he witnesses rich and varied interactions between the siblings or between one sibling and other gorillas. He appears not to be distressed by being apart from his mother, though at one point, sitting against Kigali high in a tree, and leaning back to look out upside down, Kwame makes a clear arm extension. Another gorilla may be below, positioned to see the movement, but there is no way to know because the camera is aimed at tree level. Eventually, when Kigali and Ktembe become involved in a vigorous interaction, Kwame between them, Mandara walks calmly up and takes Kwame, who moves fluidly to her.

As Kwame's social network expands, the opportunities for both making social requests and responding to them also expand. Over the next few months, his arm extensions routinely, though by no means always, are constructed as social requests, within the web of interactions themselves marked variously by co-regulation in some cases, and lack of it in others. We have seen instances in which Kwame's arm extensions are made out of sight, or possibly out of sight, of his social partner. A close look at data from the day before Kwame turned 8 months old reveals the continuation of this and some other familiar patterns, as well as hints of some new ones.

Mandara still uses her body movements to exclude Kwame from her breast area; on this day, when she did so, Kwame briefly sucked his own fingers. His siblings still show great interest in Kwame. During one social event in which Ktembe carried off Kwame, co-regulation is spectacularly absent, for Kwame expresses only distress and resistance rather mutual adjustment to Ktembe. Ktembe carried Kwame awkwardly, "walking him forward" from behind more than carrying him at some points. Kwame's face clearly expresses distress and he utters a loud scream as his lower body hits a large white cube (an enrichment object for the gorillas) and then is lifted precariously up to a ledge by Ktembe. Mandara moves in close to the pair only when the brothers separate from each other; she touches Kwame and does not interact at all with Ktembe.

Kwame makes several movements of interest at various intervals on this same morning, some that become constructed as social gesture and others that do not. First, Kwame, sitting with Mandara, watches Ktembe climb up above him, into a tree. Kwame makes a clear arm extension forward, first with palm to the side then with palm up. His eyes seem to be cast downward (from the tree) as he does this. It is unclear with whom he wishes to interact, if anyone, given that Ktembe is above, Mandara is off to the side, and the camera could not record the gorilla, if any, located beneath them. Second, facing Mandara, Kwame touches lightly around her mouth. Mandara brings her face down to Kwame and pulls him in closer; then he shifts or is shifted downward a bit against her. Third, holding a leaf, Kwame extends his arm up to Mandara's mouth area; this time his mother seems to ignore the movement. Later, Ktembe gathers Kwame from near Mandara to his ventrum, and begins to move away. Just as Ktembe is turning away, Kwame quickly extends his arm in his mother's direction, palm down. He is close enough to touch Mandara but does not. Seven seconds later, Mandara retrieves Kwame from Ktembe.

From these four movements by Kwame comes a mixed picture. In the first case, we have no way to make sense of the arm movement because its context is not clear. In the second and fourth instances, Mandara enters into the movement with Kwame so that it may be considered a social request, one with visible outcomes. In the remaining case, in which Kwame reaches toward her holding a leaf, Mandara seems either to ignore the movement or refuse to participate.

Almost 2 months later, at nearly 10 months old, Kwame makes arm extensions to Mandara's mouth or hands when she eats, with little visible response. At one point, Ktembe moves toward, and eventually a bit past, Mandara and Kwame. As he is moving past the pair, facing away, Kwame extends his arm, palm down, toward his brother (who could not have seen it). When Ktembe sits near them, adopting a more forward-facing bodily orientation, Kwame again extends his arm toward his brother, this time palm up. Ktembe may have been able to see this motion, but no visible outcome results from Kwame's movement. As before, Kwame's movements on this day are well executed as far as their form and trajectory are concerned, but are sometimes made in such a way vis-à-vis the social partner as to limit opportunities for the construction of social requests.

Kwame, then, as a young infant, sometimes makes movements so as to enable the construction of a social request that is followed by joint action. At other times, either he fails to make the movement in such a way as to allow social construction, or his social partner fails to join in. As the months go by, social requests continue to occur in fast-moving social events that comprise a mix of elements. Near Kwame's first birthday, an event occurs that illustrates this mix:

Kwame has been interacting with Ktembe but runs off toward his mother. As Kwame passes near to where Baraka sits, Baraka leans forward, reaches for and touches Kwame.

Kwame continues on toward his mother, and as he does, Baraka shifts from a seated position to leaning forward on his elbows.

Kwame walks in front of Mandara's body at the mesh, then, both arms raised high, takes a step bipedally toward Baraka and brings down both arms onto Baraka's head.

Baraka sits up again, and as he does, he lifts Kwame to him and the two gorillas play-bite and play-wrestle.

This event, a routine part of the gorillas' daily life, is not adequately described by saying that Kwame initiated play with Baraka. Certainly, Kwame's action in first raising his arms then bringing then down onto Baraka's head is playful in nature, but Kwame may not have acted in this manner had not Baraka, just shortly before, leaned toward him and contacted him. Together the partners move jointly toward play, though at one point—when Baraka lifts Kwame up—the older and stronger partner plays a more powerful role.

The gestures and body movements in this gorilla group are best seen as operating together, as part of multimodal communication. Though social gestures emerge from jointly constructed body movements, gestures should not be thought of as located at the apex of some imaginary movement hierarchy. Body movements are as vitally communicative as are the gestures, whether coupled with those gestures or on their own, a point recognized by Savage-Rumbaugh in her early study of iconicity in bonobos. Gestures alone do sometimes play a vital role, because mutually constructed arm-extension requests may be effective ways for partners to coordinate their actions. These gestures, though, are not "acquired" via dyadic shaping (ontogenetic ritualization) that is at first fluid but then stable and consistent; rather, meaning is created anew as social partners act together in a dance of movement and gesture.

As he matures, Kwame continues to use arm extensions. At about 2 and 1/2 years old, Kwame, sitting on a shelf with his mother, older brother Ktembe, and younger brother Kojo, makes two arm movements toward his mother. The first is a palm-up movement toward a white cloth that she holds, followed by a grab at the cloth (which does make contact). Ktembe had swatted the cloth across the shelf to Kwame, but Mandara had taken it away for herself, just before Kwame's arm movement. The second is a pronounced arm extension made to Mandara immediately after she mildly disciplines him, with open mouth and a slight push on his body, apparently for running into Kojo (and possibly also for hitting Kojo shortly before). His arm movement is qualitatively unlike others seen in the study in its stiffness and angle, and resembles requests for reconciliation following conflict in chimpanzees.[40] In both cases, Mandara was perfectly positioned to see the movements; immediately after the second one, she turns her head away. In neither case does overt joint action result.

At nearly 3 years, Kwame sits near Ktembe. Ktembe rises, holding onto a firehose (an enrichment object suspended across the cage). Kwame raises his arm toward the fire hose; he's sitting as he does this, but he's also pushing his body up a bit. Kwame stops his arm movement, then resumes it but in a new orientation—away from the firehose and toward Ktembe (so that his arm becomes more horizontally than vertically oriented). Kwame stands and walks semibipedally toward Kwame, and they play, while Ktembe continues to hold onto the firehose overhead. Interestingly, Kwame had made no effort to stand fully and contact the firehose. As usual, Kwame's intentions remain invisible to us, but the visible outcome, play with Ktembe, may well have been facilitated by the two brothers constructing a social request.

As Kwame matures, then, he moves from co-regulated body movement on his mother's body to a complicated mix of body movements: movements that might have been constructed as social gesture if they had been given in clear sight of the social partner; and movements that do become constructed as social gesture, some ending in joint action and others not. Over time, the co-regulation becomes generally less asymmetric. Still, co-regulation may be absent alto-gether on certain occasions. The longitudinal nature of this research will allow assessment, in the future, of Kwame's gesturing as a juve-nile, and comparisons will be made between the course of his ges-tural ontogeny and that of his younger brother's.

Though the issue of future research in African great ape social communication is discussed thoroughly in Chapter 6, before leaving the gorilla study I must acknowledge that the analysis offered here merely scratches the surface of co-regulated gesture and nonvocal so-cial communication in this group. Further qualitative analysis will deepen our understanding of the mix of symmetric and asymmetric events or of co-regulation and its absence during social communica-tion, as well as of the variation in co-regulation along varied axes of social interaction.

One possible avenue for hypothesis-testing in this gorilla group, and in other groups of African great apes, stems from research by Jaffe and colleagues on human mothers and infants. Assessing a large number of mother-infant pairs, these researchers began to sus-pect that very high levels of coordination and contingency may be suboptimal for attachment. "We hypothesize that midrange coordi-nation leaves more 'space,' more room for uncertainty, initiative, and flexibility within the experience of correspondence and contingency. Attachment outcomes are favored when the exchange transpires in an atmosphere of somewhat looser (rather than tight or very loose) coordination, 'optional rather than obligatory' contingency."[41] It may be enlightening for primatologists to compare behavioral profiles across mother-infant great ape pairs with differing intensities of co-ordination and contingency in their communication.

Some researchers might wish to carry out quantitative analysis on the gorillas at the National Zoo and other locations, perhaps to dis-cern what proportion of observed arm extensions (and other move-ments) are constructed as social requests at various ages and with various partners. How many of the gestures that were constructed by an infant and his social partners were also constructed by later-born siblings and *their* social partners would be interesting to know. More quantitative work may be useful, too, on cross-group comparison of gestural profiles in young gorillas and other African great apes.

Data on patterns of body movement and gesture as a whole can be helpful in compiling a socioemotional profile of these primates. That no events reported for the National Zoo gorillas have included Kuja, Kwame's father, in physical, playful, or intimate interaction with Kwame is not an artifact of selective reporting. Like the other gorillas, Kwame closely monitors Kuja's movements, but he also rarely comes close to Kuja. This father-son relationship seems to be one of mutual avoidance, a dynamic reflected most visibly in the tenor of Kwame's body movement around Kuja. Unsurprisingly, Kwame is more watchful and tense near the silverback male than near others in his group, but this degree of mutual avoidance between silverback and infant is not mirrored in all captive gorilla populations.[42]

"Reading" the gorillas' nonvocal communication aids in understanding group dynamics as well. The course of my study has paralleled Baraka's development into a large subadult, now at an age where young males often challenge a silverback's dominance and rule. Baraka has in fact done this in various ways, ranging from mating with Mandara to hurling objects at Kuja from close range. What may have been less predictable is the degree to which Baraka resisted Kuja during a major conflict. Despite Baraka's fear when pursued by Kuja (judged to exist on the basis of my observation of his facial expressions; his screaming; and the products of his loose bowels), Baraka refused to submit fully in the way that Kuja indicated by pushing on Baraka's limbs and body. The filmed record clearly shows this repeated resistance. Similarly, after Kojo's birth, when Kwame became a big brother and was observed repeatedly sucking his thumb near Mandara, we have visible evidence to support a contention that he wished to suck or derive comfort from Mandara's breast, from which he had been displaced at an early age.

## Summing Up

From Ladygina-Kohts's study of the chimpanzee Joni, and others like it, primatologists have long known that African great apes may express themselves to humans using body movement and gesture. More recent, detailed study reveals that body movement and gesture may be powerful avenues of social coordination for group-living captive African great apes as they interact with each other, as well. When data are recorded on film, for repeated watching and detailed analysis, it becomes easy to see that group-living African great apes spontaneously use these movements to create meaning with each other. Contingencies abound, so that the course of events changes *as* events are enacted. As in human communication, not all movements are social requests; not all potential social requests are constructed as such; and not all constructed social requests bring about joint action. Variation occurs not just with infant age or social partner but also within dyads according to a web of factors. The two social partners create meaning—or fail to create it—each time they interact.

For an anthropologist, the research opportunities and exciting discoveries associated with observing nonvocal communication in captive African great apes require that a follow-up series of questions be asked. Do wild African great apes use body movement and gesture in similar ways? If so, are these movements and gestures similarly coregulated? It is to these questions that I turn in the next chapter.

# 4

## Gesture in Wild African Great Apes

In the dense forest of the Democratic Republic of Congo, a young male bonobo leaps into a tree. He vocalizes, and is answered by other bonobos. With his right arm outstretched and his hand half-closed, he points to the undergrowth, where two groups of primatologists are attempting to conceal themselves. While pointing, he screams and turns his head toward where the other bonobos are located. When he points and calls in this manner twice more, the other bonobos approach and look toward the humans, and are soon joined by the young male.[1]

In the Central African Republic, a wild western gorilla female claps her hands together, in the same manner as humans do. Over the next few hours, most mature females in her group clap as well, with differing degrees of intensity. The group's silverback merely grunts when he hears a soft, short clap, but roars and moves around when he hears louder and longer clapping. Observing this behavior, a primatologist notes that the gorillas appeared nervous, and speculates that the clapping is a response to some unusual situation.[2]

An eastern gorilla infant, 5 months old, moves toward its mother, apparently uneasy about something. The mother extends her hand, the infant falls into it, and the mother pulls the infant in to her chest. Soon enough the infant departs, but then hurries again to its mother. Standing bipedally at the mother's side, the infant raises both arms above its head; the mother gathers the baby to her ventrum with one arm.[3]

In Tanzania, the old female chimpanzee Flo fishes for termites at a mound. Her son Figan appears restless, as if he wishes to move on (notorious for extended tool-using bouts, Flo had been fishing for 2 hours already). In fact, he *had* headed off several times, only to return when his mother did not follow. Now he approaches his little brother, Flint. Jane Goodall explains what happened next: "Adopting the posture of a mother who signals her infant to climb onto her back, Figan bent one leg and reached back his hand to Flint, uttering a soft, pleading whimper. Flint tottered up to him at once, and Figan, still whimpering, put his hand under Flint and gently pushed him onto his back."[4] When Figan left the mound area this time, Flo put down her tool and followed.

These four reports of gesture by African great apes in the wild are anecdotal. Rather than emerging from research explicitly designed to uncover patterns in gesture and body movement, or in social communication generally, these gestures were seen during general observations. Yet they hint powerfully at the role that nonvocal social communication may play in the social life of these apes in their natural surroundings. In all four cases, gesture enhanced, in some way, the coordination of social partners. When one bonobo notified some others of a source of possible danger, the apes gathered together. A silverback leader of western gorilla females apparently assessed the tension in his group by monitoring the intensity of hand clapping that he heard. Making an arms-up movement, an infant eastern gorilla was picked up by its mother. Finally, older brother chimpanzee Figan made vocalizations and movements toward Flint that resulted in Flint's climbing onto his brother's back, for a dorsal ride. (And, not incidentally, resulted also in Figan's motivating his mother, Flo, to stop termite fishing and move on.)

The movements in the last two incidents probably were constructed as social requests: The eastern infant gorilla and its mother, and the two chimpanzee brothers, together made a movement into a social request. Yet even in these cases, as in the remaining two anecdotes, making a definitive claim for co-regulated social communication is tricky because mutual adjustments of the social partners were not reported in detail. Here I confront the central challenge of this chapter: Given that little research has been done on African great ape gesture in the wild, and that the published studies on this topic typically lack qualitative detail, is it possible to do more than report a string of intriguing anecdotes? Can I support the central claims of this book, that African great ape body movement and gesture are co-regulated, and that from co-regulated events, meaning emerges?

This challenge is one of some magnitude. Gesture and body movement are rarely treated as worthy categories in reports of primate social communication. The index for Hauser's 653-page *Evolution of Communication,* published in 1996, includes no entry for "gesture" or "gestures" either in their own right or as a subcategory under "visual signals" or "nonhuman primates." By comparison, "vocal expression" and "vocal signals" each merit an entry, as does "facial expression." Under "nonhuman primates," entries related to both facial expressions and vocalizations appear.

Consulting Hauser's table of contents, one finds multiple references to facial expressions and vocalizations of primates, including 16 pages of text devoted to "facial and gestural expressions in primates." Further investigation reveals, though, that more than half of those 16 pages discuss humans alone. Of the pages that include nonhuman primates, the subject of nonvocal gestures other than facial expressions merits two sentences, and these refer to Tomasello's captive chimpanzees (under the topic of imitation).

Two volumes edited by prominent primatologists, and published by Cambridge University Press 6 years apart, provide a wealth of information on wild as well as captive great apes. According to the index in McGrew, Marchant, and Nishida's 1996 *Great Ape Societies,* "gesture" is discussed on 3 of the volume's 308 pages; 2 of these pages refer to captive apes and the third to humans. No separate listing is made for "facial expressions," though "face recognition" is mentioned. Vocalizations are discussed on over 40 pages (one 14-

page chapter in the book is "comparative studies of African ape vocal behavior.") In Boesch, Hohmann, and Marchant's 2002 *Behavioural Diversity in Chimpanzees and Bonobos,* "gesture" and "facial expression" are absent from the index. This omission is interesting given that an entire chapter is devoted to the grooming hand-clasp in Tanzanian chimpanzees, a study that I consider to fall under gestural research. Consulting the index under "vocalizations," one learns that vocal behavior is explored on 12 of the book's 276 pages.

In *Primate Cognition,* by the primatologists Tomasello and Call, great ape gesture is discussed at greater length than in any of the books noted above, perhaps because Tomasello himself carries out gestural research; in any case, most of the discussion centers on captive, including enculturated, great apes. My reading of the top scientific journals in primatology over the last decade finds little to correct this picture of inattention to gesture in wild African great apes, though occasionally an exciting exception can be found. In general, more data are published, whether in books or journals, on captive than wild African great ape gesture—a telling statement, given the paucity of gestural research in captivity. The best source of information on wild African great ape gesture today continues to be what might be termed "ape ethnographies," monographs derived from detailed long-term studies by field workers such as Schaller, Goodall, Kano, and Boesch. Such books yield rich information on body movement and gesture, even in the absence of a specific focus on nonvocal social communication.

In this chapter, I summarize much of what is known about wild African ape gesture in four behavioral contexts. Where possible, I will report on the presence of co-regulation and social construction of meaning, or at least, the potential for these to occur. The data are reviewed not exhaustively but in order to represent what may be concluded about body movement and gesture in courtship; agonism; grooming; and mother-infant behavior. I know of no better way to sort the data, but before I embark upon a review organized in this manner, I highlight one report that shows convincingly how gesture and body movement do not separate neatly into discrete behavioral categories for easy analysis.

## Rocking Gestures in Bonobos

Bonobos are the species famous for breaking the link between sex and reproduction—and for various innovative types of sexual behavior. As discussed in Chapter 3, captive bonobos coordinate with each other, using gestures, as they move together toward copulation. Kano's field work at Wamba in the Democratic Republic of Congo, then called Zaire, tells us that wild bonobos, too, gesture in the sexual realm:

A male attracts the attention of a female who is far enough away that she cannot be touched, faces her, and spreads his thighs. While exposing his erect penis, he sits or moves his squatting body up and down, forward and back, or side to side. Some males stick out their chest, and some stoop forward while they are displaying. Their hands are extended and moved in any direction according to individual preference, upward, sideways and, most often, forward, as if to beckon the female.

If the female does not respond to this first form of courtship display, the male often changes to a second form of display. He approaches the female, sits or stands bipedally, and extends his hand, lightly touching and then releasing her head, shoulder, back, or knee. His body slowly moves forward and back and side to side.[5]

Most compelling about this description is its indication of the seamless integration of various types of movement, and how the expression of this "whole package" may vary across individuals. The bonobos move their bodies up and down, forward and back, or side to side *as* they extend their hands in various directions. Different males may gesture in different ways, according to what Kano terms "individual preference." Given the absence of stable monogamous pairs in bonobos, this means that the female does not interact with just one set of gestures by one male in the sexual context. Rather, she encounters unpredictable contingencies as she attends to first one male and later another, each gesturing in his own preferred manner. The situation is even more complex than this, though, because individual males shift their gesturing as they monitor the females' response. If one bout of gesturing does not bring about the desired response from a female, a different avenue may be attempted.

Astute readers will have noticed my lapse into language at odds with DST thinking: bonobo males gesture, and females respond to the gestures. The DST interpretation would be that the male and the female together construct a gesture from the male's movement toward the female, just as in the last chapter, captive gorilla social partners were shown to construct an arm movement as a social-request gesture. DST-based analysis of filmed records would allow an understanding of the dance-like quality of bonobo courtship. One could analyze, first, the degree to which females shift their bodies, heads, limbs, facial expressions, and/or gaze *as* males make their movements toward them, and then, the trajectory of co-constructed action, which would indicate whether the partners have made meaning from a particular set of movements. In order to avoid constant repetition of the "more research is needed" refrain in this chapter, let me say it once and be done with it: only when the moment-by-moment mutual adjustment between social partners (complete with fluid coordination, missed opportunities for coordination, refusal of one partner to participate, and social ignoring by one partner of the other) becomes a part of long-term research will the co-regulated nature of African great ape gesture in the wild be better understood.

Reading Kano's description, one might predict that the males' whole-body motions (up and down, forward and back, side to side) are tightly correlated with a sexual context, so that the rocking behavior indicates sexual desire as opposed to, say, a wish for play, grooming, or some other social behavior. Data compiled by Kuroda, Kano's colleague at Wamba, tell us that the bonobos' rocking behavior is far more complex and fascinating than that. Published in a journal of the Japan Ethological Society at Kyoto University, Kuroda's report is sometimes cited in primatological literature but rarely discussed fully; it deserves to be, for its implications for understanding African great ape gesture are stunning.

Referring to the bonobos' rocking behaviors as gesture, Kuroda describes them as "a variety of motions in which the pygmy chimpanzee rocks or sways its upper body and head back and forth and/or from side to side. This also includes slow leaning backward and one time rocking of the upper body. The latter gesture sometimes appears as if the individual is sticking out its chest."[6] Kuroda's core finding is that these gestures *mean* something because the rockers' companions interpret the motions as part of a complex of factors that, taken together, imbue the motion with significance. The meaning is not "in" the rocking itself.

In order to see this more clearly, let's examine Kuroda's data in some detail. Rocking gestures were observed in seven main contexts: sex (of varied types) and courtship, demand for submissive presenting, invitation for grooming, invitation for play, mother-infant behavior, requesting permission for co-sitting and passing near another, and charging displays. Rocking brought about interactions marked by body contact or close proximity in all categories except the final one, charging. The bonobo to whom the rocking was directed might approach closely, present for some form of sexual behavior, cling, embrace, sit near—or, sometimes, ignore the rocker.

Rocking was observed in over 70 percent of courtship attempts directed by mature males to mature females, the single most frequent behavioral context with which it was associated. Immense variation in the quality of movement occurs in what might otherwise be thought a monolithic behavior. Describing actions that mirror the first type of courtship behavior reported by Kano in the opening quote of this section, Kuroda specifies that "A type rocking can be roughly divided into 4 sub-types according to the degree of rocking and arm-raising: (A1) intense rocking involving arm-raising, (A2) rocking a few times with or without arm-raising, (A3) backward leaning with one-arm-raising, and (A4) one time rocking without arm-raising."[7]

To this classification must be added the observed variation with B type courtship—apparently corresponding to the second type noted by Kano—and C type as well, in which a male simply stands quadrupedally facing a female and nods his head. Kuroda notes that various social factors—the male's age, the distance the female is from the male, the nature and speed of the female's response, and so on— bear upon which type of gesture is used. At this point it would seem just as well to give up trying to label discrete types and subtypes. Given the number of ways all these factors may be combined, the rocking gestures associated with courtship surely vary not discretely, but on a continuum.

Though males are generally penile-erected when they rock in this situation, the rocking itself is nonetheless important, as is most clearly demonstrated in cases where females cannot see the males' erections. Slight rocking by the male resulted in a second copulation by one pair of bonobos even when the male's erection was not visible to the female. In type B courtship where males walk in front of females, only the rocking is visible to the female. Two times, females made what appears to be an error in assuming that a rocking-like motion had taken place: "Young estrous females misunderstood a male's leaning on a tree trunk, as a sign for courtship. In both cases, the female rushed to the male and clung ventroventrally or crouched in presentation, but the male's penis was not erect and copulation did not occur."[8]

Though not as frequently as males, females too may use the rocking gesture. They may do so when inviting copulation with mature males or younger males, even infants (just as mature males may invite infant females), or when inviting genital rubbing with other females. Once, a juvenile male rushed to a female leaning against a tree trunk, another example, apparently, of "misreading" a mere resting posture as a rocking gesture, for the female simply ignored the youngster.

Data from behavioral contexts other than sex and courtship are critical for understanding the rocking gesture. When a male rocks more from side to side than back and forth, and hoots with erected hair but little or no arm-raising, other bonobos run away. The observer apes apparently distinguish this constellation of factors from all the other rocking gestures that bring about proximity or body contact. In fact, males who rock sidewise and hoot then go on to engage in a charging display. The argument could be made in this case that the observer bonobos simply learn by association, over time and with repeated experience, that males who have erected hair, who hoot, and who show certain kinds of body movement are about to charge. Yet, as we have seen in examining male courtship behavior, variations in rocking occur that are best considered continuous rather than discrete.

Further, when males without erect penises rock their bodies toward other males, the outcome depends on certain subtleties that are unlikely to be discrete. Slight rocking done by one male to another when the group is calm, or about to rest after a period of feeding, often results in grooming. Rocking toward another bonobo, together with a play face, leads to play. Rocking may occur when mothers and offspring are together, as well. At around 4 or 5 years of age, bonobo youngsters may whimper and rock in front of their mothers, continuing this behavior for some time if the mother does not respond. "Infants often burst into temper tantrums between bouts of such rocking. In some cases, mothers responded with slight rocking or arm-raising and the infants immediately clung to them."[9]

The critical lesson underlying Kuroda's work is that bonobo social partners together converge on a meaning for the rocking gesture. The rocking itself has no meaning. When rocking, a bonobo takes into account the identity of his partner and how that partner acts as the rocking unfolds; he may adjust his own movements *as* the other acts. When looking at another bonobo who is rocking, social partners attend to everything from the degree of rocking (slight versus more vigorous) to the partner's facial expression (play face or not?) and apparent arousal level (erect penis in males? presence of pilo-erection?). That creation of meaning occurs when bonobos communicate through co-regulated rocking is a conclusion identical to the one offered in Chapter 2 when I discussed the instance of one person saying to another, "Watch out! A tree branch is about to fall on your head!" The meaning in even such a seemingly straightforward utterance does not reside in the words. Rather, it is built up by the two people as they converse and as they assess a multitude of factors ranging from voice and facial expression to events in their shared history.

Though Kuroda himself uses the sender-receiver terminology so conventional in primatology, he reaches a conclusion that points the study of African great ape communication in unconventional directions: "The rocking gesture appears to convey clearly the rocking animals' intention to the signal receiver . . . As various rocking gestures commonly result in close access between participants, it may correspond to 'approach.' The partner is indicated by the direction of the gesture, or touching. It must be noted that the meaning of behavior changes according to combinations of participants . . . If the rocking male's penis is not erect, the meaning of the interaction changes depending on the group situation and intensity of rocking."[10]

As this passage indicates, research methodologies focusing on individual senders and receivers to the exclusion of larger social webs will draw only limited conclusions about meaning in social communication. Understanding the fascinating, subtle process of social construction of meaning through co-regulation has been subordinated to isolating the "variation by social context" that affects "senders" and "receivers."

In writing about chimpanzee social communication, Goodall notes: "Sometimes it is *only* the context that can provide the receiver with the information necessary to interpret a given signal sequence correctly. Thus in human communication, 'Go jump in the lake' means one thing when addressed by a mother to her muddy child and something quite different when it concludes a friendly argument between adults. When an adult male chimpanzee, in response to calls from across the valley, suddenly shows full hair erection, a nearby female may hurry over to him and the two may hold hands and embrace as both stare toward the sounds. If, however, the male bristles in response to the approach of a rival male, the same female is likely to rush to the safety of a tree, anticipating that there may be trouble between the two."[11]

The value of this passage rests on insights about variation that are central to Goodall's work. That she mentions variation in what "male bristling" may mean in different contexts is no surprise, given her commitment to understanding behavioral variation across individuals, and within individuals across contexts. Yet the focus in this passage is still put on two individual apes, the producer and the comprehender, and their respective roles in a social event. Kuroda's work, and DST in general, pushes us to move past variation by social context in signal production and comprehension to a full description of co-regulation by social partners.

## Courtship and Greeting Behavior

As the discussion of bonobo rocking behavior has shown, coordination and mutual adjustment is at a premium between two apes engaged in sex- or courtship-related behavior. That much of this mutual adjustment should be gesture-mediated is a reasonable prediction, given the proximity at which two potential sexual partners find themselves. Goodall describes six courtship gestures observed in a sexual context.[12] By assessing the degree to which these occur also in nonsexual situations, leading to different outcomes, we may discover whether the situation at Gombe echoes that among Kuroda's bonobos, who closely monitor a web of variables in order to construct meaning with their social partners.

Goodall describes the *bipedal swagger* as occurring when a chimpanzee, almost always male, "stands upright and sways rhythmically from foot to foot, his shoulders slightly hunched and his arms held out and away from the body, usually to the side."[13] Though this swagger is most often seen when a male is trying to court a female, a male may also adopt this posture when threatening another male of similar rank. Three times, females were observed to swagger bipedally. Two such swaggers occurred during aggressive interactions between females; the third was directed toward a mature male (no details given). Interestingly, males seem not to swagger aggressively at females, and presumably no swaggers occurred in sexual courtship between males.

It might seem then that bipedal swaggers are nearly always coupled with male courtship of females or incidents of male-male aggression, but in fact they may accompany greeting behaviors between chimpanzees as well. When Goodall describes gestures used in greeting, we begin to get a feel for the social construction of the bipedal swagger and other gestures by Gombe chimpanzees: "The particular gestures and postures displayed during a greeting depend partly on the age-sex class of the animals concerned, partly on their individuality, and partly on their mood at the time and the length of time for which they have been separated. Thus the more exaggerated gestures (such as embracing) are more likely to occur between individuals that are strongly attracted to each other (particularly if they have not seen each other for several days), than between two individuals that seldom interact socially in other ways. Swaggering and

charging prior to greeting is seen more frequently when two associations of chimpanzees meet than when one animal quietly approaches a resting group."[14] Goodall also notes that the way in which
a particular greeting unfolds between two chimpanzees may be
strongly influenced by the recent social history of the pair.[15]

Clearly, then, the bipedal swagger may be adopted in several contexts. When made outside a sexual context, it indicates, on its own,
neither aggressive intent nor desire to greet, though Goodall suggests its inclusion in a greeting ritual may introduce an aggressive element. It would be fascinating to find out whether "social construction errors" occur—whether chimpanzees, perhaps younger or less
experienced males, sometimes rush to greet a swaggering male only
to discover that he does not intend to greet at all.

Among the six courtship gestures, Goodall includes *glaring*, the directing of a fixed stare from one chimpanzee to another. Like the
bipedal swagger, the glare may be used also in threatening situations. *Branching* spans context, as well; a chimpanzee may shake a
branch from side to side or back and forward in courtship, or when
threatening other species or occasionally other chimpanzees. In the
*sitting hunch,* observed typically in adolescent males, the chimpanzee
hunches his shoulders and raises his arms in front or to the side. A
male may use this posture in an aggressive interaction with a female,
but otherwise the hunch seems tightly correlated with courtship.

Goodall mentions the final two gestures only in the context of
courtship behavior. *Tree leaping* involves a male's leaping and swinging through the branches while keeping his body upright and facing
a female. When *beckoning,* a bipedal male raises an arm level with his
head or higher, then rapidly sweeps it toward his own body, with his
hand tracing an arc in the air. This gesture, Goodall notes, resembles
the motion made by females when gathering their infants to their
ventrum. It seems to resemble, as well, the iconic motioning of the
captive gorilla Kubie to his own body when interacting with a female
(see Chapter 3).

As we would expect, Goodall describes these gestures as produced by individual chimpanzees. Whether qualitative variation, as in the degree of swagger or the arc in which the arms are raised during a sitting hunch or beckoning gesture, affects the outcome between social partners is not addressed. Goodall notes that females responded, either by running toward males or by remaining still in a crouched posture, to 82 percent of the approaches or courtship displays made by mature courting males. Some females ran away, screaming, from courting males, whereas others ignored courtship displays. If males persisted, some of these reluctant females did eventually present.

Further, in 37 of 213 observed copulations, the female solicited the male. "Typically, the female approached to within six feet, flattened herself in front of the male with her limbs flexed, and looked back at him over her shoulder. Five times the soliciting females were ignored; four of them walked away, but the fifth persisted until the male mounted and copulated with her."[16] The event in which two chimpanzees come together for copulation may thus proceed smoothly or not so smoothly, and may require persistence on the part of one social partner. No body movement or gesture is *the* indicator of sexual desire by either party. Even an erect penis, a feature that might be predicted to be unambiguously sexual, may in fact be "a confusing signal because it occurs in a variety of nonsexual contexts also, such as reunion or other kinds of social excitement."[17] Taken together, the data on Gombe courtship (and greetings) strongly suggest that the gestures involved are contingent and the communication co-regulated.

A behavior not seen at Gombe, but quite prominent at other chimpanzee sites and sometimes associated with courtship, is leaf-clipping. Leaf-clipping, first described by Nishida, occurs at Mahale when a chimpanzee picks off one or a small number of leaves, then bites the leaf to pieces by pulling the petiole from side to side in the fingers while removing the leaf blade with the incisor teeth. When the midrib and bits of the leaf blade alone remain, the leaf is dropped and another clump may be selected and worked.[18] Leaf-clipping may enhance the courtship display of male chimpanzees at Mahale. In one case reported by Nishida, an adolescent male violently shook a branch, held in one foot, while standing bipedally in a tree above an estrous female. Next, by leaf-clipping, the male made a "great crunching sound," at which point the female approached. The male slapped the tree trunk with one hand, and, when he moved toward the end of a branch, the female followed. When the male stamped the branch with one foot the female went closer to him, adopted the presentation posture, and the two copulated.

Leaf-clipping at Mahale, though, may be performed also by mature males toward females; by estrous females in soliciting copulation from males; or in play or what Nishida terms "frustrative behavior." When used in courtship, it may be integrated with other courtship movements and gestures, or may occur alone; it may be made during consortship, or outside that context. Nishida notes that the sound involved is important to leaf-clipping, but suggests that the leaf-clipping display may be more subtle than branching or stamping. In short, as with rocking the body in bonobos, here we have movements that combine with other movements and gestures in myriad ways so that the meaning of the leaf-clipping is built up by the chimpanzees interacting together.

Leaf-clipping has been observed also at other long-term chimpanzee sites (though not at Gombe), with variation in both the method of execution and the contexts in which it is performed.[19] A treasure trove of information about chimpanzee co-regulated social communication may await discovery via detailed study of leaf-clipping. Exactly how do social partners come to assign meaning to particular instances of leaf-clipping? When Mahale leaf-clippers act in a sexual way but their partners respond in nonsexual ways, or ignore the leaf-clipper altogether, what happens then? Do some Mahale chimpanzees "misread" leaf-clipping, so that communicational missteps result? Given that leaf-clipping unfolds in variant rather than stereotyped ways, even within a population, one logical next step in research is to seek contingencies in the social partners' actions during leaf-clipping.

That such variability can be reasonably expected wherever leaf-clipping occurs is suggested by Nishida's data on leaf-clipping from Mahale; by Kuroda's and Goodall's observations on variability in other aspects of chimpanzee courtship behavior; and by Kano's observation of "an unusual courtship display" by a bonobo at Wamba.[20] One day in 1991, Kano watched a low-ranked male, Mituo, court an estrous female, Miso. Earlier that same morning, Miso had mated four times with the community's alpha male. At 7:00 A.M., ten bonobos were still close to each other at their night nesting site. Mituo climbed a tree and sat on a branch above Miso. He had a penile erection but because of the apes' relative positions, it was unlikely to have been visible to the highest-ranking male in the subgroup, the second highest male in the community. At this point Miso, who was eating, ignored Mituo.

Mituo then pulled down an overhead branch, plucked off a leafy tip, and dropped it; as it fell to the ground it passed by Miso. He then dropped three more twigs in quick succession, each passing by Miso. Miso's only response was one quick look at Mituo. When Miso's 5-year-old daughter climbed up to sit in front of Mituo, the male ignored her and she soon returned to her mother. Kano describes what happened next: "Mituo stood bipedally, picked a twig from an overhead branch and dropped it. Several seconds later, he swayed himself to and fro very slowly after dropping another twig. Several seconds later, he again dropped another twig, and then swayed in the same manner. Mituo sat, shook a twig slowly for a few seconds, and released it. He repeated the same procedure. Immediately after that, Miso climbed up the tree with her infant on her back, approached and presented to Mituo who then mounted her and thrust until . . . he dismounted. Immediately after copulation, Mituo climbed down and sat, still with a penile erection while Miso remained where they

mated. About 10 seconds after, he moved down to the ground grunt-
ing softly and disappeared."[21]

Mituo's behavior differs appreciably from that of most courting
bonobo males. His leaf-dropping and leaf-shaking were performed
quietly and in a secretive way, and he did not gaze at the female during courtship as is typical. Kano's interpretation is intriguing: This
incidence of leaf-dropping behavior "is considered as a counter tactic
by the lower-ranking male to improve his mating chances" in the
presence of a higher-ranking male.[22] Similar in some ways to the
leaf-clipping at Mahale, the quiet nature of this leaf-dropping is of
great interest. I know of no other case of leaf-dropping reported
in the literature; for now the combined swaying and leaf-dropping
stands as an example of "a different way to do things" in courtship. It
indicates that two bonobos were able to construct meaning together
from body movements, gestures, and actions that are, at the least,
quite rare, if not actually unique to this particular male.

Kano acknowledges that although the majority of copulations at
Wamba are tallied as male initiated, in reality, identifying an initiator
may be impossible. Sometimes an estrous female bonobo chooses to
feed near a male, "not too close, but not too far," in Kano's wording.
"At these times, the male [pygmy] chimpanzee might be fascinated
by her swollen genitalia. Although the female would appear not to
notice the male at first, when he showed a little courtship display
movement, she would suddenly approach and present to him for
copulation. In this situation, we cannot say that the male initiated
copulation."[23] Kano does not simply mean that the female bonobo,
instead of the male, must be scored as initiating copulation. As I interpret his comment, he converges on a point made often in DST,
that outcomes do not result from one individual acting toward another but may emerge from the actions of the unit male+female, the
two social partners acting together.

A similar approach may be taken in coming to understand sexual
behavior between bonobo partners of the same sex, as in female-
female genito-genital (GG) rubbing. Kano offers, using linear terms,

a general description of what happens in GG rubbing: Female A approaches female B, then stands bipedally and extends her hand to B, bringing her face close to B's face and peering at B. If B does not respond, A may grasp B's knees or other body part, and shake her. B rolls over, spreading her thighs, and B embraces A ventrally when A mounts her. The GG rubbing then occurs.[24]

Yet we can well imagine that B is not always so passive, and might first gaze at or move toward A, just as a female may sit near a male who has shown no courtship behavior. Certainly, females vary in their approach to GG rubbing, as Kano makes clear.[25] Females who beg for an invitation to rub tend to be younger and of lower status, whereas females who simply lie down on their backs and await a mount tend to be older and higher ranking. When two females close in age GG rub with each other, they first present while lying on their backs. Awaiting clarification is the degree to which these variant routes unfold via contingencies and mutual adjustments.

Data on body movement and gesture in wild gorillas, for courtship and other behaviors, are harder to come by than those for chimpanzees and bonobos. Schaller's opinion that gorillas are "introverts, who keep their emotions suppressed,"[26] may hint at the reason. Writing for a popular audience, Schaller probably refers with this phrase to the same idea as does the primate field worker Parnell, who remarks upon gorillas' "undeniable economy of movement." Describing gorillas as "masters of nuance in close-quarters communication," Parnell believes that "up to now, we have largely missed the most sophisticated behaviors [of social communication] in the gorillas' repertoire. These may be achieved through subtle changes in body orientation or eye contact."[27] Parnell's prediction fits neatly with what is known from studies of body movement and gesture in captive gorillas (Chapter 3).

We do know that mountain gorilla females, like bonobo females, actively court and solicit males, more so in fact, in both one-male and multimale groups, than the males court the females. The gestures involved are subtle. A female may purse her lips and approach a chosen male, gaze at him, and touch him or hit the ground in front of him.[28] The quality of solicitation clearly varies between females; one female took as long as 14 minutes to complete a slow-motion approach to the male with whom she wished to copulate, whereas other females were more vigorous.[29]

In the literature, emphasis in describing gorilla courtship is put on the soliciter's actions considered apart from the solicitee's, so that it is hard to get a good sense of contingent mutual adjustment within a dyad. Harcourt and colleagues' description helps: "Once near the male after her characteristically slow and hesitant approach, the female would stand facing him with her body slightly sideways-on, as if waiting for a signal, when she would abruptly turn and back into the normal dorso-ventral copulatory position. The signal appeared to be the male's opening or raising of his arms as he prepared to hold the female around her waist in order to mount."[30] That this "signal" may actually involve contingent movements between the partners invites further study.

In courtship, social communication actually extends beyond the two sexual partners themselves. Although I have written as if courtship and copulation occurs dyadically, other group members may involve themselves and even interfere with the events surrounding copulation. In short, courtship in the African great apes proceeds along variable paths according, in part, to the body movements, gestures, and vocalizations that are made by the participants. The meaning of gestures such as the rocking of bonobos and the bipedal swagger of chimpanzees is socially constructed. In the case of some other movements and gestures, such as those in leaf-clipping, the degree to which the actions of one social partner affect the quality and trajectory of the other's actions remains less clear.

## Agonism

Agonism refers to aggressive and submissive behaviors considered together: the crouching and bobbing of a subordinant male chimpanzee is scored as agonistic by an observing primatologist, just as is the aggressive swaggering and arm-waving of the male's higher-ranking rival. Body movements and gestures associated with aggression and submission may be under as much selection pressure as those associated with courtship. Though it may be hard to imagine a tighter link than the one between copulation and reproductive success, the benefits of clear communication between social partners engaged in agonism cannot be underestimated. As shown by the data below, social events in the realm of agonism may be scripted as rarely as those in courtship; movements and gestures may help the interactants negotiate outcomes that avoid actual physical attack and risk of injury.

Data on body movements and gestures related to agonism are fairly abundant for chimpanzees, and more plentiful for gorillas than in most behavioral contexts. Schaller's descriptions of the complexity of chestbeating in eastern gorillas are classic. Only silverback males make the full chestbeating display. Schaller's lyrical recounting in *The Year of the Gorilla* of the nine component parts of this complete display deserves reading in full: the male starts to hoot softly; builds up in excitement and vigor as he stands bipedally, tears vegetation, and begins to beat his chest; runs sideways and then quadrupedally; hits and slaps at anything, ranging from vegetation to other gorillas, in his path; and ends with a "vigorous thump" on the ground with the palm of the hand.[31] Chestbeating, the most pronounced element of this complete display, is done also by females and younger males: "The open, slightly cupped hands are slapped alternately some two to twenty times against the lower part of the chest at the rate of about ten beats a second. Gorillas do not pound their chests with the fists, as is often stated, except on very rare occasions. Chest beating is not at all stereotyped in its application, and the animal may slap its belly, the outside of its thigh, a branch, a tree trunk, or the back of another gorilla. One juvenile patted the top of its head about thirty times, and once a blackbacked male lay on his back with legs stretched skyward, beating the soles of his feet. Two females did not slap their chests directly, but rotated their arms, making their breasts flap in passing. While beating its chest, the gorilla often kicks a leg into the air."[32]

The communicative importance of body posture and movement in the chestbeating display and other male agonistic displays is perhaps more obvious to the human observer than in any other type of African great ape behavior. We see this in Fossey's vivid description of conflict between Uncle Bert and Beethoven, eastern gorilla silverbacks in charge of two different groups. During a protracted interaction between the two males, Uncle Bert had been hooting, chestbeating, and otherwise displaying for nearly 2 hours when Beethoven arose and moved off. Uncle Bert at once stopped vocalizing. "He strutted up and down the ridge with such stilted and exaggerated movements that his hind legs appeared to be attached to his body by strings as they swung in arcs before hitting the ground . . . Slowly Beethoven climbed up to meet Uncle Bert, until both stood face to face, magnifying their sizes by posing in extreme strut positions with head hair erect."[33]

Chestbeating by females is carried out less frequently and less intensely than that by males. Infants may begin to beat their chests in a shaky incipient display at 4 months of age. Chestbeating is thus well entrenched in the gorilla behavioral repertoire and also variable in its quality according to age, sex, and individual preference. Although I have classed it in this section on agonism, because males engage in the chestbeating display when rival males or other groups come near, it may also be seen when gorillas play.

We know a lot about which gorillas chestbeat in which contexts; badly needed is supplemental research to assess whether chestbeating may be part of co-regulated social communication by gorillas. The primary question is how ritualized or stereotyped the chestbeating display is, given the minor variations in movements noted above. Do gorillas who have started to chestbeat, or to perform the complete silverback display, ever adjust their actions according to movements or gestures by a social partner? Alternatively, once under

way, does the chestbeating or the full display continue unaffected by
the actions of those nearby?

Some gorillas best their chests, others their thighs; some may beat
on other gorillas. Do individuals vary their choice of "beating site" on
their bodies, or others' bodies, according to what social partners are
doing? Does variation in choice of site affect the ongoing actions of
others? How does chestbeating in play differ from that in agonism,
both in quality and in involvement of the social partner? Schaller
notes that when mature males, about to give the full display, begin to
hoot and place a leaf between their lips, females and youngsters
"generally" retreat. How variable *is* the action of those nearby a gorilla engaged in chestbeating? Researchers working after Schaller
have produced data on chestbeating but have not, to my knowledge,
answered these questions. Perhaps the chestbeating display of silverback males is simply too invariant for co-regulation to play a major
role. If so, the chestbeating display would then provide a fascinating
contrast with the rocking gesture of bonobos.

As noted in Chapter 1, primatologists are now beginning to study
in detail the social behavior, including communication, of western as
well as eastern gorillas. Western gorillas chestbeat too, though this
has been described in no detail. Parnell and Buchanan-Smith recently reported an intriguing agonistic display in Nouabole-Ndoki
National Park, Congo, that they believe may occur only among those
western gorillas that visit open swamplands, or *bais*. Visual in nature, this display would probably be effective in open areas rather
than dense forest.

Nineteen western gorillas produced, over 32 months, 90 instances
of the "splash display," a catchall term that actually encompasses 10
variants of the manipulation of standing water. Three-quarters of observed splash displays occurred in three forms: the body splash, in
which a gorilla runs or jumps into water of up to a meter and a half
in depth, and one- or two-handed splashes "in which one or both
arms are raised and then brought down forcibly, the open palms

striking the water surface at a slight angle. Each of these three tech-niques generates large plumes of spray."[34]

Two-thirds of splash displays were made in an agonistic context. For silverback males, who display the most, this percentage is even higher. Further, group-dwelling silverbacks displayed twice as often as expected, whereas solitary silverbacks displayed more than four times as often. A key to the communicative nature of the splash dis-play is revealed by the statistic that solitary silverbacks were most of-ten targeted by the display, whereas adult females were only rarely targeted (and never produced the displays). Probably, then, the splashing is a way for gorilla males to intimidate their rivals, just as gorillas in ecologically different areas charge and slap the ground. Just as with the chestbeating display, it would be worth investigating how ritualized and stereotyped, or alternatively how amenable to mutual adjustment, are such splash displays.

Gorilla agonism, whether by males or females, may proceed by way of quite subtle movements and gestures, rather than through broad visual displays. Writing about eastern gorillas, Schaller noted, "Gorillas showed their dominance with a minimum of actions. Usually an animal low in the rank order simply moved out of the way at the mere approach or brief stare of a high-ranking one. The most frequently noted gesture involving bodily contact was a light tap with the back of a hand of a dominant individual against the body of a subordinate one."[35] The importance of gaze here is notable; other subtle movements and gestures in agonism include snapping mo-tions of the head and truncated charges, usually made by the gorilla moving one or two steps forward but sometimes without moving the feet at all.

Agonism among female gorillas is, in its own way, just as dramatic as that between males. Perhaps the most interesting feature of fe-male agonism is that, among Karisoke eastern gorillas at least, it oc-curs outside a strict dominance hierarchy. Most female dyads do not establish consistent dominance relationships in the sense of one female repeatedly submitting to a superior. Watts notes that dyadic interactions are characterized by bidirectionality and uncertainty of outcome, and that the quality of dyadic relationships in females ("good, bad or neutral," clearly operationalized in terms of rates of affiliative interactions) is unstable over time.[36] Females' agonistic behavior is certainly variable, not only across but also within individuals: "Females ignored some aggression; returned some, responded defensively to some by leaning aside or raising an arm, and sometimes responded submissively, or initially aggressively but then submissively."[37] Though Watts does not discuss the implications of these factors for social communication between female gorillas, as described they lead to the prediction that social partners closely monitor each other and assess movements, gestures, and vocalizations during ongoing interaction.

Agonism as expressed by wild chimpanzees involves a similar mix of the exaggerated and the subtle. Goodall presents a list of "gestures and postures of threat" observed at Gombe in order of increasing intensity and likelihood that an attack will result. At the low end are the head tip, a slight upward jerk of the chin; the arm-raise threat, a rapid raising of the forearm with bent elbow; hitting toward, with an overarm throwing movement; and flapping, rapid slapping movements in the air. Next listed are the sitting and quadrupedal hunches, two related postures, the first with arms held out from the body; swaying branches; and throwing rocks or hitting with a stick or branch. At the high-intensity end are the bipedal swagger, running upright toward another chimpanzee while waving the arms, and an outright charge. These movements may be combined with each other.

Goodall emphasizes, as she did in discussing courtship gestures, that the form of the threat depends on all the variables associated with the interacting dyad: "Thus a mild threat delivered by one chimpanzee to another of comparable rank may elicit no response at all; the same pattern directed toward a much lower ranked individual may elicit a submissive or fearful response. A juvenile without his mother typically responds to threats with more fear than if she were present. A female who would usually flee the aggressive charge of a high-ranking male may actually leap toward and hit him if he has seized and is displaying with her infant. Many females are less nervous and submissive when they are in estrus."[38] Not only, then, may female A act differently when highest-ranking male A arm-raises and branch-sways than when male B does so, she may well act differently when male A does so when she has a sexual swelling and is receptive versus when she is neither. The contingent nature of such communication is clear, and by now readers can probably devise their own suggestions for future research according to DST.

Gombe chimpanzees, when submitting to threats made by others, may present their rumps; bow, bob, and crouch; offer submissive kisses and mounts; and make various hand and arm movements including submissive touching. These terms of Goodall's provide yet another clue as to the constructed nature of meaning in chimpanzees. Movements and gestures *become* aggressive, or submissive, only in interaction, and the need for qualified terms like "submissive kissing" underscores this fact. Both dominant and subordinant chimpanzees may press the lips or teeth to the body ("kiss") another chimpanzee. As Goodall puts it, "As a submissive gesture [the kiss] frequently accompanies bowing or crouching, in which case the kiss is typically in the groin of the other individual."[39] The posture of the kisser and the quality of the movements involved as the kisser moves toward the partner, plus the location of the kiss on the other's body, all mark the kiss as submissive; its meaning is created during the interaction.

The variability inherent in presenting, bowing, and other postures is communicatively significant as well. If one chimpanzee suffers a severe attack, she may present her rump to her attacker, with four limbs completely flexed and head nearly touching the ground, while looking back over her shoulder toward the aggressor. If the attack is less severe, so too is the presenting posture. When a lower-ranking chimpanzee approaches a higher-ranking one, he may bow, adopting a posture in which the elbows are more flexed than the knees; the degree of flexion may vary according to the specific circumstance.

If one imagines an instance of agonism between two chimpanzees, it's easy to derive a picture of rapidly shifting, contingent interaction between the two as each adjusts to the other. As one pilo-erected chimpanzee, arm-raising and working himself up to a swagger, approaches another chimpanzee, the second one, if lower-ranking, may begin to flex his limbs and extend his hand to the first. As events unfold, the vocalizations, movements, and gestures of each partner shape what the other does. To this by-now familiar picture of co-regulated social communication must be added the fact that this interaction probably unfolds in the midst of shifting conditions within the party, itself an ephemeral unit of the larger chimpanzee community.

That chimpanzee agonism takes place in the context of fission-fusion movement patterns (see Chapter 1) is critical to remember for a nuanced understanding of social communication. It's not that the same two chimpanzees, one of stable low rank and the other of stable high rank, come together repeatedly through the course of a day or a week, and engage in co-regulated gestural communication. Any dyadic contingencies that occur are embedded in a dynamic community setting. Coalitions may form around two chimpanzees in conflict, with each ape seeking support from others in the same party; party membership itself constantly shifts. Over the longer term, an individual's relative rank and the quality of a social relationship between chimpanzees may be quite unstable.

In the volume *Behavioural Diversity in Chimpanzees and Bonobos,* two field researchers emphasize this fluidity in chimpanzee male-male relationships. Muller describes "the element of perpetual instability" in dominance relationships—and thus in agonism—among the males at Kibale, Uganda. "Since a high-ranking male," writes

Muller, "can never be certain what political maneuvering has occurred in his absence, it is necessary for him continually to reestablish his dominance when parties come together. This could help to explain the large proportion of aggression that takes place in the context of reunions."[40] At Budongo in the same country, adult male chimpanzees share "a long history of . . . unreliable relationships."[41] According to Newton-Fisher, as mentioned in Chapter 1, Budongo males' relationships shift repeatedly from affiliative to neutral to antagonistic in nature. The instability at all these levels would seem to increase the likelihood of social construction of meaning within any given event, because individuals' roles and their actions are unpredictable.

In many primates, agonistic interactions may be followed by a period in which the social partners come together and attempt to repair their relationship. Body movements and gestures made by chimpanzees in this context were first described by Goodall via the vocabulary of submission and reassurance. Later, de Waal discussed them in the context of reconciliation, the name he applied to post-conflict repair.[42] Assessment of the actions that constitute reconciliation reinforces the theme of this book. Submissive gestures are not signals sent back by an ape on the receiving end of aggression, but form part of a web of movements through which an outcome is jointly constructed. Goodall reports that, normally, when a subordinant chimpanzee bows or crouches, he or she is touched by the aggressor chimpanzee, and when he or she holds out a hand toward the dominant, that chimpanzee touches or holds it.[43] These observations support the idea that the subordinant and the dominant together, through their movements and gestures, arrive at a negotiated outcome.

Unsurprisingly, agonism among bonobos differs in some ways from that among chimpanzees, as de Waal describes for male displays: "A male chimpanzee appears larger than life when he raises his hair, uproots a small tree, and charges about slapping the ground with great force and energy . . . In comparison, the bonobo male's typical display looks like child's play. He will grab a branch and drag it behind him while making a brief run. There is almost no comparison with the unstoppable steam-engine display enacted by his more robust cousin."[44] The two species should not be dichotomized, however. Aggression and submission, and their attendant gestures and body movements, do occur in bonobos. Kano describes glaring and arm-waving threats, and prostration and hand-extension submissive behaviors, between adult males. During aggression, males may also carry out rump-rubbing, a behavior in which two individuals "in a 'presenting' posture direct their rear ends toward each other and press their buttocks against each other. Sometimes the positions are assumed and held motionless, but usually they are accompanied by slight rhythmical thrusting movements."[45] Females may behave aggressively in various situations, including toward their sexual partners, but I know of no extensive study of the social communication involved in these encounters or in the conflicts that occur between male and female bonobos.

## Grooming

Grooming of one's social partner is frequently observed in the African great apes. Certainly, one function of this "picking-through-the-fur" behavior of apes, using lips and hands, is hygienic, since it serves to rid the groomee's hair of insects and other debris. But anyone observing a session of grooming among free-ranging chimpanzees would grasp immediately that more than cleanliness is at issue. Some individuals may enthusiastically clap their teeth or clasp an uplifted hand of their companion while grooming. Pairs of chimpanzees may engage in relaxed mutual grooming, sometimes for prolonged periods. Individuals may approach potential grooming partners, positioning themselves in clear request postures, at times even tugging on the other's limbs to jumpstart the action. After the male chimpanzee Falstaff was attacked by a leopard at Tai in the Ivory Coast, Boesch observed nine chimpanzees grooming Falstaff for over 3 hours without interruption. His wounds were licked for 2 hours and 55 minutes. The energy and persistence that underlie these various encounters attest to the fact that grooming is a way of creating, maintaining, and repairing social bonds among the African great apes. The invitations, requests, and refusals associated with grooming are socially significant behaviors and as such are interesting subjects for the student of communication.

For assessing co-regulation, a recent analysis of the grooming hand-clasp in chimpanzees is every bit as revealing as Kuroda's report on bonobo rocking. Based on his research at Mahale, Nakamura shows that the grooming hand-clasp varies between dyads in such a way as to convey social meaning.[46] First described by McGrew and Tutin at this same site, the grooming hand-clasp occurs when two chimpanzees sit face to face, and each "extends an arm overhead and then clasps the other's wrist or hand, or both clasp each other's hand. Meanwhile, the other hand engages in social grooming" of the partner's underarm area.[47]

Presenting background information, Nakamura notes that when Mahale chimpanzees hand-clasp, mutual grooming typically ensues, though in rare cases only one partner grooms the other. If, as the grooming is beginning, one chimpanzee raises his or her hand, the partner normally responds immediately by raising his or her own hand. In many cases, however, the arm movements are so nearly simultaneous that it is impossible for observers to decide which chimpanzee "initiated"—a revelation much in keeping with Kano's finding about bonobo courtship, and with the predictions of DST regarding co-regulated social communication in general.

The grooming hand-clasp interests primatologists because of its varied distribution across long-term chimpanzee sites. Whereas chimpanzees at Mahale and Kibale often hand-clasp, this form of grooming has never been seen at Gombe, Bossou, or Budongo, and has been observed routinely in only two adult males at Tai. In all well-studied chimpanzee populations, even those where the hand-clasp is absent, however, individuals may grasp branches overhead while grooming. Nakamura compares the two types of grooming—hand-clasp and branch-clasp—at Mahale, and comes up with remarkable results and interpretation.

Of key significance is that chimpanzees do not differentiate the two patterns according to availability of branches. In some cases, they groom using the hand-clasp even when branches are readily available. Further, no individual chimpanzee specializes in either branch-clasp or hand-clasp grooming. Though Nakamura is cautious in his interpretations, he uses these facts to suggest that chimpanzees choose one form of grooming position over the other for social reasons. First, a kind of social rule may be in place, to the effect that only adults should groom with the hand-clasp, though other chimpanzees may try to do so: "Adolescent males often try to perform [the grooming hand-clasp] with adult males but are usually ignored completely. Youngsters seem to know how to perform the behaviour but do not engage in it because others do not easily accept them as partners. It is also not simply because of the physical differences between juveniles and adults, because juveniles never performed it with similar-sized juveniles."[48]

That the hand-clasp may fail to materialize even when it is invited by one social partner is of great interest. In some cases, according to Nakamura, the apes make "real mistakes"— they fail to synchronize their timing as they (in my terms) attempt to mutually construct a hand-clasp. In other cases, as already noted, failures occur because one chimpanzee simply ignores the other. And because social ignoring may take place even between adults, we have a strong hint that much more is going on beneath a possible "adult-only" social rule.

Consider two social events recounted by Nakamura. In one, an adult female raised her hand in front of an adult male. The male, however, "did not accept her solicitation but instead clasped the overhead branch. Then [the female] also took the same branch, and the two started to perform branch-clasp grooming."[49] Intriguingly, each of these adults did sometimes groom via hand-clasps, just not with each other. In the second event, the alpha male and a young adult female groomed each other using the branch-clasp method. Eventually the female stopped grooming and moved aside. Another low-ranking male arrived and sat where the female had just been. "The two males began a grooming-hand-clasp, despite the same branch being available."[50]

Reviewing his data, both quantitative and qualitative, Nakamura suggests that the hand-clasp custom may be used by the more stable dyads of chimpanzees, at least among adult-male dyads. The hand-clasp may add meaning to grooming: chimpanzees may choose to groom using the hand-clasp on the basis of partner idenity and on the circumstances of the present relationship within the pair. "What appears to be a social custom in chimpanzees may be some kind of mutual anticipation of other individuals performing in particular ways that are shaped in everyday face-to-face interactions," Nakamura concludes.[51] As his description conveys, the meaning of the hand-clasp gesture resides in the mutuality of the actions within the pair.

A follow-up, fine-grained study of hand-clasp grooming might seek answers to a host of questions. As we have seen, male chimpanzees may be fickle, and the quality of their dyadic relationships may shift over time. If a relationship shifts from affiliative to neutral or even to antagonistic, might an invitation to clasp hands during grooming be ignored by one partner even when it had in the past typically been accepted? What happens the first time that a request to hand-clasp, made to a mature male by an adolescent-turned-adult male, is accepted, following previous refusals? When a female immigrates into a hand-clasp community, does she shift from branch-clasp grooming to hand-clasp grooming over time as she forges alliances with community members? Does the quality of the mutual adjustments made between partners improve over time as a chimpanzee dyad begins to engage in hand-clasp grooming?

Chimpanzees may invite or maintain grooming through body movements and gestures even when they do not adopt the hand- or branch-clasp method. Individuals often present to the partner some part of the body—rump, back, or head—for grooming, or may hold one arm up in the air. What happens next is highly contingent. The solicited partner may start to groom, continuing for either a short or prolonged period; the grooming may be unilateral with no reciprocation, reciprocal sequentially with each partner taking a turn, or mutual right from the beginning. If the solicited partner has been grooming for a while with no sign of reciprocation in the offing, he may pause, scratch, and reposition in order to present a body part to the unforthcoming partner. At times, persistence may be necessary. At Gombe, the adult male Hugo "occasionally shook branches, hair beginning to bristle, if a lower-ranking male grooming partner ignored more typical requests. And Melissa, after six minutes of whimpering, rocking, and scratching, once actually gave old Mr. McGregor a hard shove with one foot."[52]

Grooming requests may sometimes be ignored, however. Some chimpanzees give up and retreat when no grooming is offered, and as we have seen, others may keep trying. When one chimpanzee tries to get another's attention for grooming, or wishes to nudge a partner to resume grooming that has stopped, he may pluck and groom leaves. Leaf-grooming, often accompanied by lip-smacking, often succeeds, at least at Gombe, as a strategy to solicit or resume grooming.[53]

In chimpanzees, grooming occurs during relaxed times; during tense times; between dominants and subordinants; between mothers and offspring; and in sexual situations. It is used in myriad ways to maintain and improve important social relationships. When one social partner moves toward the other and grooming results, the partners together must be alert not only to any grooming-related moves and gestures but to each other's overall current mood; their shared social history; and, probably, to the mood of the larger party or community as well. When this level of contingency is added to the various mutual adjustments each ape may make to the other's moves—especially when Nakamura's data on hand-clasp grooming are considered—grooming begins to look very much as if it involves socially constructed gestures.

Grooming is important in the expression of wild bonobo sociality as well as that of chimpanzees. At Wamba, bonobo males and females groom each other at "extremely high" rates, for instance, and most often in nonsexual affiliative situations.[54] I know of no detailed studies of the *quality* of grooming and its related body movements and gestures among wild bonobos, or among gorillas either. Eastern gorillas groom relatively infrequently, though certainly bonds may be strengthened when grooming does occur.[55] Grooming by western gorillas awaits investigation.

## Mother-Infant Behaviors

Upon first observing co-regulated body movements and socially constructed gestures between mothers and infants in captive bonobo and gorilla families, I eagerly searched the literature for information on similar behaviors between infants and their caretakers in the wild. Few such data exist, even for eastern gorillas, for which we have quite detailed reports of mother-infant behavior.[56] A bit more is known about the situation in wild chimpanzees, especially through the work of the primatologist Plooij. It's telling, however, that in Goodall's 1968 report on expressive movements and communication in Gombe chimpanzees, containing 61 pages of text, precisely two paragraphs are devoted to mother-infant communication. By contrast, 10 pages each are devoted to aggressive and submissive behaviors.

In short, Maestripieri and Call were correct to conclude, in a major review article, that mother-infant communication has rarely been studied in nonhuman primates, including the African great apes.[57] Phrased more positively, enormous potential exists for researchers to investigate co-regulated gestural communication in mother-infant dyads in all the African great apes. Infants may remain on the mother's body without a break for months after birth, and stay close to the mother both physically and emotionally for years; research already reviewed in this chapter reveals that infants may involve themselves in social construction of gestures from an early age; and data from captivity show that the mother-infant dyad itself is a likely context for significant gesturing. In other words, though it is possible that the lack of data on gesture in free-ranging mother-infant dyads reflects a genuine absence of such behavior, I consider it a highly unlikely possibility.

Gestures made during food-begging are probably the most studied in the mother-infant category. At Tai, chimpanzee mothers share with their immature offspring an amazing number of nuts cracked open with anvil and hammer. More than one-fifth of the nuts mothers crack are shared, a rate that continues for 5 years for *Panda* nuts (a particularly hard type of food) and 4 years for *Coula* nuts. Sharing, though at lower rates, continues until the offspring is 12 (for *Panda* nuts) or 8 years old (for *Coula*).[58] This lengthy period of sharing means that mothers sometimes share with two or three offspring at the same time. Energetically costly for the mother, this behavior makes possible the long period during which the immatures come to learn the nuances of nut-cracking techniques, during which they otherwise might be at nutritional risk.

In describing maternal-offspring interactions that unfold around food-sharing at Tai, Boesch and Boesch-Achermann attended to immature gestures.[59] Extending a hand, the infant may beg from the mother for a newly cracked nut, fresh from the anvil. Alternatively, he may beg for part of a nut held by the mother as she eats, or for pieces either still on the anvil or newly fallen to the ground around

the mother. Mothers may refuse any of these requests, either by giving nothing to the begger or by giving only a small portion of the
amount requested. Such outcomes vary, in part, with infant age.
When infants are about 4 years old, "mothers start to deny them access to whole *Coula* nuts from their anvils, and the infants rapidly
shift to begging exclusively for nuts from their mother's hands.
About two years later, mothers start to deny them access to *Coula*
nuts from their hands, and the infants rapidly learn to beg only for
nut remains from the anvil after the mother has taken her share.
Such changes in sharing practice often occurred quite rapidly, and
were all made on the initiative of the mothers."[60]

Does this correlation between maternal behavior and infant age
mean that little co-regulated communication goes on between
mother and infant during food-sharing, at any specific infant age? Or
does a given pair of chimpanzees together construct the infant's
movements as begging gestures, so that outcomes may vary within a
dyad even on the same day? I suspect the latter is true, but an answer
awaits data on maternal-infant sharing profiles and on the degree of
mutual adjustments made during begging within dyads.

Infants also beg for food from their mothers in populations where
nut-cracking does not occur. Interestingly, given my speculation
about maternal variability at Tai, Goodall emphasizes a "distinct difference in the generosity of the various mothers" when infants wish
to food-share.[61] Whereas some mothers will not share even the hard-
est fruits with their 3-year-olds, even though the young cannot open
such fruits until age 4, other mothers share them with offspring of
6 years. To analyze infant-begging itself, as well as other gestures
made by infants with their mothers, we may turn to reports by Plooij,
who recorded the behavioral development of infant chimpanzees at
Gombe.

In studying food-sharing between mother and infant, Plooij emphasizes a behavioral continuum that culminates in begging by the
infant. In the earliest months, an infant simply takes food from the

mother without any resistance on her part. As the infant ages, the mother begins to withdraw her hand at the infant's reach, or to hold on to her food, preventing the infant's taking it. Though the infant may persist in trying to obtain the food item in the face of maternal resistance, he will not look into the mother's face while doing so. "A change in this behaviour was first observed by the age of 9 months when the infant starts 'begging': he will touch the mother's hand or mouth and look intermittently at her face (eyes) and hand (or mouth)."[62]

A chimpanzee infant participates with her mother in food-sharing for some months, then, before beginning to beg with gestures, at anywhere from 9 to 12 and 1/2 months of age. Plooij interprets this ontogenetic sequence in a relatively standard way, concluding that the infant, in using gestures to beg, demonstrates an understanding of the role played by the mother as an agent in her world, and so begins to communicate intentionally what she might desire that agent to do. From the perspective of DST and co-regulation, some other factors need consideration. Indeed, though Plooij's account is decidedly linear, and focuses on mental processes that are not accessible to direct study, clues to another type of interpretation can be found in Plooij's data regarding the way in which infant chimpanzees come to participate more actively over time with their social partners.

Play-tickling behavior between mother and infant starts early in life. In the first 6 weeks, the infant chimpanzee is, writes Plooij, groomed and otherwise "maintained" by the mother. (I would add that co-regulated movements surely occur within the pair, especially during nursing and repositioning of the infant; see the data on captive apes in Chapter 3). Starting at 6 weeks, the maternal-infant dynamic begins to change. The infant bites whatever comes near, or touches, his face, whether a physical object or some part of another ape's body. "Soon after the onset of biting, [the mother] begins to show special attention and starts poking and tickling her infant *as a reaction to his bites*" (emphasis in the original).[63] Over the next two weeks, grasping joins biting in the infant's repertoire; he will, for instance, grasp the mother's hand as she pulls it away from him, and when he does the mother normally tickles him again. By 3 months of age, the infant limits his biting to places on the mother's body.

Gradually, over the next months, the infant not only becomes able to maintain the tickling interaction with his mother but can also, in Plooij's terms, initiate it. Plooij's writing is beautifully descriptive here: "When the mother is tickling her infant, he will 'defend' himself: if the mother tickles his belly, for instance, he will arch his back and pull up his legs so as to repel the stimulation with hands and feet. If she tickles his neck-pocket, he will bend away while bringing his hands backwards over his shoulders towards her hands or head, trying to push them away. This produces a characteristic posture. Around the age of 11 months, infant chimpanzees start to initiate play sessions by directing this posture toward their mothers or other individuals."[64]

As this passage makes clear, the inviting motion of "hands-over-the-shoulders" made toward the mother stems from earlier bodily interactions within the pair. Though Plooij terms the outcome an "initiation" by the infant to his mother (as would be expected on a sender-receiver model of social communication), infants may, at least sometimes, notice their mother's activity, degree of muscular tension or relaxation, or body, head, and gaze orientation, and act contingently in response to some shift on her part. Just as has been recognized for courtship in bonobos, and for hand-clasping in chimpanzees, it may be impossible to distinguish an initiator in this kind of situation.

In considering the "lies-down-on-back" gesture, Plooij explicitly discusses social negotiation between partners as they communicate. This gesture, for Plooij, occurs when one chimpanzee lies down on his back while keeping his head lifted and extending his arm toward a second chimpanzee toward whom he is looking.[65] Tracing the ontogeny of this gesture, Plooij notes that it may be used with very young infants. When, in the second half of the first year, infants begin to interact with partners other than the mother, these other chimpanzees adopt calm and passive postures so as not to alarm the youngster: "Apparently, the infant does not like being restrained in these situations. The only thing the older individual can do to maintain such an interaction is to lean backwards and allow the infant to walk over him and lie on top of him. It is in this context that the older individual leans backwards and extends his arm."[66] Chimpanzees as young as 12 and 1/2 months made this gesture when interacting with even younger social partners, via "social negotiation" in which the older infant finds "almost by trial and error" how to help bring about "a successful interaction." A whole account is left hidden here: Precisely how do chimpanzees at such developmentally early stages, barely over 1 year, act contingently with their younger partners to engender such an outcome? What unsuccessful outcomes preceded the successful ones in any given pair? How does the older chimpanzee come to alter its actions *as* the younger one acts?

Information about the play-tickle and lies-down-on-back gestures may be helpful in our wish to reconsider infant begging gestures. We have seen that the play-tickle invitation gestures emerge from mutual actions of two bodies. As the infant pushes on the mother (and she either pushes back or does not), and bends away from the mother (and she either bends toward the infant or does not), together they construct an outcome: some version of the play-tickle. Just as the pushing and the bending themselves do not carry meaning, neither does the action when the infant, later on, raises his hands over his shoulders toward the mother. This invitation is constructed by the pair, so that the meaning is not in the movement but in what is made socially of the movement. When an infant shifts from taking the mother's food or pulling on that food to putting out a hand for food, matched with gaze, the meaning (a request) is not in the movement but in what is made socially of the movement. What Plooij describes is more than social shaping that happens gradually but is then set in stone. We know already that some hand extensions are met with much food, others with little, and others with none, presumably even when the movements are made the same way. We know also that the lies-down-on-back gesture proceeds by "trial and error"—a term that probably masks a lot of mutual adjustment—and perhaps a similar mutual process occurs as begging gestures shift in form and quality over time.

The nuanced communication that goes on between chimpanzee mothers and infants is well illustrated by Plooij's data. Detailed qualitative analysis would be welcome for bonobos and gorillas as well, in both food-begging and other areas. When bonobo immatures beg for food, at least at Wamba, they seem to do so with some movements similar to, and others different from, those observed in chimpanzee infants. At about a half-year of age, infants at Wamba begin to put food items into their mouths and to beg from their mothers. An infant may extend a hand toward his mother's food item in her hand or mouth, but more often he will touch his mother's mouth, while sitting in her lap or clinging to her back, after she puts an item into it.[67] Bonobo infants also engage in peering during food-sharing interactions. "When peering, a pygmy chimpanzee sits or stands quadrupedally and gazes intently, from the front or side, into another's face. The actor gets close enough to almost make face-to-face contact and, with a calm facial expression, stares at the other."[68] The stare typically lasts a minute or two. Kano cautions that peering and food-begging should not be conflated, however, because peering occurs also in other contexts, including sex and play. Kano concludes that peering "seems to be begging for any kind of friendly social contact."[69] Peering, most likely, is another kind of socially constructed gesture.

Food-sharing among eastern gorillas is less pronounced than for either *Pan* species, probably because of ecological differences in diet. It will be interesting to discover whether (and how) western gorilla infants food-beg from their mothers in populations where more fruit, perhaps including hard-to-open fruit, is eaten than in eastern populations.

To judge from data on apes in captivity[70] and anecdotes from the field,[71] including the second pair of anecdotes that opened this chapter, coordination of travel between mother and infant would be a fruitful arena for studying co-regulated social communication and constructed meaning. In short, in mother-infant communication research, there is a crying need for a change in the units of analysis. A shift from scoring initiation of behavior by infant to mother (and vice versa), or exchange of signals between a sender infant and receiver mother (or vice versa), toward seeing the mother-infant pair as a whole unit in constant relationship, continually constructing meaning in their daily lives, would bring rich rewards to the study of African great ape social communication.

## Summing Up

Taken together, the data from courtship, agonism, grooming, and mother-infant behavior in wild chimpanzees, bonobos, and gorillas provide compelling support for the view that co-regulated social communication is neither an artifact of the captive environment nor confined to a few extensively studied groups of wild African great apes. Some of the most convincing data come from field work by the Japanese, an intriguing fact given the history of association between Japanese primatology and skilled qualitative research. Kuroda's study of rocking gestures in bonobos and Nakamura's focus on social meaning in the grooming hand-clasp among chimpanzees point us toward a future in which the nonvocal social communication of the African great apes is understood far more comprehensively than at present.

Mutual creation of meaning may not occur with all African great ape body movements and gestures. Field reports indicate that neither the chestbeating display of silverback gorillas nor the leaf-clipping behavior of chimpanzees is stereotyped or simple in its execution. It is not yet clear, though, whether the individuals performing these actions adjust to the actions of their partners, so that contingencies and unpredictabilities result. It would be folly (and poor science) to *assume* that body movements or gestures among wild African great apes are co-regulated, with their meaning constructed during social interaction. To learn more, a new type of research program is needed. Before tackling issues related to future research, though, I devote a chapter to evolutionary questions. In it, I consider the significance of the African great ape data for understanding the social construction of meaning by hominids.

The western gorilla Kwame, 3 and $\frac{1}{2}$ years of age, sucks his thumb. (Courtesy of Lucinda Baker.)

Two western gorillas : Kojo, 1 and $\frac{1}{2}$ years of age, rides dorsally on his mother, Mandara. (Courtesy of Lucinda Baker.)

Kojo, at 1 and ½, descends from the back of his mother, Mandara. (Courtesy of Lucinda Baker.)

Bonobos at Wamba, Democratic Republic of Congo. At the upper left, a male infant bonobo extends a hand toward an adult female's foot. At the lower left, this female extends that foot, probably in response to the infant's own gesture. In the photo above, the infant examines the female's sexual swelling. This sequence illustrates what may be considered a gestural request on the part of the infant. Though the female's back is to the infant at the moment the first photo in the sequence was taken, Ellen Ingmanson's interpretation is that the female was aware of the infant's movement (and probably of other of his movements made just before this photo was snapped), resulting in a coordinated social event. (Courtesy of Ellen Ingmanson.)

Chimpanzees at the Yerkes Primate Field Station, Atlanta: A female named Georgia (right) approaches the dominant male Jimoh. In describing this photo, Frans de Waal writes, "Dancing is a dialogue in which the body movements of each partner affect those of the other." (Courtesy of Frans de Waal, from *My Family Album*, Berkeley: University of California Press, 2003.)

# 5

## The Evolution of Gesture

For an anthropologist, one of the delights of studying African great apes is the dual significance of such research. To learn more about nonvocal social communication of the chimpanzees, bonobos, and gorillas is to gain knowledge about the way complex, fascinating animals live their lives. By attending closely to the ways these apes relate to each other and construct social meaning together, humans can learn about other ways of being on this planet. By studying chimpanzees *as* chimpanzees, and not primarily as humans' closest relatives or as a kind of evolutionary freeze frame through which we may peek into our own past, we can learn that human ways are not the only ways for sentient, socioemotional creatures to interact. We can better appreciate the vital creatures alive in the world today, and use that knowledge to help them as they face unprecedented perils—especially at the hands of our own species, as in the devastating bushmeat trade in which great apes are killed, sold, and consumed for food (see Chapter 6).

Yet to ignore the evolutionary value of research on the African great apes would amount to missing an opportunity. In the 1950s and 1960s, anthropologists in the United States, Britain, and Japan began to set up field sites around the globe to study nonhuman primates in order to illuminate the lives of early human ancestors. Ever since, the African great apes have held a special place in the science of reconstructing human evolution. Baboons or other monkeys, and

nonprimate mammals such as dolphins and elephants, certainly relate to each other socioemotionally. They may construct social meaning as they communicate. That such other creatures would do these
things—participate in the dynamic dance as described in this book—
to the same degree as the African great apes seems unlikely to me,
but this hypothesis remains untested (see Chapter 1). What remains
absolutely clear is that the African great apes are closer to us evolutionarily than are any other animals on earth. For anthropologists
this means that they hold special significance in the theoretical
realm.

For two and a half centuries, since the time of the French philoso-
pher Etienne Bonnot de Condillac, theories proposing that human
language may have originated in the gestural rather than vocal mode
have come in and out of favor. Condillac himself envisioned a type of
sign language as the first stage in the evolution of human communication, leading eventually to speech.[1] Writing in the eighteenth century, well before the scientific world knew much about the African
great apes or their evolutionary connection to humans, Condillac
naturally did not focus on primates other than humans. In more recent work, gestural-origins theorists have been able to use information about the African great apes to bolster their case that human ancestors first used gesture and only later developed speech.

In this chapter, I contend that even the most up-to-date gestural
theories tend to underestimate—ironically enough—the body movements and gestures of the African great apes, and that this situation
has important implications for anthropological modeling of the evolution of language. Material in this chapter is organized around three
major questions: How do modern-day gestural theorists portray the
communicational abilities of the African great apes? In what ways do
these portrayals need amendment, and should data on captive and
enculturated, as well as wild, apes factor in to any such revisions?
How can this amended picture help us understand the unified role
of gesture and speech among humans? In considering this final

question, I review briefly a subset of recent work on gesture in human social communication, in order to highlight ways in which human gesture differs from African great ape gesture. This review will bring into focus those aspects of gesture that have evolved since the evolutionary split between the African great ape and human lineages.

## Gestural Theories: The Role of African Great Apes

As recently as the 1970s, anthropologists thought it likely that humans last shared a common ancestor with the African great apes shortly before 14 million years ago. A fossil from Asia, called *Ramapithecus,* was then considered a likely candidate to represent the first hominid, or human ancestor. It was estimated to have lived 14 million years ago, indicating that the divergence between African apes and hominids must have occurred earlier. As it turned out, however, *Ramapithecus* was an ancestor of the orangutan, not a hominid at all.

Technical advances in molecular anthropology sealed the fate of such an old "split date" for African apes and hominids. Comparison of interspecies proteins led to a consensus within anthropology that humans and the African great apes last shared a common ancestor at about 7 million years ago.[2] (When I use the term "common ancestor," I refer specifically to the ancestor of the African great apes and hominids. Other common ancestors existed, such as the ones for chimpanzees, bonobos, and humans, but not the gorilla; humans and all great apes, including the Asian orangutan, and so on).

Estimates of a precise date of divergence between the African great ape lineage and the human lineage do vary slightly, and the discovery in 2002 of a hominid in Chad dated to about 6 or 7 million years ago[3] has raised new questions: If hominids had evolved by 7 million years ago, how then could a relatively generalized ancestor of chimpanzees, bonobos, gorillas, and hominids have lived at this same time?

After all, what it means to posit a common ancestor is to say that before 7 million years ago, there *were* no chimpanzees, no bonobos, no gorillas, and no human ancestors. Only a single undifferentiated African great ape–like species lived at that time. Could such a creature, living right around 7 million years ago, evolve into the Chad hominid, living at 6 or 7 million years ago? An absence of fossil finds representing a common ancestor of African great apes and humans has only increased the uncertainty inherent in the molecular evidence.

Whether the common ancestor lived at 7 or 8 million years ago, or even slightly longer ago, is of no real importance to gestural-origins theories. It is enough to know that humans are related mostly closely to African great apes of all the primates, and that humans were literally one creature with the African apes at some relatively recent point in our evolutionary past. Yet it would be a mistake for gestural theories to make too much of what Marks calls "the most overexposed factoid in modern science," our great genetic similarity to apes.[4] That humans share about 98 percent of our DNA with the African great apes is repeated ad infinitum in TV documentaries and popular science writing. Often the implication is that humans share not only 98 percent of our DNA but also 98 percent of our essence—our capabilities, our identity as a species—with the African great apes. No one is better than Marks at unpacking what the genetic percentages actually do and do not mean: "The very structure of DNA compels it to be no more than 75% different, no matter how diverse the species being compared are. Yet the fact that our DNA is more than 25% similar to a dandelion's does not imply that we are over one-quarter dandelion."[5] Marks goes on to explain clearly to the nongeneticist precisely *why* the genetic data do not translate into humans "being 98% chimpanzee," and I recommend his analysis.

But let's return to gestural-origins theories, the premise of which (from my perspective, focused on the African great apes) is as simple as it is evolutionarily sound: If the social communication of modern-day African great apes relies heavily on gesture, compared to vocalizations, the likelihood is increased that human language was gestural rather than vocal in its origins. That this logic is sound does not mean it is entirely without risk. As biological anthropologists acknowledge, the African great apes have experienced about 7 million years of evolution on their own, apart from the human lineage; we cannot know when their reliance on gestural skills might have evolved. These skills might have originated only recently, owing to selection pressures that developed after the "split point" with hominids. If biological anthropologists debate *how* to model evolution of human behavior using African great apes, they nonetheless accept the basic premise that such modeling is reasonable, despite the risks. How, then, do gestural-origins theories deal with the social communication of African great apes? I will focus on the three that I judge to be foremost among the detailed and influential theories of the last 30 years, those by Hewes; Corballis; and Armstrong, Stokoe, and Wilcox.

In 1973, Hewes published a seminal article in the journal *Current Anthropology* that is often credited with reviving, in the modern day, the serious examination of gestural origins for language. Hewes chided scholars who try to reconstruct language origins by assessing the function of language in modern hunter-gatherer and other human societies. He posited instead a gradualist thesis: "Unless we reject an evolutionary approach, we must assume that protolanguages were simple and restricted, unlike any spoken natural language."[6] Hewes distanced himself explicitly from theorists, prominent among them Noam Chomsky, who suggested that language might have arisen solely from a mutation. Hewes found the mutation idea "simplistic and hardly more plausible than the idea that language is a gift of the gods."[7]

For Hewes, hominid protolanguages were likely gestural in origin: "It is argued that a preexisting gestural language system would have provided an easier pathway to vocal language than a direct outgrowth of the 'emotional' use of vocalization characteristic of nonhuman primates."[8] In order to explain a shift, later in human evolution, to the vocal mode as primary, Hewes invoked two notions. The so-called mouth-gesture hypothesis claimed that the lips, mouth, and tongue could essentially imitate hand movements; research in sound symbolism suggested the existence of semantic-phonetic universals (for instance, that sharp items are more likely to be associated with t or k sounds whereas soft and smooth things are linked with l or m sounds). These ideas for explaining the shift from gesture to vocal language strike today's reader as quite vague, and even Hewes himself acknowledged that they "still leave most of the postulated transformation from a gestural to a vocal language unexplained."[9]

My concern, however, is not with Hewes's explanation of a shift from gestural to vocal communication, but with his treatment of the communicational abilities of African great apes. To support his central contention that gestures provided an easier pathway to language evolution, Hewes first discussed work with what are now called enculturated chimpanzees, those raised in a heavily human-oriented environment. Reviewing the language-like accomplishments of chimpanzees such as Washoe with American Sign Language (ASL) and Sarah with plastic symbols, Hewes concluded that early hominids (the australopithecines) might have made similar achievements.[10] That humans tutored Washoe, Sarah, and other chimpanzees like them does not disqualify these apes from use in evolutionary reconstructions, Hewes believed, though australopithecines might have taken millions of years, in contrast to several years for the tutored apes, to master "simple sign languages."

Hewes noted that all chimpanzees behave in ways that are likely "the substrate for gestural language": they make arm and hand gestures, engage in attention orientation, produce facial expressions and body postures. While stating clearly that little was yet known (in the early 1970s) about such nonvocal communication in chimpanzees, whether in the wild or in captivity, he did contrast chimpanzees'

nonvocal and vocal communication. The vocalizations of chimpanzees (or of any other primate) were not, Hewes wrote, good candidates for a starting point toward language because they are quite involuntary, "mainly 'emotional' and only meagerly propositional."[11]
Here Hewes fit squarely within the perspective of mainstream primatology of the time, when it went unquestioned that nonhuman
primate vocalizations indicated only the caller's arousal level or current emotional state, perhaps fear (at an approaching predator) or excitement (when sighting a tree full of fruit). So-called propositional
behavior or environmental reference, the ability to refer specifically
to some aspect of the external environment, was thought to be a
uniquely human ability, "aside from such minor examples as the dif-
ferential alarm calls of vervet monkeys."[12] The important aspect of
chimpanzee gestures, for Hewes, was precisely how they differed
from nonhuman primate vocalizations. Gestures are "voluntary and
based on higher-level cognitive analyses of situations primarily ap-
prehended visually."[13]

Hewes's ideas were given "CA treatment," meaning that *Current
Anthropology* editors invited other scholars to write critical comments
that would be published along with the original article. The commentaries are intriguing for their range of opinions, not only about
Hewes's gestural thesis specifically but also about the communicative significance of gesture generally. Washburn knew of no evidence
to suggest that gestural communication was any more important for
the evolution of human communication than for the natural behavior of chimpanzees. Given his conclusion that the gesture systems of
nonhuman primates "are adequate for only very limited communication, unless taught by human beings who are using a sound code,"
his commentary amounted to a dismissal of Hewes's thesis.[14]

By contrast, Gardner, who with his wife was responsible for the
early breakthroughs of Washoe in using a form of ASL to communicate with humans, supported a gestural thesis for origins of language. Washoe, he noted, "accompanied a few of her signs with char-

acteristic unvocalized sounds that made these signs intelligible to an observer who could not see her," and the chimpanzee Viki, trained by other researchers to try and enunciate human words, "accompanied each of the spoken words in her small repertoire with a characteristic gesture that made the words intelligible to an observer who could not hear her."[15] This information, that a signing chimpanzee used sound, and a vocalizing chimpanzee used gesture, certainly indicates that enculturated apes may spontaneously use gesture to enhance clarity of communication. That it indicates *primacy* of gesture in an evolutionary sense is not clear to me, but for Gardner, this spontaneous mixing of auditory and visual behavior added great support to Hewes's main thesis.

Most interesting of all, for my purposes, are some challenges to Hewes's stated contrast between gestures and vocalizations. In assessing the claim that nonhuman primate vocalizations are meagerly propositional, Gardner implied that Hewes had fallen prey to a double standard: "To the extent that human beings also emit sounds that are prominent and repetitious and that are readily observable at a distance, this statement applies to the calls of human as well as nonhuman primates."[16] In other words, Gardner wished the spontaneous utterances of humans to be assessed in the same ways as are the spontaneous utterances of chimpanzees. Suzuki too wanted to rethink a focus on emotional vocalizations versus cognitive gestures. A chimpanzee field worker, he recognized that it isn't necessary to construct "emotional" communication as somehow inferior to propositional communication: "I think it is indispensable for communication, however, that all the individuals involved share the same emotional base. Thus we should not exclude the emotional aspect of the question. Chimpanzees' vocal activities are fully developed as a means of expressing their emotions."[17]

Commentaries on Hewes's theory thus offered some skepticism about a view of primate vocalizations as emotional but not propositional. Not for another decade, however, would skeptics have a full arsenal of data at their disposal. As more and more field projects yielded data on social communication, primatologists began to realize that vocal calls of a number of nonhuman primate species are indeed propositional in nature.[18] Most of these were found to occur in monkeys, not the African great apes, however. Were African great ape vocalizations irrelevant, after all, for evolutionary reconstructions? Information began to emerge in the 1990s that helped shed new light on this issue.

For a good example we may turn to the best-studied chimpanzee vocalization, the pant-hoot. A loud, long-distance call, the pant-hoot is made by males when they rejoin associates (in the ever-constant fission and fusion process within a community), when meeting unfamiliar chimpanzees, when displaying, upon sighting rich food sources, when capturing prey, and when recruiting male allies.[19] At Tai, Boesch and his co-workers noted that each male chimpanzee's pant-hoot was uttered with idiosyncratic features of voice intonation and rhythm, and thus was distinct from the pant-hoots of others. Typically stable over time, any individual chimpanzee's pant-hoots *may* be quite sensitive to shifts in social events: "When [the male chimpanzee] Le Chinois disappeared in February 1984, Macho changed his formerly rather atypical pant-hoot sequence, so that within three weeks he used exactly the same 'hooaa' sound that Le Chinois had used. We were so confused that for many weeks we checked whether Le Chinois had come back. At the same time in 1984, shortly after four adult males had disappeared, Brutus stopped producing his typical long series of rapid hoots, and instead made shorter series of slower hoots. Thereafter, Falstaff, the oldest male of the community, started to imitate Brutus' long series of rapid hoots exactly, and he used them, until his death in 1987."[20]

These Tai observations attest to the fact that chimpanzees may change the structure of their pant-hoots voluntarily, in response to a shifting social environment. Data from Mahale show that male chimpanzees there too may alter the structure of their pant-hoots, this time when chorusing with other males in a process termed call convergence. During chorusing, males alter both the structure of their pant-hoots and the timing. Convergence occurs dyadically rather than to a single "ideal call" exemplar.[21] That is, the two chimpanzee partners *each* adjust their calling, rather than one shifting to match the call of another, or several chimpanzees shifting to match the call of a high-ranking male. In its mutual adjustment, this process is tantalizingly similar to co-regulation in gestural communication.[22]

None of this information about the propositional and nonfixed nature of nonhuman primate vocalizations was available to Hewes in 1973, of course. Fast forward to the year 2002, though, and we find, paradoxically, an even greater reliance on a contrast between nonhuman primate gestures and vocalizations in the origins theory put forth by Corballis. Like Hewes, Corballis asserts that the vocal calls of nonhuman primates make poor candidates for the building blocks of language precisely because their features set them apart from gestures.

Corballis's intent is to explain the emergence, late in human evolutionary history, of the "essential feature of modern expressive language": that "the vocal component can function autonomously and provide the grammar as well as the meaning of linguistic communication."[23] His central task is to show how a system evolved in which meaning and grammar are embedded in vocalizations that themselves derived from gestural origins. He does so by positing a series of steps that occurred throughout human evolution. The baseline gestural communication of nonhuman primates encountered intense selection pressure once bipedalism arose in the early hominids. Manual gesture continued to be primary in human evolution until quite late, when a mutation allowed, for the first time, control of both the hands and of vocalizations to reside in a single cerebral hemisphere. Finally, cultural convergence kicked in, allowing hominids to realize that sound alone might be sufficient for language.

My key concerns in evaluating Corballis's ideas, as with Hewes's, involve his portrayal of the social communication of African great apes. Echoing Hewes, he finds few examples of referential (propositional) primate calls—a mere two in chimpanzees (and these are only tentatively classed as referential). Even more critical is the issue of voluntary control. "Movements of the hands and arms can be controlled by the higher centers of the cerebral cortex, while vocalizations are largely (if not completely) controlled by more primitive subcortical areas. This means that hand movements can be *intentional*, flexibly programmed on-line, as it were, to respond to novel situations, whereas vocalizations are largely tied to fixed situations."[24]

Though Corballis acknowledges that some primate vocalizations, including the pant-hoots of chimpanzees, can be modified, he admits only narrow modification, in the timing of calls and not in the actual sounds uttered. Boesch's data, reviewed above, provide an immediate challenge to this point; individual chimpanzee males do respond vocally to novel situations. When one male goes missing, another may adopt the first male's pant-hoot, completely altering his original pant-hoot. It is worth noting, in fairness to Corballis, that we do not know whether the Tai chimpanzees—or chimpanzees elsewhere—pant-hoot when not in an aroused emotional state. When Corballis maintains that nonhuman primate vocalizations are "largely fixed and tied to specific situations or emotional states,"[25] he relies explicitly on Goodall's famous observation that chimpanzees find it almost impossible to produce a sound in the absence of the appropriate emotional state.[26] How *invariably* true is Goodall's observation? Answering this question would help us understand the contrast between chimpanzee vocalizations and gestures. Though Corballis is wrong about the details of pant-hoot modifiability, he may be right about a tight link between emotional state and at least some vocalizing in the African great apes.[27]

Close scrutiny reveals some further problems with Corballis's statements about the African great apes. When he notes that chimpanzees and bonobos have elaborate tool cultures (chimpanzees do; by almost any definition, bonobos do not); that gorillas live on a simple vegetarian diet (western gorillas' diet varies from eastern gorillas', and neither is described accurately as simple); or that the famous language-using gorilla called Koko is a male (she's a female), little damage ensues to his specific thesis. When he misunderstands African great ape social communication, and indeed the apes' social life generally, more harm is done, as can be seen in two particularly egregious statements.

First: "One reason to suppose that [autonomous speech] emerged late is that dramatic anatomical changes were necessary to convert our forebears from primates capable only of involuntary grunts and cries to fully articulate humans."[28] As I have written elsewhere,[29] that Corballis would repeat this old canard about the nature of nonhuman primate communication is disappointing and all too reminiscent of misleading statements by Pinker about chimpanzees that "hoot and shriek."[30] Seventeen years before Corballis published his book, Steklis concluded that any characterization of nonhuman primate vocal communication as involuntary and emotional was outdated.[31] Steklis's conclusion has been widely cited and, with new data, extended, as we have seen.

Second: "Animals in the wild simply do not have much to communicate about" and specifically, "in the natural world of the bonobo, there may simply have been too few objects and actions worth talking about for grammar to emerge."[32] If we leave aside the arguable focus here on the central importance of grammar as a separate defining feature of language, no African great ape field worker, indeed no one acquainted with the complexities of the fission-fusion social life of bonobos and chimpanzees, could find these statements to be plausible. A review of Chapter 4's data on communication in free-ranging bonobos and chimpanzees confirms this sense of implausibility. Given that the meaning of bonobo rocking behavior is constructed socially, in that it varies as partners negotiate social outcomes; given that the chimpanzee hand-clasp in grooming varies according to social histories between partners as well as present conditions; given that male chimpanzees are fickle, with constantly shifting loyalties (and shifting behaviors), it is untenable to suggest that these apes have nothing about which to communicate. (And I have not even considered what they might wish to communicate about regarding the location of ripe fruit, or the need to coordinate in hunting, or innumerable other matters.)

For that matter, how likely is it that gorillas, who live in cohesive small groups rather than in fission-fusion communities, have nothing about which to communicate? That animals as intelligent as gorillas share such close quarters on an hourly basis no doubt results in selection pressures for skilled social communication. Female eastern gorillas vary their body posture and vocalizations as they engage in dyadic interactions that prove to be unstable over the short as well as the long term. Male western gorillas engage in spectacularly communicative water displays. Isn't it clear that these gorillas have found something worth communicating about?

In sum, African great apes use flexible vocalizations as well as co-regulated gestural communication, a situation that renders suspect any strict dichotomizing of their vocalizations and gestures. Corballis shares with Hewes an unwarranted elevation of the significance of gesture at the expense of vocalizations. Unlike Hewes, Corballis wrote at a time when data were available to undermine such a proposed dichotomy. As should be obvious from earlier chapters, my unease with this dichotomizing stems not from a disavowal of the idea that gestures are significant, even primary, in the evolution of language. In fact, I believe Hewes and Corballis to be on the right track with their major claims.

Most current scholarship in language origins relies on what Ingold refers to as the standard model, which sees language as a system of rules and representations that are "inscribed in the minds of its speakers and transmissible as a body of information, from one generation to the next, independently of its instantiation in those acts of speaking and listening for which it is a prerequisite."[33] In this model, language is described as a thing apart; meaning is found in the syntax-rich, patterned sentences generated by one human mind and sent to a receiver for decoding. Meaning is divorced from social interaction, because it is generated within the mind. In other words, the standard model's depiction of language concords with the information-processing model of communication and differs dramatically from the DST view. In arguing against the standard model, Ingold captures perfectly the DST perspective on spoken language: "Speaking is not a discharge of representations in the mind but an achievement of the whole organism-person in an environment; it is closely attuned and continually responsive to the gestures of others, and speakers are forever improvising on the basis of past practice in their efforts to make themselves understood in a world which is never quite the same from one moment to the next."[34]

A key realization is that both Hewes and Corballis break with the standard model. Both reject the idea of language-as-rules-in-the-head, and seek instead an evolutionary explanation for the meaning-making that characterizes language in social beings. As I have shown, though, their views rest on inaccurate assumptions about the fundamental evolutionary platform represented by the African great apes—apparently owing to lack of available data in the earlier case, and to ignorance of these data in the later case. Twinning the evolutionary perspective of Hewes and Corballis with an accurate portrayal of the African great ape platform in social communication should, then, result in a compelling approach to the origins of language. Some of what I have in mind can be found in *Gesture and the Nature of Language* by Armstrong, Stokoe, and Wilcox.

Like Hewes and Corballis, Armstrong and his co-authors wish to reconstruct an evolutionary history for language in our species: "We are arguing that language arose out of gestural communication primarily within emerging hominid extended families."[35] Two insights are central to their endeavor. First, Armstrong and colleagues do not dichotomize vocalizations and gestures; in fact, vocalizations, including human speech, are merely classed as auditory gestures and manual movements as visible gestures. Armstrong and colleagues do note at one point that "as far as can be determined" primate vocalizations "tend to be tied to particular stimuli."[36] But much less is made of this contrast, already so tentatively offered, than in the scenarios put forth by Hewes and Corballis. When features of chimpanzee language-like behavior are summarized by Armstrong and colleagues, no hard-and-fast contrasts between chimpanzee vocalization and gesture are included.[37]

In short, though Armstrong and colleagues embrace the notion of gestural origins, their ideas do not require that primate vocalizations differ dramatically from primate gestures. Owing to their unified view of gesture, the authors have no need to posit a mechanism to explain a switch from gestural to vocal language; language always has been, and always will be, gestural. What, then, could account for the evolution of human language from an African great ape platform?

This question brings us to Armstrong and colleagues' second innovation, a focus on the "pattern congruity between visible gesture and syntax."[38] Only keen students of sign languages could have arrived at this notion. Stokoe pioneered the study of American Sign Language as a language equivalent in every way to spoken languages, and both Armstrong and Wilcox have scholarly reputations in the analysis of signed languages. As they put it, "the sign language word has the structure of a miniature sentence: *what is active* is the agent or subject or "S," and *what it does* is the action of the verb or "V."[39] In other words, when people sign words today, they are essentially *doing syntax*. Early hominids would have gradually developed syntax in tandem with their gesturing, as they came to notice the structure inherent in their movements. *Gesture and the Nature of Language* thus provides an evolutionary explanation for syntax that is embodied: "The key to building syntax incrementally is the discovery of *relationships* within symbols, and that embryo sentences are already inherent in simple visible gestures."[40]

The important evolutionary action, then, occurred in visible gesture; it led to a realization about relationships between elements of a manual utterance, which in turn led to other linguistic insights, from which syntax as we know it emerged. Armstrong and colleagues provide much more detail than can be included here about the precise path by which human language might have evolved from the starting point of gesturing African great apes. The critical point is that their theory invites complementary scholarship from the study of the apes themselves.[41] The apes in *Gesture and the Nature of Language* are significant to evolutionary reconstructions, and not because their vocalizations lack reference or voluntary control. Restore to these apes their full abilities for embodied meaning-making (as explained in Chapters 3 and 4), and we find ourselves traveling down a much different path than the one envisioned by Hewes or Corballis.

## The Evolution of Co-Regulated Social Communication

Data that demonstrate the co-regulated nature of the African great apes' social communication make a powerful addition to theorizing about the origins of language. To see why, let's start with a point made by the biological anthropologist Matt Cartmill. If language (or any other complex phenomenon) is considered unique to humans— as is often the case—then its evolution must remain mysterious.[42] In order to understand how it may have originated and developed, one must be willing to define language in such a way as to permit a search for its precursors in nonhumans, and to see, across different species, fundamental regularities in behavioral patterns that might indicate such precursors. For instance, to exclude a priori as language any communication system that lacks the specific type of syntax found in human-uttered sentences dooms the quest for evolutionary understanding right from the start.

Cartmill's work shows just how critical it is for evolutionary explorations to define co-regulated and creative social communication in nonanthropocentric terms. When this is accomplished, the data lead to twin conclusions. Bonobos, chimpanzees, and gorillas have a great deal to communicate about, and they do so often in contingent, creative ways that result in socially created meanings between partners. Further, the meaning that is socially created depends critically on past social histories as well as on present conditions.

With this new perspective, it becomes possible to work toward a reformulation of the African great ape platform upon which many theories of language origins are based, and the evolution of social construction of meaning begins to seem a little less mysterious. Of primary importance is a shift in the unit of analysis, from the discrete gesture to the co-regulated social relationship. It is vital to know which individuals make which movements (arm-waves; chestbeats; head nods; clasped hands; and so forth). Yet this knowledge adds up only to a crude starting point, for the heart of the matter involves the transformation of these movements into social gestures that mean something to the interactants. For this reason, the practice by some language theorists of listing in chart form which apes make which gestures ("trait listing")[43] can be only a preliminary tool to motivate the investigation of social construction of meaning.

One outcome of this revision in the African great ape social platform is a heightened realization of what hominid social communication, too, was probably all about. Often, hominid communication is tied to the enhancement of a type of social cooperation that is narrowly, even aridly, imagined. Corballis, for instance, sees locational signaling, or "indicating where predators or prey were lurking," as of greatest important to hominids.[44] Given their silent nature, manual gestures would pose a lowered risk of detection, compared to vocal calls, for hominids who attempted to avoid becoming prey. Perhaps it is unsurprising that hominids should be reduced to one-dimensional figures, battling for their survival in challenging environments. Years ago, Landau brought to paleoanthropology's attention the mythic structure of scenarios about the evolution of our species.[45] In most reconstructions of how we became human, heroic figures battle some environmental pressure, overcoming it through mastery of a new skill or by developing a new ability. The earliest hominids located food in harsh environments by foraging bipedally; the first *Homo* overcame various environmental challenges via innovative tool-making; and so on. No wonder, then, that hominid social communication is often reduced to a mechanism for enhancing or accelerating the heroic achievement of major milestones in our prehistory.

A result of our "upgraded" African great ape platform for social communication, then, is the conclusion that hominids almost certainly communicated in a co-regulated way, grounded in their socioemotional connections with each other. Even without knowing the specifics of their social organization, we may speculate that hominid males and/or females exhibited shifting loyalties when choosing allies, and so became embroiled in conflicts based on jealousy or vengefulness; that hominid juveniles played with each other joyfully, laughing and having fun; and that hominid mothers felt affection or love for their children. For hominids, as for African great apes, survival would have been only one aspect of life.

A greater effort should be made to ground language-origins theories in up-to-date information about African great ape behavior. Although it is true that gestural research has been comparatively neglected among wild populations, the data presented in Chapter 4 show that a serious combing of primary sources yields much useful information. I find puzzling the proclivity of some language-origins theorists to focus exclusively or nearly exclusively on captive and enculturated African great apes. Nowhere in Pinker's famed book

*The Language Instinct,* for example, nor in his more technical article with Bloom,[46] does he analyze wild chimpanzee vocal or gestural signals. Wild chimpanzees are described as "strong, vicious wild animals" that "hoot and shriek,"[47] but are considered no further. (For *why* Pinker chose this path, that is, for discussion of how this focus on captive apes supports his language-origins thesis, see my earlier work.)[48]

Clearly, the significance of ape gestural behavior derives from what the apes actually do in their day-to-day lives, rather than from what they cannot do vocally. The more thoroughly the routine behavior of African great apes, living in a variety of environments, can be described, the better off our theories will be.

In selecting the language-origins theories by Hewes, Corballis, and Armstrong and co-authors, I confined my review to scenarios that have, first, focused heavily on gestural behavior and, second, influenced thinking in a number of disciplines. Casting the net wider, let us consider some theories that move us closer to the two correctives suggested here: acknowledgment that the African great apes engage in co-regulated social communication and create meaning as they interact, and inclusion of data from wild populations.

## Bringing Children into Language-Origins Theories

Selection pressures for social cooperation or cohesion among hominids appear commonly enough at the heart of language-origins theories; sometimes they are coupled with a focus on gesture. Parker and Gibson see as critical to language origins the need for early hominids to share with their close kin information about hidden foods, via a "gestural protolanguage." For Parker and Gibson, the key event in the hominid lineage was the shift, after the split with African great apes, to primary dependence on obtaining embedded food by using tools (also called extractive foraging with tools). They write obliquely about close social relationships among relatives: "During a long apprenticeship period, juvenile protohominids depended on their mothers and other close kin to share food with them, to help them open embedded foods, and to act as models for extractive foraging." Foraging-related selection pressures, then, pushed hominids toward an "increased tendency for voluntary combination and coordination of gestures and their use to refer to objects and events."[49] Writing alone, Parker emphasizes that language can be seen as a means for social manipulation, both in the present and in the evolutionary past.[50]

Appreciation of the significance of social relationships for primates, especially for mother and infants, informs scenarios such as these. Yet they are not "fleshed out" in the way that I am advocating here. Attention to another pair of language-origins theories yields the welcome conclusion that hominid socioemotionality has not, after all, been completely neglected.

Borchert and Zihlman make an explicit plea for reinserting "the social interaction between hominid babies and their mothers, siblings and peers" into the record of language-origins theorizing.[51] They bring to bear data from chimpanzees and bonobos, in both the wild and enculturated settings, as well as from modern-day human children, to consider the question of how the survival of hominid youngsters might have been enhanced via shifts in their communication with adults.

Writing in 1990, Borchert and Zihlman noted the rich repertoire of gesture and body movements in wild chimpanzees. This repertoire, though it extends to interactions between adults and offspring, as in food-begging, lacks the "Gestural Complex of *communicative pointing, showing and giving,* and *ritual requesting*" that is prevalent between human children and their caretakers (a complex also mentioned by Parker and Gibson). A large literature, reviewed by Zihlman and Borchert and more recently by Blake,[52] attests to the strong motivation of children to participate with their parents and other caretakers in jointly viewing, handling, or playing with objects in their world, and suggests that such joint referencing plays a role in helping the child learn language. This gestural complex, I contend, is often socioemotional. The child may experience a strong desire to enter into a shared experience with caretakers, and joy when this comes about or frustration when it does not.

Given that this gestural complex is absent in the wild African great apes, what clues from primate studies can be found to its origins? In answering this question, Borchert and Zihlman make good use of data from enculturated apes, particularly those from Savage-Rumbaugh's research.[53] The chimpanzees Sherman and Austin were given a keyboard with language-like symbols, and a series of intriguing problems to solve. They began, without specific training, to manifest some behaviors of the so-called gestural complex. They were able to request, using symbols, specific tools from each other in order to carry out a cooperative task, then hand over the tool requested; the apes did this in such a way as to show beyond doubt that the symbols had come to *represent* the tools for them. Sherman and Austin began "to point spontaneously at objects while naming them at the keyboard, seemingly for the purpose of engaging caretakers in social interactions." Most significantly, "No genetic change was required for these two chimpanzees to traverse important steps in the ontogeny of language. The transition occurred because researchers provided a special kind of social environment."[54]

The situation is even more interesting with the bonobo Kanzi because, unlike Sherman and Austin, he was studied from infancy in just this kind of special environment. As is well known, Kanzi was near his mother, Matata, while she was trained (not very successfully) on various linguistic tasks by Savage-Rumbaugh and co-workers. Kanzi himself, however, was not trained on any tasks. As Borchert and Zihlman say, before the age of 1 year "Kanzi had acquired a very rich gestural repertoire. Around age ten months, he began *pointing communicatively* in order to make requests for objects, to make known his desire to be carried from one place to another, and to initiate joint activities and games."[55] Even before his involvement with research-related tasks, then, Kanzi showed some evidence of the gestural complex identified for human children.

Though Matata will be remembered as a less than brilliant pupil in terms of her own language training, her role in Kanzi's communicative development was immense. Once again the 10-month mark in Kanzi's life was critical; at around this age, he began to use eye contact, gestures, and vocalizations in communicating with his mother. Savage-Rumbaugh, and in turn Borchert and Zihlman, suggest that this ability emerged because Matata had by that time attributed intentionality to Kanzi's movements and calls.[56] Borchert and Zihlman seem to suggest that the quality of Kanzi's communication with his mother would not be found in wild bonobos. In Kanzi, then, we have an ape who demonstrates some linguistic ability, and does so, like Sherman and Austin, without any genetic change from his wild counterparts—but also, *unlike* Sherman and Austin, without any training. Remarkably, Kanzi has both produced and comprehended symbolic utterances—the first by using lexigrams on a keyboard, the second by listening to spoken English. The question remains, though, whether Kanzi's so-called intentional communication *with his mother* would not be found among wild bonobos or in other African great apes, wild or captive.

In relating Savage-Rumbaugh's work to the issue of language origins, Borchert and Zihlman write, "Matata's maternal style, we believe, also suggests one of the earliest key steps taken by early hominid mothers in the phylogenetic emergence of language."[57] They consider Matata's behavior to represent a species difference, because they consider bonobos to be more socially inclined in certain ways than are chimpanzees and gorillas. Though admitting they do not know whether Matata is a typical bonobo mother, they predict that early hominid mothers would have interpreted their infants' actions as if they were intentional, as Matata did with Kanzi.

Vital to this picture is the increased infant vulnerability that accompanies the development of bipedality. Once bipedalism arose, Borchert and Zihlman contend, clinging ability was probably lost. Lacking an opposable toe, hominid babies would not have retained the ability to cling with their feet as ape infants do. Hominid babies would thus be favored to communicate differently than do African great ape infants. Natural selection would have favored infants "who were more successful at using vocalizations to manipulate their mothers' behavior. Vocal symbolic tool-using may have increased infants' protection from predators and may have ensured them a reliable supply of food, water, warmth, affection, social interaction and cognitive stimulation."[58]

Details of Borchert and Zihlman's thesis may be flawed. Given that the skeletal adaptations of the early hominids indicate that they were able to climb trees as well as walk bipedally on the ground, is it really so clear that infant clinging ability would have been lost early in human evolution? Parker suggests, in fact, that only later with *Homo erectus*'s commitment to full terrestrial bipedalism would clinging have been lost. This would mean that "[*Homo erectus* infants] may have been the first hominid infants who spent time off their mothers' bodies, lying on their backs."[59]

Further, the data from captivity (Chapter 3) indicate that some unenculturated African great ape mothers behave with their young infants *as if* their infants' movements were intentionally communicative. Captive gorilla mothers, for instance, help construct their infant's arm extensions as social requests. Perhaps Matata's behaviors with Kanzi are unique neither to that pair nor to that species. More research on what African great apes can and cannot do gesturally might suggest what hominid mothers did that no other primate mothers could do, and that led to development of the showing, giving, and ritual requesting of objects that take center stage in human caretaker–infant interactions.

Still, Borchert and Zihlman do well to point language-origins theorists toward socioemotional interactions between hominid mothers and their babies. Their thesis, unfortunately, has garnered relatively little recognition; Falk cites it not once in a lengthy article on this same topic.

Falk too considers the vulnerability of hominid infants to be a key point in language-origins theorizing. Like Borchert and Zihlman, she notes that the advent of bipedalism would have meant the loss of infants' clinging to their mothers' bodies. She adds that even if modern human babies could somehow cling to their mothers' bodies, "it would be difficult for mature human infants to 'ride' unaided for extended lengths of time on backs that are habitually oriented vertically rather than horizontally. Infant carrying is therefore entirely up to the human mother (or a substitute) and, as any mother will attest, growing babies soon become heavy."[60] Given that the first hominid bipeds were also oriented vertically, this point is significant for evolutionary reconstructions. Coupled with the observation that monkey and ape infants vocally protest separation from their mothers, it leads us to the crux of Falk's theory: "Presumably, early hominin babies were no happier at being separated from their mothers than are anthropoid infants today, and would have been increasingly likely to vocalize distress during the period of evolution when active infant riding was lost and babies were put down periodically so that mothers could forage."[61] This shift in turn would have led to more "distal" mother-infant communicative exchanges and eventually to what Falk terms "full-fledged multimodal motherese" that moved away from the affective and into the referential realm. (With "motherese," Falk refers to infant-directed speech, or ID, as discussed in Chapter 1.)

"Multimodal" is a key term for Falk. Though the bulk of her attention relates to the role played by shifts in infant vocalizations, Falk integrates gesture into her theory at every stage. Citing Plooij (see Chapter 4) among others, she notes that ID gestural communication appears to be much richer in chimpanzees than does ID vocal communication. Like Borchert and Zihlman, she makes use of observations made of Matata's and Kanzi's gestural interactions. In describing how modern human infants interact with their caretakers, she includes a variety of modes of expression. "Because communication with infants involves tactile and visual as well as auditory stimuli, interest is growing in multimodal motherese that involves gesture, facial expressions, and touching of infants in addition to vocal utterances."[62] Even as she concentrates on vocalizations in modeling distal communication between the generations, then, she leaves room for gestures—making special mention of enhanced sensitivity to facial expressions.

Challenges can be made to the fine points of Falk's theory as they were to Borchert and Zihlman's. As already noted, Parker suggests that only later with *Homo erectus* did distal communication play an important part in mother-infant exchanges. Second, the sequential nature of Falk's vocal scenario—affective first, referential second—is arguable, given the referentiality in some nonhuman primate vocalizations. Minor challenges aside, Falk's theory, like Borchert and Zihlman's, is ripe for coupling with data on the co-regulated social communication of the African great apes in order to produce an accurate picture of the platform for the origins of language. African great ape mothers and their infants contributed to this evolutionary platform a highly nuanced and multimodal system of social communication in which each partner attends to the contingencies and unpredictabilities inherent in the events in which they participate. Sometimes, to be sure, their vocalizations and gestures occur in ritualized contexts and lead to predictable outcomes. But often, predictability is absent. African great apes, starting from infancy, gradually come to participate with their social partners in dance-like social communication, and become very practiced at adjusting their own actions to the actions of others as they construct meaning together.

Selection pressures during early hominid evolution would have worked on variation in abilities related to co-regulation and social construction of meaning as well as on variation in abilities related to the production of certain vocalizations or gestures. Humans have a long evolutionary history not just of gesturing but of constructing gestures socially, an ability that evolved as part of our proclivity for co-regulated social communication.

## A Note on African Great Ape–Human Communication

Any scenario concerned with evolution must naturally include consideration of African great apes living under natural circumstances, exposed directly to the pressures of natural selection. As Chapter 3 attests, data on spontaneous social communication in captive groups may support key points in gestural origins theories, and help raise new questions for future research. The language-origins theories reviewed here, though, suggest that it would be a mistake to exclude from consideration research on apes whose communicative or problem-solving behavior is directed primarily toward humans.

Three research projects showcase how much may be learned about social communication in this context. Gomez recounts problem-solving activities by the captive female infant gorilla Muni, as she interacted both with objects and with people. Gomez wanted to discover whether Muni could take into account that humans, unlike objects, may both act spontaneously and react to events as they unfold. Supporting his conclusion that Muni did in fact understand the social nature of humans, Gomez provides descriptive accounts of events in which Muni communicated with a person. In his descriptions, "G" stands for gorilla (Muni) and "H" for human: "A swing hanging from a tree, a favorite toy for Muni, is raised too high for her to reach it from the ground. G tries various approaches (all . . . through objects), but her efforts are unsuccessful. She gives up for a while. But as soon as H stands by the swing, G approaches him, lifts her arms toward H, and looks at his eyes. G 'freezes' her posture without trying to climb up H. *Only when H begins to take her in his arms does G actively collaborate in the lift.* Once in H's arms, G turns to the swing and reaches it" (italics added).[63]

Gomez categorizes events such as this one as proof that Muni intentionally communicates with a human. Another way to express what happened is to say that the arm-raise movement made by Muni becomes a social gesture—and indeed, an effective one—when her human companion entered into interaction with her. Clear hints of co-regulation exist, for Muni began to participate in being raised up only *as* the human moved to raise her.

Similar co-regulation can be noted in communication between the chimpanzee Panzee and human companions, as studied by C. Menzel. Reared by Savage-Rumbaugh and colleagues, Panzee knows how to communicate with humans using lexigram symbols, and has grown up with English spoken in her environment. Wishing to study her memory skills, Menzel carried out 34 experimental trials over a study period of 268 days.[64] In each trial, an experimenter hid a different test object (some food and some nonfood items) outdoors at a distance from, but in view of, Panzee. Panzee then experienced a delay, sometimes only a few minutes and sometimes overnight, before next encountering a human. Never asked or prompted for any information, Panzee was allowed to interact with this second person, always someone who knew nothing about the hidden object's location (and in most cases had no idea that a trial was under way at all).

Results are striking, not only for Menzel's own interest in chimpanzee memory but also for ours in co-regulation. Panzee, using vocalization, gesture, or the symbols on her lexigram board, first captured the uninformed person's attention: "Panzee then covered her eyes with her hand [Menzel notes elsewhere in his article that this action is for Panzee associated with a hide-and-seek game], held her arm extended in the direction of the tunnel leading outdoors, moved to the tunnel, and went outdoors. If the person did not follow, then Panzee came back inside, again gestured 'hide,' beckoned, and pointed outdoors with her arm extended. Once both Panzee and the person were outdoors, Panzee beckoned manually and moved to the edge of the enclosure. She sat facing the object, at the closest possible position. She extended her index finger through the cage wire and jabbed it in the direction of the object. She prompted the person to search the terrain by gesturing 'hide,' by pointing manually toward the object location with her index finger extended, by giving low vocalizations, and by staring toward the location, with interspersed looks toward the person."[65]

Menzel all but deploys the term "co-regulation" in his description of Panzee's behavior! Panzee clearly adjusted her own actions in concert with what the human was doing: "Panzee kept pointing, showed intensified vocalization, shook her arm, and bobbed her head or body, as the person got closer to the site. Once the person found the object, Panzee stopped pointing manually outside the enclosure and stopped gesturing 'hide.'"[66] Panzee's strategies were effective; the uninformed persons successfully located all 34 hidden objects. On only 3 of the 268 days in the testing period did Panzee urge the person to search for an item when, in fact, no object had been hidden. (I direct readers interested in African great ape memory to Menzel's accounts for the many details I have omitted here.)

Working also with captive chimpanzees, Leavens and colleagues have studied the abilities of great apes to point, a subject of considerable confusion in the existing literature. Leavens and colleagues review a variety of published claims about ape pointing, including that apes do not point at all; that apes do not point with the index finger unless explicitly trained; that apes do not point with any understanding that their actions may influence a social partner; and that apes point only when interacting with humans and not with each other.[67] Each of these statements is wrong. Apes point spontaneously, and sometimes with each other, though judging from what we know at this stage, they do so more often with the whole hand than with the index finger, and more often in captivity than in the wild.

In the most recent experimental work by Leavens and colleagues, two researchers participated in hidden-food trials administered to chimpanzees at the Yerkes Primate Research Center in Atlanta, Georgia.[68] In one experiment, two buckets were inverted near the chimpanzees' cages. After one person placed a banana either atop a bucket (visible condition) or beneath a bucket (hidden condition), a second person, the experimenter, arrived and addressed a single chimpanzee subject by name. Any communicative behavior on the part of the subject during a visible-condition trial resulted in the experimenter giving the banana to the chimpanzee. In the hidden condition, the experimenter tried to discern the banana's location by reading the chimpanzee's gestures and postures. The chimpanzee was given the banana whether or not she or he communicated the banana's location accurately—either immediately, if the chimpanzee indicated the correct bucket, or slightly later if the person had to locate the banana under the second bucket. Each subject received only one trial in each condition.

The chimpanzees' gestures were significantly associated with the presence of the experimenter. Sixty-two chimpanzees made 101 gestures during these trials; all but one of these occurred during the approach or after the arrival of the experimenter. The chimpanzees gestured both to the experimenter and to the buckets—in the latter case, significantly more often to the baited than to the unbaited buckets. After analyzing, on video, details of the chimpanzees' gestural production, Leavens and colleagues concluded that the chimpanzees effectively communicated to an ignorant human the location of hidden food, and that their gestures were referential in function.

As with Gomez's and Menzel's work, the goal of Leavens and colleagues' research goes well beyond gesture production, to consider various cognitive issues. In this case, presumably because results are presented statistically for so many chimpanzees instead of only one, the form of the gestures is not described other than as arm-extensions or points. No qualitative information hints at the presence or absence of co-regulation between chimpanzee subject and human experimenter. Still, this work supports Gomez's and Menzel's in showing the efficacy of chimpanzee gestural behavior, especially pointing, in interaction with humans.

Another group of research projects goes under the rubric "ape-language research." The African great ape linguistic projects involve bonobos (Kanzi and his half-sister Panbanisha); chimpanzees (Lana, Washoe, Sarah, Sherman, and Austin) and a gorilla (Koko).[69] The significance of these projects inheres not in the size of the vocabulary acquired by any individual ape; nor in the patterns that might indicate incipient syntactical abilities in their utterances; nor in any other so-called feature of language. Their power rests instead in the co-regulated social relationship at the heart of any results that are achieved.

By definition, the enculturated African great apes enjoy close social relationships with humans. Personal observation of the intimate tie that may be forged between an African great ape and a human has no doubt influenced my thinking on this topic. When conducting research at Georgia State University's Language Research Center (see Chapter 3), I encountered the famous "linguistic ape" Kanzi. Though I studied Kanzi's behavior only when he was a visitor to the enclosure of his mother and half-sisters, the nature of his relationship with ape-language researcher Savage-Rumbaugh was at times quite visible to me. Science writers often note that Kanzi enjoys walks or car rides with Savage-Rumbaugh, or shares food with her. What translates only with difficulty to the printed page is the emotional tenor of these interactions, the alert focus each (one bonobo, one human) has relative to the other, and the excitement and pleasure that ensues in their spending time together. I remember clearly a time during which Savage-Rumbaugh spent the bulk of her hours with Panbanisha instead of with Kanzi. One day during this period, Kanzi heard Savage-Rumbaugh's voice coming over the hand-held radio of a staff member working nearby. Kanzi's alert orientation and excited vocalizing—absent when he heard voices other than Savage-Rumbaugh's—told me much about their relationship.

By all accounts, foremost among them Fouts's about his years with Washoe,[70] a similar bond is present between apes and humans in other linguistic projects. This emotional connection has, of course, engendered criticism by skeptics. As the argument goes, this emotional intimacy leads the researcher inevitably astray, away from scientific objectivity. The researcher is then susceptible to over-analyzing or overinterpreting any utterances by the apes. Savage-Rumbaugh's own view is that her interactions with Kanzi and Panbanisha allow her to become "more proficient . . . at entering into the bonobos' world."[71] Meshing of worlds through shared interactive routines may be, as Shanker and I have written,[72] the key that permits the gradual development of linguistic production and comprehension in enculturated African great apes.

Savage-Rumbaugh writes of meaning in a way instantly recognizable to DST theorists. "Meaning cannot exist in words any more than it can exist in the smile, the eye-flash of understanding, the subtle posture. Meaning can exist only in the patterning of these things, and the patterning exists not within one individual but between individuals."[73] The enculturated African great apes show us that meaning may exist in the patterning between individuals even when the social partners in question come from two different species. Embedded here is a larger point for language-origins theorizing.

As we have seen, co-regulated social communication may be enhanced when two social partners are emotionally engaged in some way. Given that co-regulation is dependent on close attention to subtleties and contingencies, and on mutual adjustment to another's actions, it is surely meaningful for evolutionary reconstructions that individual bonobos, chimpanzees, and gorillas so easily enter into emotional relationships with individual humans. The African great ape's emotional system, and the human's, are both labile and recruitable. Under the right conditions, when faced with a social partner with a different set of skills, co-regulation and mean-making proceed apace (however imperfectly, as always may be the case, even in humans). That African great apes can do this attests to their long evolutionary history of participating spontaneously in co-regulation and meaning-construction with diverse members of their own species—potential rivals or allies or sexual partners, hesitant juveniles or playful infants. The African great apes attend, as we have seen so many times, not to discrete "signals" and "messages" but to the contingent events unfolding all around them.

Hominids, then, were probably well equipped to participate in coregulated social communication with those group members who were in some way slightly advanced in terms of communicational skills, whether because of natural variation or of mutation. Armstrong and colleagues, for instance, predict that some early hominids would have been more adept than others at recognizing the embryonic syntactical patterns in visible gesture. These individuals might well have begun using gesture in innovative ways. Borchert and Zihlman, and Falk, predict that some early hominid mothers, when putting down their vulnerable infants in order to forage or carry out other activities, would more readily have used some form of infant-directed speech or elaborated form of infant-directed multimodal communication.

The African great ape platform described here suggests that this variation across hominid individuals was important *socially* as well as *genetically*. Others in the hominid group would have been well equipped to adjust their own actions to the variant communicational abilities being displayed. As the theorist Burling realizes, the enculturated African great apes' abilities to comprehend human utterances (whether vocal or gestural) are meaningful for understanding how language originated. "The priority of comprehension over production suggests that when a few individuals began to produce increasingly wordlike signs, others would have been able to understand them."[74] Add to this a focus on co-regulated social communication in African great ape dyads, families, and groups, and we have the beginnings of a solid theory of language origins.

My interest in this chapter, though, is not to construct yet another entry in the game of language-origins theorizing. Instead, I have tried to elucidate the nature of the African great ape platform on which reasonable theories for the origin of language may be constructed. One final issue remains. What is the role of gesture in human social communication in the present day? In other words, what is the current product of the millions of years of "evolutionary action" in the gestural mode?

## Modern Human Gesture

Predictably, given the variable ways in which gesture and social communication may be defined, no agreement exists about the relationship between gesture and speech. Iverson and Thelen identify three views.[75] In the first, gesture and speech are separate communication systems; gesture merely supports speech. When gestures are produced, perhaps when someone cannot find the words to articulate his thoughts, they are assumed to have no effect on speech production or on the cognitive processes underlying speech. Thus the influence is unilateral because speech may affect gesture, but gesture does not affect speech.

In the second view, the link between gesture and speech is reciprocal, so that gesture may affect speech as well as the other way around. The link, however, is limited; the production of gesture is seen to activate the memory so that the sought-for word may be articulated after all.

Gesture and speech constitute a single system in the third view, the unified perspective mentioned earlier in this book, and the one informing Armstrong and colleagues' gestural theory. The unified view has been explained well by McNeill, who emphasizes that "speech and gesture must cooperate to express the person's meaning. A conception of language and gesture as a single integrated system is sharply different from the notion of a 'body language'—a communication process utilizing signals made up of body movements, which is regarded by its believers as separate from and beyond normal language."[76] The unified view is compatible with the premises of DST, especially in its recognition of a relationship deeper than mere mutual influence between gesture and speech.

Two avenues of inquiry in recent research on human gestural

communication bolster the unified view. First is a body of work, best exemplified by McNeill's and Goldin-Meadow's research, showing that gesture may yield real insight into what people are thinking. Hand gestures, facial expressions, and body movements, as Goldin-Meadow notes, have traditionally been assumed to reflect the speaker's feelings, with speech assumed to be the medium used for expressing concepts and thoughts. In producing data that counter this assumption, Goldin-Meadow and McNeill also strengthen the idea that gesture and speech are fundamentally linked. (Note the interesting parallel here to research showing that nonhuman primate vocalizations are not, as so long assumed, entirely about the emotional state of the caller.)

Most compelling are data that show precisely how gesture may give us access to others' thoughts, access not available from verbal utterances. McNeill's *Hand and Mind* is chock full of examples of this phenomenon, specifically related to gestures that exhibit images. One involves a woman retelling an event. Saying, "she chases him out again," the storyteller makes (after the word "she" and during the rest of the utterance) an iconic gesture in which her hand appears to swing an object through the air. Here, "speech conveys the ideas of pursuit and recurrence while gesture conveys the weapon used (an umbrella); both speech and gesture refer to the same event, but each presents a somewhat different aspect of it."[77]

This basic idea is explored brilliantly by Goldin-Meadow and colleagues in their study of how children express their understanding of math concepts. Children sometimes convey two very different ideas about some math problem, one through speech and one through gesture. Goldin-Meadow reports on a 6-year-old boy who says that when one of two identical rows of checkers is spread out farther than the other, the number of checkers actually changes. The number of checkers in the spread-out row is, in the child's words, "different because you moved them." At the same time, however, the child "moves a pointing hand back-and-forth between the two rows, pairing the first checker in row 1 with the first checker in row 2, and so on. The child speaks about how the checkers were moved, but he has also noticed—not necessarily consciously—that the spread-out row can be aligned with the untouched row. This insight is one that the child expresses only through his hands."[78]

Conflict between speech and gesture is not an age-specific phenomenon. When 9-year-olds were asked to explain their solution to a math problem such as: $4 + 5 + 3 +\_\_\_ = + 3$, Goldin-Meadow again found mismatches between speech and gesture. "For example, a child says, 'I added 4 plus 5 plus 3 plus 3 and got 15,', demonstrating no awareness of the fact that this is an equation bifurcated by an equal sign. Her gestures, however, offer a different picture: she sweeps her left palm under the left side of the equation, pauses, then sweeps her right palm under the right side. The child's gestures clearly demonstrate that, at some level, she knows the equal sign breaks the string into two parts."[79]

Mismatches such as these—which occur at all ages and in numerous contexts outside math reasoning—characterize the behavior of people who are in some transitional phase in their learning. Children who produce a lot of mismatches as they explain some incorrect belief are more likely to benefit from instruction on that task than other children, Goldin-Meadow reports. This finding has obvious implications for education. Goldin-Meadow's most significant finding may be that ordinary people—people not trained in speech or gestural analysis or in education—pick up on and interpret the gestural parts of the mismatches. In the example of the 6-year-old boy and the checkers, an adult noted the one-to-one correspondence pointed out by the boy's hand. "Ordinary listeners can thus take advantage of the unique insight gesture offers into the thoughts speakers have, but do not express in words. . . . If gesture can play this type of role in spontaneous interaction, learners may be able to shape the day-to-day input they receive just by moving their hands."[80] This conclusion is wholly predictable from an evolutionary perspective on co-regulated social communication.

Goldin-Meadow clearly sees a link between gesture and cognitive change, and returns once again to the boy and his checkers to make her point. She notes that the ease with which his hand was able to pair up the two sets of checkers may facilitate an eventual realization that the number of checkers does not change when a row is spread out. McNeill, too, writes at length about the ways gesture may impact thought, and includes examples from children.[81]

Both Goldin-Meadow and McNeill use gesture to unlock and explore interior mental processes. But how does gesture enable or retard visible social coordination in human dyads, triads, and subgroups? Though this aspect of gesture has been studied less well than have mental processes (see Chapter 1), some studies do adopt a focus on coordinated behavior, with compelling results.

Data analyzed by the Goodwins, Charles and Marjorie, support the idea that speakers and listeners together construct meaning as each adjusts to the other's speech and gesture. C. Goodwin's perspective on the construction of sentences comes straight out of DST: "Sentences in natural conversation emerge as the products of a process of interaction between speaker and hearer . . . [who] mutually construct the turn at talk."[82] Though C. Goodwin's focus is the spoken sentence, when marshalling data for co-construction he relies heavily on gaze. Microanalysis of data shows that the speaker actually reshapes his sentence as he talks—not in a premeditated way but in response to the contingencies involved in gaze-mediated interactions with the social partners.

Writing with M. Goodwin, C. Goodwin includes hand gestures as well as gaze in an analysis of co-constructed communication. In a central example, the speaker stops partway through a sentence, searching for a word. She makes a hand gesture after this self-interruption. Through microanalysis, the Goodwins show that active participation by the listener in the speaker's search for a word would have been inappropriate during the silence. Not only had the speaker gone silent, but she had also dropped her gaze and made what is called "a thinking face," two key visible indicators of her engagement in her own mental search. When making the gesture, however, she shifts her gaze up again; the listener's co-participation "is now not only appropriate, but sought by the speaker." The gesture "occurs at the moment when a change in co-participation status is occurring and the recipient's aid in the search [for a word] is requested."[83]

Visible shifts in interaction between children and caretakers are brought about by gestures as well. As the review by Falk indicates, studies of gestural motherese are on the rise.[84] Fivaz-Depeursinge and Corboz-Warnery move well beyond a dyadic verbal focus to look at holistic co-regulated communication in triads. They have studied the body movements, gestures, and vocalizations in what they call "the primary triangle," the mother-father-child nuclear family. (As an anthropologist, I cannot help noting that such a family configuration would not be recognized as primary in most societies around the world, but that is a separate issue.) The human infant is often considered to be preadapted for dyadic interactions, but Fivaz-Depeursinge and Corboz-Warnery wish instead to study the family as a unit, not merely as a series of dyads. In this goal, they echo the work of Murray Bowen, who wrote decades ago about families as systems, and whose theories continue today to influence clinical family therapy.[85]

Fivaz-Depeursinge and Corboz-Warnery study play in the triad "because it is the purest form of affective communication unmediated by objects."[86] Like the Goodwins, they rely on microanalytic methods, focusing on play routines structured in part by the researchers themselves. They want to see how "partners are able to communicate specific affects to each other by means of vocalizations and brief movements of the face, hands, head, and body—movements that are contingent and resonant with each other." The microprocesses at the heart of such communication are "most clearly revealed by 'false steps,' 'errors,' or 'miscoordinations.'"[87] These miscoordinations in turn are made obvious to the researchers when families participate in the so-called Lausaunne triadic play task, consisting of four parts: one parent interacts with the baby while the other parent waits on the periphery; the other parent now interacts with the baby, while the first parent observes; all three family members play together; and the two parents interact together, with the baby on the periphery. Left up to the parents are decisions about how to orient the seat in which the infant rests, which parent plays first, when to carry out the switch in which parent assumes the active role, and when play should end.

Microanalysis allows assessment of miscoordination and repair during the transitions between component parts of the triadic play task. Just as an understanding of co-regulated social communication would predict, the results show tight linkage between the movements of the family members within each triangle system. Some primary triangles negotiate their inevitable moments of miscoordination fluidly, whereas others are less successful. To make this point clearly, I will contrast the actions of the families of infant Xerxes and infant Tania, as they change from the two-plus-one to the three-together configuration in the play task. (Only the actions that seem to me most relevant are reported here.)[88]

Xerxes's mother has been the active parent in the two-plus-one stage. She and Xerxes are very involved in a game, and the father looks on closely. When the mother is about to begin another round of the game, the father moves forward. At the same instant, both the father and Xerxes look away. "These cutoff signals finally register with mother; she stops the game and sits up." After some other brief activity, the two-plus-one is "definitively dismantled," but the transition to the three-together phase includes a miscoordination. Here is what happens: "Having turned his body slightly inward, father is ready to reengage. He sits up, leans toward Xerxes, and extends an arm to touch him. But mother does not follow up. She keeps on looking off, her head on her hand, as if having left the field of action. So father calls again for her to join in. . . . in a soft and warm voice, glancing at her. She begins to lean forward, turning her body to mirror father's position. Both look at the baby, leaning forward, their shoulders aligned as they call for him. Xerxes starts shifting his face toward his parents." The mother's temporary disengagement did not shut down this family's transition; the father simply calls to the mother, and she rejoins the moment.

A different picture emerges from scrutiny of Tania's family's transition. In this case, the father is the active partner in the two-plus-one phase. At one point, Tania, sitting in a sagging posture in the infant seat, reorients to her father while sucking on a belt. "There is no game and the affective tone is tense and negative." The mother, from the periphery, cuts in to ask Tania, "Is it good?" Tania immediately looks away. Thus the mother's action, which may have been intended to move the family toward the three-together stage, interrupts the action between Tania and her father. "During the next period, the parents intensify the miscoordinations. They stick to their antagonistic positions, father increasing his caresses and mother calling again on Tania." The parents seem entrenched; finally the father sits up and proposes playing together. Rather than a repair, however, what comes next is further miscoordination. Tania reorients toward her father, who greets her and leans forward, leaving out the mother, who in turn makes no effort to participate. "The family returns to the initial state . . . The phases are determined by delayed and contradictory moves of the three partners, as if they were tied together by their very aversive moves."

Fivaz-Depeursinge and Corboz-Warnery's microanalytic approach reveals much about how families coordinate, or fail to coordinate, their actions. For these researchers, gestures are just one part of the seamless web of co-regulated communication within a family. Their perspective is quite close to the one I have adopted in studying captive African great apes, with allowances made for interspecies differences in communication and for inevitable methodological divergences. Highlighting their approach also highlights continuity between the co-regulated communication of African great apes and humans. This continuity coexists with discontinuity, however. No gesture researcher, to my knowledge, denies that humans use gesture in more varied and complex ways than do the apes.

What form is this discontinuity thought to take? Research on this question is very much still in its infancy. Those who study African great apes are unlikely to hypothesize that spontaneous gestures by their subjects yield special information about ape thought processes in the way that Goldin-Meadow and McNeill have done for human children. Aside from the issue of whether the math tasks of Goldin-Meadow's research or the story-telling of McNeill's work could be adapted for research with apes, apes have no "speech output" that researchers can readily understand and contrast with observed gestures. Researchers instead tend to score spontaneous gestures and compare their use across species.

Tomasello and Camaioni identify four areas in which gesture use by human infants departs significantly from gesture use by chimpanzees, first acknowledging that the gestural communication of chimpanzees resembles that of human infants in some ways.[89] Chimpanzees gesture intentionally, for instance, meaning that the gestures are learned socially and applied flexibly.

First, human infants gesture triadically. According to Tomasello and Camaioni, chimpanzees gesture only dyadically. That is, the naturally occurring gestures of chimpanzees do not include those used "to attract the attention of another to some outside entity," such as an object or another organism. Further, human infants use gesture declaratively, "to direct the attention of others to an outside object or event, simply for the sake of sharing interest in it or commenting on it."[90] Chimpanzees use gestures only imperatively, to request actions from others. In making these two contrasts, Tomasello and Camaioni refer to the gestural complex—pointing, showing, and giving—that characterizes interactions between human infants and their caretakers, already encountered in my discussion of language-origins theories. Routine use of the gestural complex is thus considered unique to humans.

Third, human infants make gestures at a physical remove from their social partners, whereas chimpanzees gesture mostly when they are in direct physical contact with others. (In Tomasello and Camaioni's terms, the chimpanzee "signaler" and "recipient" are in contact.) Chimpanzees may also gesture in anticipation of contact, but this practice still differs from the practice of human infants, who learn distal gestures early and only relatively rarely gesture when in contact with others. Last, human babies learn their gestures by social imitation, whereas chimpanzees rely only on ontogenetic ritualization, the learning process discussed in Chapter 3. Recall that Tomasello uses his own longitudinal data on captive chimpanzee gestures to suggest that chimpanzee youngsters "acquire" gestures by a gradual (but finite) process of social shaping within a pair. In this way, their social learning is quite different from the imitation of which all humans, including infants, are capable.

Tomasello and Camaioni conclude that "the overwhelming majority of chimpanzee gestures may be seen as dyadically intended imperatives, that is, attempts to direct the attention or behavior of another to the self."[91] Some primatologists challenge this conclusion, and a look back at the data from African great apes suggests why. Humans use the gestural complex in more elaborated ways than do chimpanzee or other African great ape infants. In certain situations, though, African great apes point spontaneously to objects or other organisms. Certainly, a good number of the gestures reported for captive and wild African great apes takes place in the absence of either physical contact or anticipation of physical contact. Social requests constructed by infants and their mothers, for objects or food, provide a good example.

Tomasello and Camaioni recognize that African great ape play gestures may be made from a distance, but emphasize that their typical apparent goal is physical contact between two animals. Food-begging gestures, they go on to say, may violate the suggested interspecies contrasts. In food-begging, the "'palm-up gesture' is triadic—a request to another chimpanzee for food—and is somewhat distal since the signaler is not touching the recipient."[92] Still, food-begging is carried out with the social partners at close proximity. In any case, Tomasello and Camaioni clearly consider it exceptional within the chimpanzee gestural repertoire.

Some primatologists believe that the African great apes are capable of more social imitation than they are credited with by Tomasello.[93] Certainly, when enculturated apes are brought into the equation, the contrasts made by Tomasello and Camaioni break down. The bonobo Kanzi and other "linguistic apes" do use the gestural complex, for instance. My own concern is that the terms of debate about differences between African great ape and human gestural communication should not neglect the comparative *quality* of the communication as it takes place between social partners.

Only when systematic qualitative research considers the event between social partners as the unit of analysis will a comparative perspective on gesture bear full fruit. Because social communication is not about the sending and receiving of messages that are coded as to meaning, we must look further than individual production and comprehension of gestures. It is not enough to know which human body movements and gestures may have evolved from precursors in the apes, or to classify gestures as dyadic versus triadic, distal versus proximate, learned via shaping versus learned via imitation. New questions might include: In what ways is co-regulated social communication with gesture more elaborated in humans than in the African great apes? Are humans more attuned to the contingencies and unpredictabilities inherent in social communication than are the African great apes, so that humans notice, and adjust to, their partners' actions more readily? How does the process of miscoordination and repair in the African great apes compare to that in humans?

## Summing Up

Anthropologists will be able to model the origins of language with greater clarity when the African great ape evolutionary platform is constructed to reflect the apes' true social, communicational abilities. Co-regulated social communication regularly takes place between African great ape social partners as they move their bodies, construct gestures, and vocalize. This type of social communication probably evolved before the split between African great apes and hominids. Fleshing out the African great ape platform by attending to the socio-emotionality underlying co-regulated social communication can only enhance the starting point for theories about the origins of human language.

Comparative research into African great ape and human gestural communication may show us more clearly the significance of human gestural behavior today. That gesture is not just about arousal state, but equally is not just an aid to cognition, suggests a variety of research projects for the future. Longitudinal qualitative research into social coordination and meaning-making through gesture in both African great apes and humans is an area wide open for study. In the final chapter, I look in a more detailed way at the future of such research.

# 6

# Imagined Futures

$A$T an international symposium convened in 1996 and sponsored by the Wenner-Gren Foundation for Anthropological Research, two well-known researchers of African great ape behavior traded intriguing comments. When William McGrew suggested the establishment of a journal devoted to ape ethnography, Christophe Boesch nicknamed such an enterprise "The Journal of Irreproducible Results." Reading this exchange in *The Beast on the Table* by Sydel Silverman,[1] Wenner-Gren's president at the time of the symposium, I found myself in a quandary.

My immediate urge was to interpret the exchange, and Silverman's brief commentary on it, through my own perspective on a tension in current primate studies. This tension revolves around the question of what constitutes good scientific methodology. It engenders debate about different methods, often seen as alternatives: qualitative versus quantitative data collection and analysis, "thick" longitudinal description versus statistical treatment of the data. Though good methodology texts dutifully insist that researchers can and should combine a multiplicity of methods, often, in current primate behavior studies, the quantitative alone is valued far more than is the qualitative (see Chapter 2). In this light, McGrew's suggestion for a new journal may be read to champion inclusion, in the array of accepted primatological methods, of longitudinal qualitative analysis, detailed description of ape social events, and so on. Boesch's invoking the nickname that he did may, by contrast, be seen to indicate his concern about the scientific validity of such an approach. After all, scientific results are reproducible results—aren't they?[2] Silverman's parenthetical interpretation of McGrew's term "ape ethnography" too becomes interesting, for she glosses it merely as "natural-history notes."

Unfortunately for my incipient analysis, lessons derived from the dynamic systems approach to social communication rushed back to me at this point. I hadn't been present at the symposium to witness the McGrew-Boesch exchange. If, as DST claims, meaning doesn't reside in words but is created by social partners through interaction, could I really know from Silverman's minimalist reporting what Boesch intended by his reply? Had it been said playfully or sarcastically? With a smile, or with a snort? How serious was McGrew in the first place, and what did he mean by ethnography? Is Silverman's glossing of the term a paraphrase of McGrew, or her own interpretation, and in either case, is it accurate?

Given that no microanalysis of this conversation has been done, I'll analyze it no further. I do wish to analyze some deeper issues that underlie my initial interpretation of the reported conversation, focusing not on what McGrew or Boesch might have intended, but instead on some related issues that touch directly on the future of research into African great ape body movement and gesture.

## Looking Back

Let's revisit, first, the major arguments I have made in support of the idea that the social lives of the African great apes can be better understood by thoroughly exploring their nonvocal communication. Five central points have formed the heart of these arguments. First, the African great apes, both in captivity and in the wild, engage in social interactions that are marked by gesture and body movements. They masterfully read others' nuanced actions, and produce movements of their own, some quite subtle and others entirely obvious, that others may see. In their moment-by-moment mutual adjustments and fluidity, these interactions can be termed *co-regulated* because they are highly unpredictable and contingent, reminiscent of a dance between two highly attuned partners.

Second, African great ape social partners may create meaning *as* they participate in co-regulated social communication. When the interaction is co-regulated, rather than predictable or fixed in nature, meaning may emerge from the actions of the social partners. The meaning derives not from individual movements or utterances but is constructed socially.

Third, the social communication of the African great apes often results in heightened coordination of individuals' behavior (involving miscoordinations along the way, at times). Movements and gestures help bring about a shift within a pair or subgroup; because "coordination" in this context implies no particular outcome, the result may involve anything from affiliation to conflict. Youngsters discover early that when they move their bodies, heads, or limbs in certain ways, often with certain facial expressions and while vocalizing, they help bring about shifts in the social dynamic.

Fourth, analysis of African great ape social communication can be advanced when researchers concentrate on visible outcomes between partners rather than on the number, form, or function of the gestures themselves. A dance *could* be studied by counting the number of leg extensions, head turns, or pirouettes per individual, but what could be learned from such an exercise? After all, if meaning is created when partners act together, it becomes untenable to then expect that a certain arm gesture or body posture could have meaning in itself, apart from the social event in which it is embedded. Further, by focusing on visible outcomes, it is possible to study issues of importance to cognition while avoiding reliance on inferences about how apes mentally represent the world—a crucial step for those observing apes outside strictly experimental contexts. Qualitative methods, combined with quantitative ones when the research question requires it, provide a superb way to approach the study of visible outcomes.

Last, the validity of theorizing is greatly strengthened when the above points are incorporated into scenarios about the origins and evolution of language. The social co-regulation and meaning-making that we may observe in gorilla, bonobo, and chimpanzee dyads and subgroups today was probably present in the common ancestor of humans and African great apes and available for natural selection and mutation to act upon at the dawn of the human lineage.

The theory and methods of dynamic systems thinking offer an exciting avenue by which study of African great ape nonvocal communication might be approached. What remains to be considered are specific ideas for future research.

## Looking Ahead: The Goualougo Chimpanzees

The five points just summarized cry out for new methods, or perhaps more accurately, a new *mix* of methods, in studies of African great ape social communication. Underlying such a mix would be questions that are also new, or at least infrequently asked. As one of the epigraphs for this book notes, the conservationist and gorilla researcher George Schaller once remarked that asking different questions will create a different animal. Analyzing co-regulated social communication when it is present, and figuring out under which conditions it is absent, may help us to describe different African great apes, in Schaller's sense.

Let's imagine primatologists studying a social group of African great apes, and what "different questions" they might ask about social communication. The group is new to science, rather than from an established field site (where research methodologies are also likely to be well established) such as Gombe, Mahale, or Tai for chimpanzees, Karisoke for eastern gorillas, or Wamba for bonobos. Given that never-before-known-about "pockets" of African great apes are still occasionally discovered, we can, surprisingly enough, use a real-life rather than imaginary example that fits these criteria. In 2003, the researchers Morgan and Sanz reported results from two field seasons' observations on chimpanzees of the Goualougo Triangle, located at the southern end of the Nouabale-Ndoki National Park in northern Congo.[3] The researchers are fairly certain that the chimpanzees had had no, or very minimal, contact with humans ever before.

The Goualougo Triangle chimpanzees were first brought to the attention of the scientific world by the Wildlife Conservation Society's Michael Fay, during his 1990 survey of forest elephant populations.[4] Fay and his colleague Marcellin Agnagna came across chimpanzees who, to their considerable surprise, observed them curiously, rather than fled from them. When Morgan, chosen by Fay, returned and set up a field camp in the Triangle in 1999 (to be joined by Sanz later), the chimpanzees were still fearless and curious. The Triangle area is located 34 miles from Bomassa, the nearest village; between the two exist only dense forest and swampland. Residents of Bomassa say that they visited the Triangle for the first time in 1993, when Fay led his now-famous trek through Congo and Gabon to document the importance of preserving the region and its incredible biodiversity (including chimpanzees and gorillas). But the most compelling evidence that these apes have remained undisturbed comes from the behavior of the chimpanzees themselves.

The Goualougo chimpanzees responded to the initial presence of Morgan and Sanz quite differently than chimpanzees at other locations have, in previous years, responded to the arrival of researchers. Elsewhere, chimpanzees apparently became sensitized to the correlation between human presence and activities such as poaching, hunting, and destruction of the habitat. As a result, they were wary of humans. Curiosity rather than wariness, however, was the most common response from 84 percent of the Goualougo chimpanzees in their initial 5 minutes of contact with Morgan and Sanz. The apes stared at the humans; crouched and moved to see them better; slapped tree trunks and threw branches at them; and made what are described as "inquisitive" vocalizations.

Speaking to the media, Sanz noted, "Such an overwhelmingly curious response to the arrival of researchers had never been reported from another chimpanzee study site. Researchers have occasionally described encounters with apes who showed curious behaviors toward them. However, these encounters were rare and usually consisted of only a few individuals."[5] By contrast, nervousness on the part of the chimpanzees was the rarity at Goualougo. In only 12 percent of the human-ape encounters did the chimpanzees depart or hide from, climb away from, or ignore the human observers.

Two further features of these initial encounters are noteworthy. The average encountered lasted over 2 hours (136 minutes, to be precise), with some lasting as many as 7 hours, ending only when the humans elected to leave—at which point the chimpanzees sometimes followed them. Morgan and Sanz witnessed the chimpanzees using tools, and engaging in relaxed social behaviors. Field workers who spent *years* habituating their study subjects well enough to see such events must have heard these reports with envy.

Serious ethical concerns exist in this situation. All indications are that the Goualougo chimpanzees would be easy to habituate, given their ready acceptance of Morgan and Sanz. Full habituation, however, might have dire consequences in a part of the world where so many apes fall prey to the bushmeat trade. If the chimpanzees' tendency to trust humans is exacerbated by habituation to researchers, that would make them ripe targets for poachers or hunters because they would not flee. In fact, a danger exists now, even before habituation. Once the trusting attitude of these chimpanzees is known locally, they are likely to come under increased threat. The Wildlife Conservation Society, well aware of this possibility, intends to protect the chimpanzees.

I will assume that intense behavioral research on these chimpanzees would benefit, not harm, them. Observing this population, primatologists find themselves with an astonishing opportunity to ask new questions about social communication, beginning as early as the habituation process. After all, habituation is essentially about social communication between the observers and the observed, though these roles may be fluid at times, as when the curious Goualougo chimpanzees peered at and followed the researchers. How the chimpanzees adjust to the humans' movements, vocalizations, and gestures, and how the chimpanzees adjust to each other's movements, gestures, and vocalizations in the presence of humans, are valid and intriguing topics of study.

Smuts has described this process in an account about wild baboons. Noting that the term "habituation" implies that the baboons adapted to her while she herself stayed the same, Smuts writes, "the reverse is closer to the truth. The baboons remained themselves, doing what they always did in the world they had always lived in. I, on the other hand, in the process of gaining their trust, changed almost everything about me, including the way I walked and sat, the way I held my body, and the way I used my eyes and voice."[6] In this particular passage, Smuts overlooks the possibility that her presence may have affected the baboons just as much as theirs affected her. She nonetheless remarks upon "subtle responses" of the baboons to her presence, including directing their gaze at her, and the tendency of mothers "to issue calls and direct stern looks at their infants to signal them to return to mom, just in case the dangerous human moved any closer."[7] Were these actions by the baboons part of a "dance" with Smuts, in that they adjusted themselves to her actions? Or were they, instead, merely examples of "signals" sent by "producers" (the baboons) to a "receiver" (Smuts)? Another of Smuts's observations clues us in to an answer: "Instead of avoiding me when I got too close, they started giving me very deliberate dirty looks, which made me move away. This may sound like a small shift, but in fact it signaled a profound change from being treated as an *object* that elicited a unilateral response (avoidance), to being recognized as a *subject* with whom they could communicate. Over time they treated me more and more as a social being like themselves, subject to the demands and rewards of relationship."[8]

In sum, Smuts and the baboons can be seen as elements in a system, elements whose actions affected each other's. I do not mean to advocate that researchers attempt to interact intimately with nonhuman primates during the habituation phase of research (or afterward). We should nonetheless realize that habituation of monkeys and apes, especially the African great apes, proceeds between fellow primates who are adapted to "read" the nuances of body movements, gestures, and vocalizations that emerge from their ongoing interactions.

Let's fast-forward in our scenario of the Goualougo chimpanzees, and assume that habituation is now complete. From the point of view of primatology and anthropology, the most exciting research is still ahead: discovery of what the chimpanzees do spontaneously with each other, once no longer concerned with human presence to any serious degree. Needed here, too, are currently atypical approaches. The sampling techniques employed most routinely at present focus on one ape at a time. This may involve the researcher either following one ape, scoring what it does with others, or else recording in quick succession the behavior of a series of apes, so that the behavioral state and location of first one ape then another is scored in order to get data on group activity and behavioral synchrony. What happens when sampling focuses instead on the social event itself, with events filmed for later analysis?

The idea would be to film social events in a great variety of circumstances, for later analysis of mutual adjustments, unpredictabilities, and contingencies, and comparison of outcomes (including coordination and miscoordination). Admittedly, a research program of this nature carries its own challenges and risks. How, for instance, should researchers decide what constitutes a social event? Given the role of past social history in shaping a current interaction, how do we parse the stream of behavior in order to decide the bounds (onset and offset points) of a social event? Further, how should the filmer frame the unfolding action? If two gorillas interact and a third is nearby, it is prudent to film the third in case his or her movements affect the primary pair, but what of the gorilla 5 meters away? Might subtle movements in that gorilla's body or even his gaze affect the primary pair? Careful consideration of these questions can, I believe, lead to well-designed research protocols.

Through this approach, we would discover where and when, in this population of chimpanzees, co-regulated nonvocal social communication occurs, and where and when it is absent. Under what circumstances do the chimpanzees adjust their body movements, gaze, limb or head gestures, and facial expressions as they act together to produce visible outcomes? When a "bank" of filmed social events is created, it becomes possible to assess when chimpanzees act more fluidly and creatively, and when they act more rigidly and in ritualized ways. Do the body movements and gestures in a grooming, sexual, or aggressive encounter always unfold the same basic way when two specific chimpanzees come together? Or does such an encounter unfold variably between the partners over time, unless a third, dominant ape is present, whereupon the encounter becomes less contingent and more predictable?

Do the movements and gestures in aggressive events turn out to be more often ritualized, across the board, than those in affiliative events? Or perhaps aggressive events are more stereotyped when occurring between animals of disparate social ranks, and more fluid when the chimpanzees are closer in rank? How do behavioral outcomes differ when interactions are co-regulated versus when they are not? When certain types of interactions appear to be contingent and unpredictable, are the outcomes more variant—within partners over time, and across partners per unit of time—than when interactions are not co-regulated, as I would predict?

These questions are, by definition, comparative. What a creative social event looks like, versus a ritualized one, can only be known once a large number of social events, involving chimpanzees of different ages, sexes, ranks, and social histories, is analyzed. Information on the chimpanzees' social histories would not be available at the project's outset. Thus research would be limited at first to assessing in what way the co-regulated creativity depends on individuals' age, sex, rank, and perhaps temperament, and their recent interactions with fellow community members.

A skeptic might suggest that I too readily describe African great ape social communication as creative. Indeed, I have discussed numerous examples in which creativity rather than rigidity occurs. Yet I hope by listing some questions for future study, I have clarified my position. Primatologists need to test hypotheses, species by species and population by population, in order to discover where and when co-regulated social communication and creativity occur routinely, and where and when they are absent or seen rarely. This suggestion, though basic, may be one of the most critical of this chapter.

Another goal for the future is a broadly comparative research program, extending beyond the African great apes. Comparing the co-regulated and socially constructed nonvocal communication in the African great apes to that of some African monkeys, say the baboons and macaques, is an obvious place to start. My prediction that the African great apes show enhanced creativity and social construction of meaning, and thus are an appropriate platform for modeling origins of language, could then be tested directly.

## Ape Ethnography Revisited

Application of sociocultural anthropology's practice of ethnography to the kind of study of the African great apes envisioned here is an exciting goal. My definition of this term probably differs somewhat from McGrew's. Whereas his major interest involves understanding the cultural adaptations of a variety of nonhuman primates, so that his use of the term "ethnography" is tied closely to his interest in uncovering culture in monkeys and apes,[9] mine embraces an approach rather than a research issue. Still, it is useful to frame the approach that I have in mind with reference to social communication.

Hypotheses in the study of ape ethnography could be formulated as suited to the interests of the researcher, then tested with a mix of qualitative and quantitative data. One area ripe for hypothesis-testing is the ontogeny of body movement and gesture, and, by extension, the ontogeny of meaning-making between social partners. Suppose the questions of interest were these: To what degree are the earliest mother-infant interactions characterized by co-regulation, with attempts by one or both parties to repair miscoordination and misreading of each other's movements? Do African great ape mothers respond to their infants' early arm and leg extensions as if those movements were communicative? Do the very same movements within a single pair lead to different visible outcomes at different times?

Research on these questions would begin with clear operationalization of terms (what are arm and leg extensions? what is "communicative"?). Interactions between mothers and infants would be filmed at regular intervals from birth through the end of infancy, at a minimum. Quantitative work would yield the ratios of fluid to miscoordinated interactions; maternal imbuing of infant communicative intent to its absence; and one type of outcome versus another. Shifts in these ratios within one pair, and statistically different ratios across pairs, would be meaningful. Yet, the heart of the analysis would be the detailed account of the *quality* of the interactions: Did one ape adjust its movements *as* the other was still moving? Did gaze shift as well as body and limb orientation? At what point did the pair move toward a negotiated outcome, or did that point never come? What happens as infants age, and as other dynamics in the group shift?

In group-living African great apes, interactions must be analyzed "beyond the dyad." Often, social communication is studied between mother and infant, two sexual partners, two grooming partners, two allies, or two rivals. The African great apes engage in more complex interactions, however. DST-based projects have made some progress in studying how mutual adjustment unfolds in "triangles," as in Fivaz-Depeursinge and Corboz-Warnery's laboratory study of human mother, father, and baby as they play together (see Chapter 5), or Christine Johnson's zoo research into bonobo social-tool use (see Chapter 2). The analysis is exponentially more complicated once a third (or fourth and fifth) individual is added, but rigorous analysis of spontaneous (as well as laboratory-induced) events is possible.

Long-term detailed analysis of social events, with a focus on the co-regulated dance between social partners in an emotional system, represents a genuine departure from primatology's conventional reliance on statistical analysis of signals produced and received. Qualitative and quantitative analysis would proceed in a balanced way determined by the research questions asked. Such a new mix qualifies as one component of what Latour calls a well-articulated primatology.

Bruno Latour coined this term after attending a Wenner-Gren international symposium, the same type of gathering at which McGrew and Boesch debated the merits of ape ethnography. In this case, Wenner-Gren participants came from all fields of animal behavior (not just primatology) and included science analysts (those who study scientists and how they do science). Latour was much taken by remarks made by a well-known primatologist who has, in recent years, turned to the behavioral study of sheep. Latour uses them to explain the excitement he felt when the symposium participants began to consider (and construct) together new ways of doing science: "One sentence by Thelma Rowell will clearly exemplify the alternative model that was slowly seeping into our discussions. Speaking about her new study on sheep, she stated one of her 'biases' in the following way: 'I tried to *give* my sheep the opportunity to behave *like* chimps, *not* that I believe that they would be like chimps, but because I am sure that if you *take sheep for boring sheep* by opposition to intelligent chimps they *would not have a chance'"* (Latour's emphasis).[10] Rejecting the idea that Rowell's perspective amounts to a bias, Latour heralds it as an opportunity to reveal what sheep really do by connecting two disparate phenomena.

When scientists seek such connections in order to better understand the animals they study, according to Latour they make articulated propositions. "'Boring sheep are boring sheep' is an inarticulate proposition since it repeats tautologically what a sheep is, as if refusing to enter into a connection with anything else. 'Sheep are intelligent chimps' is an articulated proposition since it offers to establish a connection between two completely different entities that will give meaning to both . . . The first sentence is a repetition—A is A. The second is, to use a philosophical term, a predication—A is B—that is, something else, on which it now depends to gain its meaning."[11]

Because Latour wants to open up primatology to new approaches, and free researchers from constricting assumptions, I admire his attempt a great deal. My own imagining of primatological futures overlaps in spirit with his, but suggests a less fixed path. I don't wish to give gorillas, chimpanzees, or bonobos the opportunity to act like animals other than gorillas, chimpanzees, or bonobos. All too often, African great ape behaviors are judged against a human standard. When that happens, and ape gesture is relentlessly compared to human gesture, or ape vocalizations to human language, almost inevitably the ape behaviors are judged "less than" the human behaviors. The nature and richness of what African great apes do becomes lost in a thicket of comparison.

Well-articulated propositions can be created not only when connections are sought between differing entities (sheep and chimpanzees, or chimpanzees and humans), but also, and perhaps more important, when connections between social partners in a single system are recognized. When two chimpanzees are seen as internally related parts of a system, it becomes possible to see a dynamic dance emerging. This in turn fits Latour's notion that we are allowed to say new things in well-articulated settings.

## The African Great Apes in Crisis

Observing the National Zoo gorillas, I become enthused when I notice two young brothers come together in play after one extends an arm toward the other, or when I see the adult female move from behind the subadult male, around to his side, immediately after he extends one leg slowly back toward her. When I point out to other people these gestures, I am occasionally asked whether attention to such fine detail of body movement and gesture is beneficial to science. Are these minute movements and gestures really significant?

My answer is, naturally, yes. To judge from the social outcomes that result from these movements and gestures, these actions are important to the apes themselves, whether in the wild or captivity. The observed movements and gestures are just the visible tip of the iceberg, the most obvious indicators that co-regulated social communication may occur between social partners. This book has told the story of how wild and captive African great apes may construct meaning with each other, and why their ability and proclivity to do so is important for modeling the origins of human language.

The importance of gorilla nonvocal social communication to research pales, however, beside a fact increasingly at the center of consciousness of any person who cares deeply about these magnificent animals. Gorillas, chimpanzees, and bonobos are in imminent danger of extinction. All African great ape species are listed as endangered in the U.S. Endangered Species Act of 1973, and all are listed as threatened with extinction in the Convention on International Trade in Endangered Species of Wild Fauna and Flora (CITES).

The illegal commercial bushmeat trade is, without question, the primary threat to African great ape populations. The Bushmeat Crisis Task Force supplies a concise explanation for this phenomenon: "In Africa, forest is often referred to as 'the bush,' thus wildlife and meat derived from it is referred to as 'bushmeat'. This term applies to all wildlife species, a number of which are threatened and endangered species used for this meat. Though habitat loss is often cited as the primary cause of wildlife extinction, commercial hunting for the meat of wild animals has become the most immediate threat to the future of wildlife in the Congo Basin in the next 5–10 years and has already resulted in widespread local extinctions throughout West Africa."[12]

According to Butynski, Africa is losing its forests, the home of many ape populations, faster than any other continent. The rate of forest loss in some African countries is enough of a danger, all on its own, to consign great apes to extinction should it continue. According to a report issued by the United Nations in late 2002, less than 10 percent of the habitat now used by the African great apes will remain undisturbed in the year 2030 if the current rate of road building, mining, and related development is allowed to continue.[13] Considering that the threat of habitat destruction is secondary to the threat of the bushmeat trade, this statistic is sobering indeed. And the picture only gets worse. Butynski cites Rose's estimate that between three and six thousand African great apes are killed *annually* from the trade in meat alone. "Whatever the number," Butynski writes, "the informed consensus is that this activity is out of control and unsustainable, and it continues to spread and accelerate."[14]

Habitat destruction and the bushmeat trade are intimately entwined, with the logging industry as the point of connection. As succinctly put by Butynski: "Logging roads, logging trucks, and guns enable the ape meat trade." He explains further: "Hunters work full-time to supply ape meat to logging company workers, to expanding agricultural communities, and to people in distant towns and cities. This trade is conducted without adequate medical or veterinary precautions, legal controls, regard for wildlife protection laws, or scientific and management information. Where they occur, the chimpanzee and gorilla are often among the most sought after species."[15] In other words, the problem goes far beyond one in which indigenous peoples hunt the apes for food because they lack options for feeding their families. The problem is driven by the actions of international corporations.

As with any tragedy involving deaths of great numbers of individuals, the full implications can be grasped only when one looks beyond the statistics. That bushmeat hunting kills three thousand chimpanzees, bonobos, and gorillas per year, possibly even six thousand per year and sixty thousand per decade, can only be fathomed by allowing oneself to think hard about the individual animals who die. Thousands upon thousands of gorillas, for example, every bit as smart, playful, and socially communicative as the ones I observe at the National Zoo, wind up as beef on humans' dinner tables. When I watch the two young gorilla brothers tumbling and wrestling through piles of hay in their indoor cage, or down a grassy slope in their outdoor enclosure, I remember the multitudes of gorillas in West Africa who will not live long enough to do so.

The power of anecdotes that describe the social lives of the African great apes may be put to use in this grim situation. I have taken care (see Chapter 2) to distinguish longitudinal, detailed qualitative research from the collection of anecdotes, one-time observations of interesting events. Anecdotes focus researchers' attention on newly discovered or rare phenomena, and may lead to hypothesis-testing and to greater appreciation for variation in behavior. Chapter 4 opens with anecdotes because they give nonprimatologists a quick glimpse into the complex social world in which African great apes live. Anecdotes can also compel people to understand both what the African great apes are losing when their families and social groups are disrupted by the bushmeat trade and habitat destruction, and what we humans are losing as they die.

Consider two anecdotes, each noted by an experienced researcher.

For the first, we travel to Kibale, Uganda, to witness, through the observations of the primatologist Richard Wrangham, the behavior of an 8-year-old chimpanzee named Kakama. While traveling with his community, Kakama carried around with him a small log. He cradled it, and retrieved it when it fell from his location high up in a tree. Wrangham writes, "The log's meaning to Kakama emerged when he made sleeping nests. His first nest was an ordinary one, in which he lay on his back with his limbs in the air, his log held over him, playing the airplane game . . . His second nest was an odd one. It was smaller than usual and in a strange place—in the fork of a tree rather than in the comfortable outer twigs. It looked like a toy nest. After making it, he first put the log in it. He sat next to it for two minutes before climbing in himself, rather awkwardly because the nest was small."[16]

The persistent and tender quality of Kamaka's actions toward the log, which occurred when Kakama's mother was pregnant and sleeping a lot, is noteworthy. Intriguingly, Kakama is the only chimpanzee observed so far to make a nest for another chimpanzee. At 5 years of age, he made a ground nest for a 1-year-old chimpanzee, carried the infant to the nest, and placed her inside. On several occasions he was also observed embracing an infant for up to an hour. Armed with this contextual knowledge, Wrangham concludes, "Kakama is unusually drawn to the young, it seems. And when there wasn't any infant around to look after, he invented one."[17]

Wrangham's claim that a chimpanzee created an imaginary companion moves us well away from the realm of visible outcomes and squarely into the realm of intentionality. Still, the quality of Kakama's actions is visible. His actions echo behaviors observed in other African great apes in captivity, usually females. Tamuli, a bonobo who was unable to reproduce, stretched a squirrel across her belly in apparent imitation of maternal infant-carrying (Chapter 3). Two captive gorillas displayed "behaviors resembling maternal behavior patterns applied to objects such as stones, shoes, balls, pieces of cloth, and even a rubber doll. These patterns usually involved plac-ing the objects between arm/armpit region and sides/chest, or on the neck or the top of the back area while standing on all fours, usually followed by walking while keeping the object in balance, but readjusting it with the hand if necessary."[18] That no play faces or play vocalizations were recorded during these actions by the goril-las supports the speculation that they invented social partners to in-teract with.

A second anecdote comes from the San Diego Zoo, where Ingmanson observed a complex interaction between three brothers housed in a group of seven bonobos. Two of the males were young adults, Kevin (age 12) and Kalind (age 10); the third, Kak, was youn-ger (age 7). Though Kalind was younger than Kevin, he was, ac-cording to Ingmanson, beginning to try and assert dominance over his brother. On this particular day, the two older brothers engaged in visible rivalry for dominance. "The tension between them was obvi-ous, affecting the entire group," Ingmanson notes.[19] Kak appeared to monitor his brothers' activity closely, but stayed well back from the action.

When zoo staff provisioned the bonobos with their usual after-noon browse (leafy branches), the action heated up. After a female bonobo made off with a large chunk of the browse, Kevin took most of the rest. Tension between Kevin and Kalind increased, with Kalind's frustration expressed through vocalizations and pilorection. Soon, a fight broke out between the two. Events unfolded too rapidly for Ingmanson to derive a clear account, but in the end, Kalind gath-ered the browse and walked away from Kevin. He sat down to eat, making the chirping vocalizations that accompany a pleased mood in bonobos. "All of this occurred in no more than 15–20 seconds. Kevin remained where he was sitting, with his shoulders and head slumped—the picture of dejection. At this point Kak exhibited what I took to be empathy. Kak approached Kevin, placed his right hand on Kevin's shoulder, and looked him straight in the eyes for about 3 seconds. Kak then walked over to Kalind, sat by his side and groomed him."[20]

Though Ingmanson is careful to term this incident one of "apparent" empathy on Kak's part, she does not underplay the importance of what she saw: "For me, this was one of those moments when as a researcher you are astounded by what you are observing."[21] As she points out, Kak, with his actions, went beyond simply acknowledging a change in the relative status of the two brothers. "My impression was that Kak clearly understood not just the change in status, but how Kevin would feel about it." Just as with Wrangham's interpretation of Kakama and the log, evidence is available to support Ingmanson's perspective, none more convincing than Boesch and Boesch-Achermann's report of community members' actions toward a young male chimpanzee when his sister was killed by a leopard (Chapter 2).

"Spectacular" is a good adjective to describe both Wrangham's and Ingmanson's observations. Each anecdote reveals a surprising event, or series of events, that is almost certainly rare in African great apes' lives. This very rarity is what makes the reports anecdotal in the first place. Carrying out systematic qualitative research, primatologists would encounter events like these only very occasionally. These anecdotes demonstrate the cognitive complexity and the socioemotional depth of the African great apes. At the same time, they cause us to realize just how much we have yet to learn from these animals, especially about co-regulated social communication. Had these events been filmed, detailed analysis might answer some intriguing questions. How did the bonobo Kevin act when Kak gazed into his eyes and laid a hand on his shoulder? What had happened between Kevin and Kalind during the fight, and perhaps more important, just afterward? As for the chimpanzee Kakama and his log, given that the "social partner" in this case is an inanimate object, different questions arise. Did Kakama intensify his actions with the log when rebuffed by his mother, or at times when she appeared particularly weary or indifferent to him? Or are his actions with the log independent of anything that happens in his "real" social relationships?

Finally, these brief glimpses into the lives of the African great apes move us emotionally, I hope, enough to prevent the loss of this way of being in the world. Research into co-regulated social communication between African great ape social partners amounts to more than an indicator of how intelligent are our closest relatives, and more than a direction to follow in tracing the origins of language in the primate lineage. It forces us to recognize how much these animals depend, in order to thrive, on emotional connections in their intact families and social groups. These socioemotional connections cannot be sustained when ape populations are severely disturbed by human activity, and when so many apes are dying.

We must not fail the African great apes now, as they face unprecedented dangers. I urge you to contact the organizations listed here in order to learn more, and to donate your effort, time, and money to save these creatures.

Bushmeat Crisis Task Force
8403 Colesville Rd., Suite 710
Silver Spring, MD 20910–3314
www.bushmeat.org

Jane Goodall Institute
8700 Georgia Ave., Suite 500
Silver Spring, MD 20910–3605
www.janegoodall.org

African Wildlife Foundation
1400 Sixteenth St., Suite 120
Washington, D.C. 20036
www.awf.org

# Notes

## 1. Social Communication as Dance

1. J. Mizenko, Shall we dance? ballroom dancing and the benefits of the Alexander technique at *www.omplace.com/articles/Alexander_Technique.html*.

2. 1993.

3. Interview with Ted Koppel, televised August 1, 2002, *Up Close*.

4. Ibid.

5. Bakhurst and Shanker 2001:9.

6. Greenspan (1997:35) notes that the child's emotions were equally elided in a Piagetian account of development.

7. E.g., Vygotsky 1986 [1934].

8. Attributed to the pediatrician D. W. Winnicott and cited by Small 1998:35.

9. Fogel 1993:54–57.

10. Fogel, personal communication.

11. From Papousek 1995:64; I use her translation from the original German.

12. Mead 1934 as cited by Lock 1980:25.

13. Griffin 1997:492.

14. See Fernald 1992.

15. See Fogel 1993 and Fivaz-Depeursinge and Corboz-Warnery 1999 for examples.

16. 1974.

17. Trevarthen 1999:190; see other chapters in this same volume.

18. Ibid., 193.

19. See the review by Blake 2000:92.

20. Fogel 1993:78–79.

21. Ibid., 79–80.

22. Iverson, Capirci, Longobardi, and Caselli 1999:72.

23. I take the transcription word for word from Nyland 2001, although I use "child" and "caregiver" instead of Nyland's coding symbols.

24. 1999.

25. Birthdates and other details about this gorilla group are given in Chapter 3.

26. Reconciliation after aggression is a common phenomenon in many primates, and occurs in certain contexts in gorillas; see Watts 1995.

27. Boesch and Boesch-Achermann 2000; the following quote is from p. 109.

28. Newton-Fisher 2002:125.

29. Ibid., p. 125.

30. Butynski 2001:3–4.

31. 1999:51, though Parker recognizes three species of chimpanzees and only one or possibly two species of orangutans.

32. Tanner and Byrne 1999:228.

33. Gibson and Jessee 1999:193.

34. Reviewed by Gibson and Jessee 1999.

35. Gibson and Jessee 1999:200–201.

36. Reader and Laland 2002.

37. Ibid., 4439.

38. For reviews see Byrne 1995 and Parker 1996.

39. See Ottoni and Mannu 2001.

40. See Goodall 1990, Boesch and Boesch-Achermann 2000, and de Waal 2001; contra Turner 2000, who mistakenly concludes that apes tend to develop comparatively few social ties.

41. I follow here the scheme of Kappeler and van Schaik 2002.

42. Details about these sites found in Boesch and Boesch-Achermann 2000 and Mitani, Watts, and Muller 2002.

43. 1965:394.

44. Reynolds and Reynolds 1965:394–395.

45. Mitani, Watts, and Muller 2002:10; see Goodall 1965:452–453.

46. Tetsuro Matsuzawa, personal communication (email August 10, 2003).

47. Kano 1992:70; though Kano was referring to bonobos when he wrote, this general description is equally apt for chimpanzees.

48. Boesch and Boesch-Achermann 2000:88.
49. Data from the review by Mitani, Watts, and Muller 2002.
50. See Wrangham 1980 for the classic formulation of this theory.
51. 2002:22.
52. Goodall 1986.
53. Personal communication (email August 10, 2003).
54. Boesch and Boesch-Achermann 2000:107.
55. Ibid., 150.
56. Ibid., 108.
57. Doran et al. 2002.
58. McGrew 1992; Whiten et al. 1999.
59. De Waal and Lanting 1997:70.
60. Kano 1992.
61. De Waal 2001:130.
62. Boesch and Boesch-Achermann 2000:108.
63. White 1996:30.
64. White 1996, Boesch 1996:111.
65. Boesch and Boesch-Achermann 2000:108.
66. De Waal 2001:132.
67. Anestis 2003.
68. De Waal 2001:131.
69. Furuichi and Hashimoto 2002.
70. De Waal and Lanting 1997:79–80.
71. Kano 1992:176.
72. White 1996:34.
73. Ibid.
74. Ellen Ingmanson, personal communication.
75. Ibid.
76. White 1996:34.
77. Kano 1992:91.
78. Ibid.
79. De Waal and Lanting 1997:66.
80. Ellen Ingmanson, personal communication.
81. 1996.
82. Cited in Schaller 1964:5.
83. Robbins, Sicotte, and Stewart 2001; for a popular account of the decades of research at Karisoke and Dian Fossey's role in it, see Weber and Vedder 2001.

84. Robbins 1995, 2001.
85. Gerald-Steklis and Steklis 2001.
86. Robbins 1995.
87. Watts 1995.
88. Yamagiwa 1996:94.
89. Yamagiwa and Kahekwa 2001.
90. Ibid., 115.
91. E.g., Fossey and Harcourt 1977.
92. E.g., Tutin and Fernandez 1985, Doran and McNeilage 2001.
93. Jones and Sabater-Pi 1971, Remis 1994, cited by Parnell 2002.
94. 2001:136.
95. Parnell 2002.
96. Ibid., 202.
97. Ibid., 203, and see Parnell's useful discussion of differences among multimale and age-graded male gorilla groups.
98. See Melson 2001.
99. I wish to sidestep here the issue of human creation of and interaction with artificial life, robots, and so on.
100. Kenneth Frampton quoted in "Polishing Up a Well-Cut Gem," Julie Iovine, *New York Times*, June 6, 2002.
101. Strum and Fedigan 2000 summarize this change over time.
102. And see King 1999 for previous statements about ape-human continuity.

## 2. Gesture and Dynamic Systems Theory

1. 1996:6.
2. Hailman 1977:52, in Hauser 1996:7.
3. 1986.
4. King and Shanker 2003.
5. 1993:170.
6. 1965:544.
7. Maestripieri, Ross, and Megna 2002:219.
8. 1999:275.
9. Gouzoules, Gouzoules, and Marler 1984.
10. Thanks to Charles Hogg for this example.
11. King 1994.
12. E.g., Fragaszy and Visalberghi 1996, Rapaport and Ruiz-Miranda 2002, Maestripieri, Ross, and Megna 2002.

13. E.g., Blake 2000.

14. Taylor is a linguist; see Taylor 1997.

15. Of course, it is probably more accurate to say not that I hadn't *encountered* such ideas but that I hadn't *absorbed* them; my professors or mentors, or books I'd found, may well have exposed me to such ideas.

16. Waldrop 1992:13.

17. Ibid., 64–65.

18. Ibid., 65.

19. Bertalanffy 1968.

20. Fitch, Neubauer, and Herzel 2002.

21. Ibid., 414.

22. Shanker and King 2002; see Fogel 1993 for discussions of creativity in co-regulation.

23. Proust 1981:333.

24. 1986:30.

25. Tanner and Byrne 1999:216.

26. Tomasello, Call, Warren, Frost, Carpenter, and Nagell 1997:231.

27. See Armstrong, Stokoe, and Wilcox, chap. 2, for a review.

28. Sheets-Johnstone 1999:155.

29. Goldstein and Fowler 2003:161.

30. Ibid., 162.

31. Sheets-Johnstone 1999.

32. Parr, Hopkins, and de Waal 1998.

33. Schmidt and Cohn 2001.

34. Ekman and Keltner 1997.

35. 2001.

36. Lyons et al. 2000.

37. Greenspan and Shanker in press.

38. De Waal 2001.

39. Hauser 1996:246–248.

40. Johnson 2001.

41. Tomasello and Call 1997.

42. Johnson 2001:168–170.

43. I am particularly grateful to Melanie Bond in this regard.

44. Schaller 1965:344.

45. In writing this section, I was indebted to Willow Powers for her insights about methodology in cultural anthropology.

46. Bernard 2002.

47. Small 2001.

48. Shostak 2000.

49. Briggs 1970:7.

50. 1998:2.

51. Barth 2002:31.

52. Ibid.

53. I don't deny that debate does occur, but it goes on without the intense need to justify the basic qualitative approach that can be found in some other fields.

54. Fish 2000:553.

55. See Fogel 1993, Thelen et al. 2001, Greenspan and Shanker in press, and Bronfenbrenner 1979.

56. Rumbaugh and Washburn 2003:xv.

57. Ibid., 256.

58. Ibid., 55.

59. In this section I rely on Strum and Fedigan's 2000 history of North American primatology, which I recommend to readers who want a much more thorough treatment.

60. Strum and Fedigan 2000:8.

61. Ibid., 25.

62. Ibid., 34.

63. Goodall 1990.

64. Goodall 1986.

65. Goodall 1990.

66. Asquith 2000.

67. Ibid., 170.

68. Strum 2000:491.

69. 1997.

70. Mitchell 1997:151.

71. Byrne 1997:138.

72. Ibid., 1997:150.

73. But see Burton 1994.

74. Bunk 1998:10.

75. De Waal 1989.

76. De Waal 2001.

77. Savage-Rumbaugh, Shanker, and Taylor 1998.

78. Boesch and Boesch-Achermann 2000:248–249.

79. I am grateful to Alan Fogel for uttering, at a critical turning point, the phrase "the rigor is in the comparison" (personal communication, October 4, 2002).

80. Altmann 1974.

81. Johnson and Oswald 2001:456–457.

82. See Kohler and Gumerman 2000.

83. See the journal *Family Systems* from the Bowen Center for the Study of the Family, Washington, D.C..

84. Vinson Sutlive pointed this out to me, for which I am grateful.

85. Bateson 1972:319.

86. Ibid., 317.

87. Ingold 2000:18.

88. I rely on Ingold 2000 for this account.

89. Ingold 2000:260.

90. Goodwin 1979.

91. Hutchins 1995:226.

92. E.g., Bonvillian and Patterson 2002, Rendall and Vasey 2002.

93. Fogel 1993:56–57.

94. Hinde 1985:109.

95. Ibid., 110.

96. 1998.

97. Owren and Rendall 1998:301.

98. Hinde 1985:109.

99. Owren and Rendall 1998:303–304.

100. Slavoff 1997.

101. Savage-Rumbaugh comes closest to what I have in mind here; many of her publications are cited throughout this book.

102. Bonvillian and Patterson 2002.

103. Bonvillian and Patterson 1999.

104. Jensvold and Gardner 2000; see Savage-Rumbaugh 1999, Shanker and King 2002.

## 3. Gesture in Captive African Great Apes

1. 1999.

2. Published in English as Ladygina-Kohts 2002.

3. Ibid., 196.

4. Ibid., 68.

5. Ibid., 40–49.

6. Ibid., 50.

7. De Waal 2000:vii.

8. See the chapters in Beck et al. 2001, particularly Teleki 2001.

9. Goodall 2001:xx.

10. Amman 2001.

11. Fouts 2001:207.

12. De Waal 2001:247.

13. See Rumbaugh and Washburn 2003; similar comments apply to the orangutan Chantek.

14. Menzel 1979:367, 370.

15. Savage-Rumbaugh, Wilkerson, and Bakeman 1977.

16. Ibid., 108.

17. Tanner and Byrne 1999:220.

18. Ibid., 230.

19. I am very grateful to Joanne Tanner for sharing her filmed data, as well as information from her doctoral thesis, Tanner 1998.

20. Tomasello and Call 1997:247.

21. Pika, Liebal, and Tomasello 2003.

22. Tomasello et al. 1997.

23. Tomasello 1999:43.

24. Tomasello et al. 1997:247.

25. King and Shanker 2003.

26. Pika et al. 2003:107.

27. Tanner and Byrne 1999:230.

28. Ibid., 230–231.

29. Ibid., 231.

30. E.g., de Waal 1988.

31. Savage-Rumbaugh and Lewin 1994.

32. Savage-Rumbaugh et al. 1998:61.

33. See King 2002 for analysis of the development of Elikya's dorsal riding on her mother.

34. Thanks also to Elizabeth Groneweg for research assistance in the first months of this study.

35. See the papers in Strum and Fedigan 2000.

36. See Wootton 1997 for an account of the development of gestural requests in a human child.

37. Altmann 1980.

38. E.g., Yerkes and Tomilin 1935 and many succeeding reports.

39. See Fogel 1993.

40. Thanks to Gabriel Waters for discussing this point with me.

41. Jaffe et al. 2001:107.

42. Personal observation, Animal Kingdom, Disney World, Florida, May 2003.

## 4. Gesture in Wild African Great Apes

1. Vea and Sabater-Pi 1998.
2. Free-living gorillas clap to communicate 1989.
3. Schaller 1963.
4. Goodall 1971:109.
5. Kano 1992:140.
6. Kuroda 1984:128.
7. Ibid., 129.
8. Ibid., 130.
9. Ibid., 132–33.
10. Ibid., 134–135.
11. 1986:139.
12. Goodall 1968.
13. Ibid., 336.
14. Ibid., 366.
15. Goodall 1986:367.
16. Goodall 1968:361.
17. Goodall 1986:447.
18. Nishida 1980.
19. Whiten et al. 1999.
20. Kano 1997, available at *http://mahale.web.infoseek.co.jp/PAN/4__1/contents.html*.
21. Ibid.
22. Ibid.
23. Kano 1992:140–141.
24. Ibid., 190–191.
25. Ibid., 193.
26. Schaller 1964:209.
27. Personal communication via email from Dr. Richard Parnell, September 29, 2001.
28. Sicotte 2001.
29. Fossey 1983:188.
30. Harcourt, Stewart, and Fossey 1981:272.
31. Schaller 1964:218.

32. Ibid., 217.
33. Fossey 1983:68.
34. Parnell and Buchanan-Smith 2001:294.
35. Schaller 1965a: 346–347.
36. Watts 2001:221–223.
37. Watts 1994:348.
38. Goodall 1986:318.
39. Goodall 1968:350.
40. Muller 2002:121.
41. Newton-Fisher 2002.
42. De Waal 1989.
43. Goodall 1968:352.
44. De Waal and Lanting 1997:30–31.
45. Kano 1992:178.
46. Nakamura 2002.
47. McGrew and Tutin 1978:238.
48. Nakamura 2002:80.
49. Ibid., 78.
50. Ibid., 79.
51. Ibid., 82.
52. Goodall 1986:391.
53. Ibid.
54. Kano 1992:186.
55. Robbins 2001:39.
56. E.g., for eastern gorillas, see Fossey 1979, Fletcher 2001.
57. Maestripieri and Call 1996.
58. Boesch and Boesch-Achermann 2000:209.
59. Boesch and Boesch-Achermann 2000.
60. Ibid., 212–213.
61. Goodall 1986:372.
62. Plooij 1978:120.
63. Ibid., 114.
64. Ibid., 115–116.
65. Ibid., 117.
66. Ibid.
67. Kano 1992:165.
68. Ibid., 200.
69. Ibid.

70. See especially King 2002.
71. E.g., van de Ritj-Plooij and Plooij 1987.

## 5. The Evolution of Gesture

1. Condillac 1746 [1947].
2. Marks 2002.
3. Brunet et al. 2002.
4. Marks 2002:13.
5. Ibid., 5.
6. Hewes 1973:6.
7. Ibid.
8. Ibid. 12.
9. Ibid., 10.
10. Gardner and Gardner 1969; Premack 1971.
11. Hewes 1973:6.
12. Ibid., 20.
13. Ibid., 7.
14. Washburn 1973:18.
15. Gardner 1973:13.
16. Ibid.
17. Suzuki 1973:17–18.
18. Hauser 1996:520–521.
19. Mitani and Nishida 1993, Goodall 1986.
20. Boesch and Boesch-Achermann 2000:235.
21. Mitani and Gros-Louis 1998.
22. King and Shanker 2003.
23. Corballis 2002:186.
24. Ibid., 46.
25. Ibid., 29.
26. Goodall 1986.
27. But see the brief review in Leavens 2003.
28. Corballis 2002:138.
29. King 2003.
30. Pinker 1994:342.
31. Steklis 1985.
32. Corballis 2002:37, 39.
33. Ingold 2000:393–394.

34. Ibid., 401.
35. Armstrong, Stokoe, and Wilcox 1995:223.
36. Ibid., 152.
37. Ibid., 217.
38. Ibid., 83.
39. Ibid., 89.
40. Ibid., 161.
41. See also Burling 1999.
42. Cartmill 1990.
43. Corballis 2002, Blake 2000.
44. Corballis 2002:99.
45. Landau 1984.
46. Pinker and Bloom 1990.
47. Pinker 1994:335, 342.
48. King 1999.
49. Parker and Gibson 1979:373, 374.
50. Parker 1985.
51. Borchert and Zihlman 1990:15.
52. Blake 2000.
53. Savage-Rumbaugh 1986, Savage-Rumbaugh and Lewin 1994.
54. Borchert and Zihlman 1990:29, 29–30.
55. Ibid., 30.
56. See Lock 1980 on the guided reinvention of language in humans.
57. Borchert and Zihlman 1990:30.
58. Ibid., 34.
59. Parker 2000:301.
60. Falk in press.
61. Ibid.
62. Ibid.
63. Gomez 1990:339.
64. Menzel in press.
65. Ibid.
66. Ibid.
67. Leavens, Hopkins, and Thomas 2004.
68. Ibid.; see also Leavens and Hopkins 1999.
69. See the references in Wallman 1992.
70. Fouts 1997.
71. Savage-Rumbaugh 1999:182.

72. Shanker and King 2002.

73. Savage-Rumbaugh 1999:178.

74. Burling 1999:343.

75. Iverson and Thelen 1999.

76. McNeill 1992:11.

77. Ibid.

78. Goldin-Meadow 1999:422–423.

79. Ibid., 423.

80. Ibid., 426.

81. See especially McNeill 1992, chapter 9.

82. Goodwin 1979:97–98.

83. Goodwin and Goodwin 1986:71.

84. Falk in press.

85. Bowen 1978; see the journal *Family Systems* published by the Bowen Center for the Study of the Family, Washington, D.C.

86. Fivaz-Depeursinge and Corboz-Warnery 1999:xiv.

87. Ibid., 66, 16.

88. The full accounts are on pp. 87–91 (Xerxes) and pp. 96–98 (Tania) of Fivaz-Depeursinge and Corboz-Warnery.

89. Tomasello and Camaioni 1997.

90. Ibid., 10.

91. Ibid., 12.

92. Ibid., 11.

93. See Byrne and Russon 1998.

## 6. Imagined Futures

1. 2002.

2. See Savage-Rumbaugh 1999 for an interesting discussion of this point.

3. Morgan and Sanz 2003.

4. Quammen 2003.

5. Press release, Washington University in St. Louis, March 11, 2003.

6. Smuts 2001:295.

7. Ibid.

8. Ibid.

9. McGrew 2001.

10. Latour 2000:367.

11. Ibid., 374–375.
12. Bailey, Stein, and the Bushmeat Crisis Task Force 2002:1.
13. Environment News Service 2002.
14. Butynski 2001:27.
15. Ibid., 26.
16. Wrangham 2000:34.
17. Ibid.
18. Gomez and Martin-Andrade 2002:259.
19. Ingmanson 2002:282.
20. Ibid., 283.
21. Ibid.

# Bibliography

Altmann, J. 1974. Observational study of behavior: sampling methods. *Behaviour* 49:227–267.

———1980. *Baboon Mothers and Infants*. Chicago: University of Chicago Press.

Amman, K. 2001. Bushmeat hunting and the great apes. In *Great Apes and Humans: The Ethics of Coexistence*, ed. B. B. Beck, T. S. Stoinski, M. Hutchins, T. L. Maple, B. Norton, A. Rowan, E. F. Stevens, and A. Arluke, pp. 71–85. Washington, D.C.: Smithsonian Institution Press.

Anestis, S. F. 2003. Genito-genital rubbing as a female bonding strategy in a group of captive chimpanzees *(Pan troglodytes)*. *American Journal of Physical Anthropology* Supplement 36:59.

Armstrong, D. F., W. C. Stokoe, and S. E. Wilcox. 1995. *Gesture and the Nature of Language*. Cambridge: Cambridge University Press.

Asquith, P. 2000. Negotiating science: internationalization and Japanese primatology. In *Primate Encounters: Models of Science, Gender, and Society*, ed. S. C. Strum and L. M. Fedigan, pp. 165–183. Chicago: University of Chicago Press.

Bailey, N. D., J. T. Stein, and the Bushmeat Crisis Task Force. 2002. Great Apes and Bushmeat. Online fact sheet at www.bushmeat.org.

Bakhurst, D., and S. G. Shanker. 2001. Introduction: Bruner's Way. In *Jerome Bruner: Language, Culture, Self*, ed. D. Bakhurst and S. G. Shanker, pp. 1–18. London: SAGE Publications.

Barth, F. 2002. Toward a richer description and analysis of cultural phenomena. In *Anthropology Beyond Culture*, ed. R. G. Fox and B. J. King, pp. 23–36. Oxford: Berg.

Bateson, G. 1972. *Steps to an Ecology of Mind*. Chicago: University of Chicago Press.

Beck, B. B., T. S. Stoinski, M. Hutchins, T. L. Maple, B. Norton, A. Rowan, E. F. Stevens, and A. Arluke, ed., *Great Apes and Humans: The Ethics of Coexistence*. Washington, D.C.: Smithsonian Institution Press.

Bernard, H. R. 2002. *Research Methods in Anthropology: Qualitative and Quantitative Approaches*. 3rd ed. Walnut Creek, CA: AltaMira Press.

Bertalanffy, L. V. 1969. *General Systems Theory: Foundation, Development, Applications*. New York: George Braziller.

Blake, J. 2000. *Routes to Child Language: Evolutionary and Developmental Precursors*. Cambridge: Cambridge University Press.

Boesch, C. 1996. Social grouping in Tai chimpanzees. In *Great Ape Societies*, ed. W. C. McGrew, L. F. Marchant, and T. Nishida, pp. 101–113. Cambridge: Cambridge University Press.

Boesch, C., and H. Boesch-Achermann. 2000. *The Chimpanzees of the Tai Forest: Behavioural Ecology and Evolution*. Oxford: Oxford University Press.

Bonvillian, J. D., and F. G. P. Patterson. 1999. Early sign-language acquisition: comparisons between children and gorillas. In *The Mentalities of Gorillas and Orangutans*, ed. S. T. Parker, R. W. Mitchell, and H. L. Miles, pp. 240–264. Cambridge: Cambridge University Press.

———2002. A new paradigm? comment on Shanker and King. *Behavioral and Brain Sciences* 25 (5):621–622.

Borchert, C. M., and A. L. Zihlman. 1990. The ontogeny and phylogeny of symbolizing. In *The Life of Symbols*, ed. M. L. Foster and L. J. Botscharow, pp. 15–44. Boulder: Westview.

Bowen, M. 1978. *Family Therapy in Clinical Practice*. New York: Jason Aronson.

Briggs, J. 1970. *Never in Anger: Portrait of an Eskimo Family*. Cambridge: Harvard University Press.

———1998. *Inuit Morality Play: The Emotional Education of a Three-Year-Old*. New Haven: Yale University Press.

Bronfenbrenner, U. 1979. *Ecology of Human Development: Experiments by Nature and Design*. Cambridge: Harvard University Press.

Brunet, M., F. Guy, D. Pilbeam, H. T. Mackaye, A. Likius, D. Ahounta, A. Beauvilian, C. Blondel, H. Bocherens, J.-R. Boisserie, L. De Bonis, Y. Coppens, J. Dejax, C. Denys, P. Duringer, V. Eisenmann, G. Fanone, P. Fronty, D. Geraads, T. Lehmann, F. Lihoreau, A. Louchart, A. Mahamat, G. Merceron, G. Mouchelin, O. Otero, P. P. Campomanes, M. Ponce De Leon, J.-C. Rage, M. Sapanet, M. Schuster, J. Sudre, P.

Tassy, X. Valentin, P. Vignaud, L. Viriot, A. Zazzo, and C. Zollikofer. 2002. A new hominid from the Upper Miocene of Chad, Central Africa. *Nature* 418:145–151.

Bunk, S. 1998. Interdisciplinary study of nonhuman primates gains ground. *The Scientist* 12 (10):10,13.

Burling, R. 1999. Motivation, conventionalization, and arbitrariness in the origin of language. In *The Origins of Language: What Nonhuman Primates Can Tell Us*, ed. B. J. King, pp. 307–350. Santa Fe: School of American Research Press.

Burton, F. D. 1994. In the footsteps of Anaximander: qualitative research in primates. In *Strength in Diversity: A Reader in Physical Anthropology*, ed. D. A. Herring and L. K. W. Chan, pp. 77–102. Toronto: Canadian Scholars' Press.

Butynski, T. M. 2001. Africa's great apes. In *Great Apes and Humans: The Ethics of Coexistence*, ed. B. B. Beck, T. S. Stoinski, M. Hutchins, T. L. Maple, B. Norton, A. Rowan, E. F. Stevens, and A. Arluke, pp. 3–56. Washington, D.C.: Smithsonian Institution Press.

Byrne, R. W. 1995. *The Thinking Ape: Evolutionary Origins of Intelligence.* Oxford: Oxford University Press.

———What's the use of anecdotes? distinguishing psychological mechanisms in primate tactical deception. In *Anthropomorphism, Anecdotes, and Animals*, ed. R. W. Mitchell, N. S. Thompson, and H. L. Miles, pp. 134–150. Albany: State University of New York Press.

Byrne, R. W., and A. E. Russon. 1998. Learning by imitation: a hierarchical approach. *Behavioral and Brain Sciences* 21:667–721.

Cartmill, M. 1990. Human uniqueness and theoretical content in paleo-anthropology. *International Journal of Primatology* 11 (3):173–192.

Condillac, E. B. 1746 [1947]. Essai sur l'origine des connaissances humaines, ouvrage ou l'on reduit a un seul principe tout ce concerne l'entendement. In *Oeuvres philosophies de Condillac.* Paris: Georges Le Roy.

Condon, W. S., and L. S. Sanders. 1974. Neonate movement is synchronized with adult speech: interactional participation and language acquisition. *Science* 183:99–101.

Corballis, M. C. 2002. *From Hand to Mouth: The Origins of Language.* Princeton: Princeton University Press.

De Waal, F. B. M. 1988. The communicative repertoire of captive bonobos *(Pan paniscus)*, compared to that of chimpanzees. *Behaviour* 106:183–251.

————1989. *Peacemaking among Primates.* Cambridge: Harvard University Press.

————2001. *The Ape and the Sushi Master.* New York: Basic Books.

————2002. Foreword. In *Infant Chimpanzee and Human Child,* ed. F. B. M. de Waal, pp. vii-ix. New York: Oxford University Press.

De Waal, F. B. M., and F. Lanting. 1997. *Bonobo: The Forgotten Ape.* Berkeley: University of California Press.

Doran, D. M., W. L. Jungers, Y. Sugiyama, J. G. Fleagle, and C. P. Heesy. 2002. Multivariate and phylogenetic approaches to understanding chimpanzee and bonobo behavioral diversity. In *Behavioural Diversity in Chimpanzees and Bonobos,* ed. C. Boesch, G. Hohmann, and L. F. Marchant, pp. 14–34. Cambridge: Cambridge University Press.

Doran, D. M., and A. McNeilage. 2001. Subspecific variation in gorilla behavior: the influence of ecological and social factors. In *Mountain Gorillas: Three Decades of Research at Karisoke,* ed. M. M. Robbins, P. Sicotte, and K. J. Stewart, pp. 123–149. Cambridge: Cambridge University Press.

Ekman, P., and D. Keltner. 1997. Universal facial expressions of emotion: an old controversy and new findings. In *Nonverbal Communication: Where Nature Meets Culture,* ed. U. Segerstrale and P. Molnar, pp. 27–46. Mahwah, NJ: Lawrence Erlbaum.

Ellis, A., and G. Beattie. 1986. *The Psychology of Language and Communication.* London: Weidenfeld and Nicolson.

Environment News Service. 2002. Future grim for world's great apes. *http:// ens-news.com/ens/sep2002/2002–09–03–01.asp.*

Falk, D. 2000. *Primate Diversity.* New York: W.W. Norton.

————In press. Prelinguistic evolution in early hominids: whence motherese? *Behavioral and Brain Sciences.*

Fernald, A. 1992. Human maternal vocalizations to infants as biologically relevant signals: an evolutionary perspective. In *The Adapted Mind,* ed. J. Barkow, L. Cosmides, and J. Tooby, pp. 391–428. New York: Oxford University Press.

Fish, J. M. What anthropology can do for psychology: facing physics envy, ethnocentrism, and a belief in "race." *American Anthropologist* 102:552–563.

Fitch, W. T., J. Neubauer, and H. Herzel. 2002. Calls out of chaos: the adaptive significance of nonlinear phenomena in mammalian vocal production. *Animal Behaviour* 63:407–418.

Fivaz-Depeursinge, E., and A. Corboz-Warnery. 1999. *The Primary Triangle: A Developmental Systems View of Mothers, Fathers, and Infants.* New York: Basic Books.

Fletcher, A. 2001. Development of infant independence from the mother in wild mountain gorillas. In *Mountain Gorillas: Three Decades of Research at Karisoke,* ed. M. M. Robbins, P. Sicotte, and K. J. Stewart, pp. 154–182. Cambridge: Cambridge University Press.

Fogel, A. 1993. *Developing through Relationships: Origins of Self, Communication, and Culture.* Chicago: University of Chicago Press.

———2003. Lessons from our infancy: relationships to self, other, and nature. In *Social and Cognitive Development in the Context of Individual, Social, and Cultural Processes,* ed. C. Raeff and J. B. Benson, pp. 219–233. London: Routledge.

Fossey, D. 1983. *Gorillas in the Mist.* Boston: Houghton Mifflin.

Fossey, D., and A. H. Harcourt. 1977. Feeding ecology of free-ranging mountain gorillas. In *Primate Ecology,* ed. T. H. Clutton-Brock, pp. 415–449. New York: Academic Press.

Fouts, R. 2001. Darwinian reflections on our fellow apes. In *Great Apes and Humans: The Ethics of Coexistence,* ed. B. B. Beck, T. S. Stoinski, M. Hutchins, T. L. Maple, B. Norton, A. Rowan, E. F. Stevens, and A. Arluke, pp. 191–211. Washington, D.C: Smithsonian Institution Press.

Fouts, R. S., and R. Rigby. 1997. *Next of Kin.* New York: William Morrow.

Fox, E. A., A. F. Sitompul, and C. P. van Schaik. 1999. Intelligent tool use in wild Sumatran orangutans. In *The Mentalities of Gorillas and Orangutans,* ed. S. T. Parker, R. W. Mitchell, and H. L. Miles, pp. 99–116. Cambridge: Cambridge University Press.

Fox, R. G., and B. J. King. 2002. Introduction: beyond culture worry. In *Anthropology beyond Culture,* ed. R. G. Fox and B. J. King, pp. 1–19. Oxford: Berg.

Fragaszy, D. M., and E. Visalberghi. 1996. Social learning in monkeys: primate "primacy" reconsidered. In *Social Learning in Animals: The Roots of Culture,* ed. C. M. Heyes and B. G. Galef, pp. 65–84. San Diego: Academic Press.

Free-living gorillas clap to communicate. 1989. *Gorilla Journal* 13:11.

Furuichi, T., and C. Hashimoto. 2002. Why female bonobos have a lower copulation rate during estrus than chimpanzees. In *Behavioural Diversity in Chimpanzees and Bonobos,* ed. C. Boesch, G. Hohmann, and L. F. Marchant, pp. 156–167. Cambridge: Cambridge University Press.

Gardner, R. A. 1973. Comment on article by Hewes. *Current Anthropology* 14:13.

Gardner, R. A., and B. Gardner. 1969. Teaching sign language to a chimpanzee. *Science* 165:664–672.

Gerald-Steklis, N., and H. D. Steklis. 2001. Reproductive benefits for female mountain gorillas in multi-male groups. *American Journal of Primatology* 54 (S1):60–61.

Gibson, K. R., and S. Jessee. 1999. Language evolution and expansions of multiple neurological processing areas. In *The Origins of Language: What Nonhuman Primates Can Tell Us*, ed. B. J. King, pp. 189–227. Santa Fe: School of American Research Press.

Goldin-Meadow, S. 1999. The role of gesture in communication and thinking. *Trends in Cognitive Science* 3 (11):419–429.

Goldstein, L., and C. A. Fowler. 2003.Articulatory phonology: a phonology for public language use. In *Phonetics and Phonology in Language Comprehension and Production: Differences and Similarities*, ed. N. O. Schiller and A. Meyer, pp. 159–207. Berlin: Mouton de Gruyter.

Gomez, J. C. 1990. The emergence of intentional communication as a problem-solving strategy in the gorilla. In *"Language" and Intelligence in Monkeys and Apes*, ed. S. T. Parker and K. R. Gibson, pp. 333–355. Cambridge: Cambridge University Press.

Gomez, J. C., and B. Martin-Andrade. 2002. Possible precursors of pretend play in nonpretend actions of captive gorillas *(Gorilla gorilla)*. In *Pretending and Imagination in Animals and Children*, ed. R. W. Mitchell, pp. 255–268. Cambridge: Cambridge University Press.

Goodall, J. 1965. Chimpanzees of the Gombe Stream Reserve. In *Primate Behavior: Field Studies of Monkeys and Apes*, ed. I. DeVore, pp. 425–473. New York: Holt, Rinehart and Winston.

———1968. A preliminary report on expressive movements and communication in the Gombe Stream chimpanzees. In *Studies in Adaptation and Variability*, ed. P. Jay, pp. 313–374. New York: Holt, Rinehart and Winston.

———1971. *In the Shadow of Man*. Boston: Houghton Mifflin.

———1986. *Chimpanzees of Gombe: Patterns of Behavior*. Cambridge: Harvard University Press.

———1990. *Through a Window*. Boston: Houghton Mifflin.

———2001. Foreword: problems faced by wild and captive chimpanzees: finding solutions. In *Great Apes and Humans: The Ethics of Coexistence*, ed. B. B. Beck, T. S. Stoinski, M. Hutchins, T. L. Maple, B. Norton, A. Rowan, E. F. Stevens, and A. Arluke, pp. xiii–xxiv. Washington, D.C.: Smithsonian Institution Press.

Goodwin, C. 1979. The interactive construction of a sentence in natural conversation. In *Everyday Language: Studies in Ethnomethodology,* ed. G. Psathas, pp. 97–121. New York: Irvington Publishers.

Goodwin, M., and C. Goodwin. 1986. Gesture and coparticipation in the activity of searching for a word. *Semiotica* 62:51–75.

Gouzoules, S., H. Gouzoules, and P. Marler. 1984. Rhesus monkey *(Macaca mulatta)* screams: representational signaling in the recruitment of agonistic aid. *Animal Behaviour* 32:182–193.

Greenspan, S. 1997. *The Growth of the Mind and the Endangered Origins Of Intelligence.* Reading, MA: Addison-Wesley.

Greenspan, S., and S. G. Shanker. In press. *The First Idea.* New York: Perseus.

Griffin, E. 1997. *A First Look at Communication Theory.* 3rd ed. New York: McGraw Hill.

Hailman, J. 1977. *Optical Signals: Animal Communication and Light.* Bloomington: Indiana University Press.

Harcourt, A. H., K. J. Stewart, and D. Fossey. 1981. Gorilla reproduction in the wild. In *Reproductive Biology of the Great Apes,* ed., C. E. Graham, pp. 265–279. New York: Academic Press.

Hauser, M. 1996. *The Evolution of Communication.* Cambridge: MIT Press.

Hewes, G. W. 1973. Primate communication and the gestural origins of language. *Current Anthropology* 14 (1–2):5–24.

Hinde, R. A. 1985. Expression and negotiation. In *The Development of Expressive Behavior: Biology-Environment Interactions,* ed. G. Zivin, pp. 103–116. New York: Academic Press.

Hutchins, E. 1995. *Cognition in the Wild.* Cambridge: MIT Press.

Ingold, T. 2000. *The Perception of the Environment.* New York: Routledge.

Ingmanson, E. 2002. Empathy in a bonobo. In *Pretending and Imagination in Animals and Children,* ed. R. W. Mitchell, pp. 280–284. Cambridge: Cambridge University Press.

Iverson, J. M., O. Capirci, E. Longobardi, and M. C. Caselli. 1999. Gesturing in mother-child interactions. *Cognitive Development,* 14:57–75.

Jaffe, J., B. Beebe, F. Feldstein, C. L. Crown, and M. D. Jasnow. 2001. Rhythms of dialogue in infancy. *Monographs of the Society for Research in Child Development* 66 (2):1-132.

Jensvold, M. L. A., and R. A. Gardner. 2000. Interactive use of sign language by cross-fostered chimpanzees *(Pan troglodytes)*. *Journal of Comparative Psychology* 114:335–346.

Johnson, C. M. 2001. Distributed primate cognition: a review. *Animal Cognition* 4:167–183.

Johnson, C. M., and T. M. Oswald. 2001. Distributed cognition in apes. In *Proceedings of the 23rd Annual Conference of the Cognitive Science Society,* ed. J. D. Moore and K. Stenning, pp. 453–458. Edinburgh: Human Communication Research Centre.

Kano, T. 1992. *The Last Ape: Pygmy Chimpanzee Behavior and Ecology.* Stanford: Stanford University Press.

———1997. Leaf-dropping sexual display exhibited by a male bonobo at Wamba. *Pan Africa News* 4 (1), available at *http://mahale.web.infoseek.co.jp/PAN/4__1/contents.html.*

Kappeler, P. M., and C. P. van Schaik. 2002. Evolution of primate social systems. *International Journal of Primatology,* 23:707–740.

Kendon, A. 1972. Some relationships between body motion and speech. In *Studies in Dyadic Communication,* ed. A. Siegman and B. Pope, pp. 177–210. New York: Pergamon Press.

King, B. J. 1994. *The Information Continuum: Social Information Transfer in Monkeys, Apes, and Hominids.* Santa Fe: School of American Research Press.

———1999. Viewed from up close: monkeys, apes, and language-origins theories. In *The Origins of Language: What Nonhuman Primates Can Tell Us,* ed. B. J. King, pp. 21–54. Santa Fe: School of American Research Press.

———2002. On patterned interactions and culture in great apes. In *Anthropology beyond Culture,* ed. R. G. Fox and B. J. King, pp. 83–104. Oxford: Berg.

———2003. Alternative pathways for the evolution of gesture. *Sign Language Studies* 4:68–82.

King, B. J., and S. G. Shanker. 2003. How can we know the dancer from the dance? the dynamic nature of African great ape social communication. *Anthropological Theory* 3 (1):5–26.

Kohler, T. A., and G. J. Gumerman. 2000. *Dynamics in Human and Primate Societies: Agent-based Modeling of Social and Spatial Processes.* New York: Oxford University Press.

Kuroda, S. 1984. Rocking gesture as communicative behavior in the wild pygmy chimpanzees in Wamba, Central Zaire. *Journal of Ethology* 2:127–137.

Ladygina-Kohts, N. N. 2002. *Infant Chimpanzee and Human Child: A Classic 1935 Comparative Study of Ape Emotions and Intelligence,* ed. F. B. M. de Waal. New York: Oxford University Press.

Landau, M. 1984. Human evolution as narrative. *American Scientist* 72:262–268.

Latour, B. 2000. A well-articulated primatology: reflections of a fellow traveler. In *Primate Encounters: Models of Science, Gender, and Society,* ed. S. C. Strum and L. M. Fedigan, pp. 358–381. Chicago: University of Chicago Press.

Leavens, D. A. 2003. Integration of visual and vocal communication. *Behavioral and Brain Sciences* 26 (2):232.

Leavens, D. A., and W. D. Hopkins. 1999. The whole-hand point: the structure and function of pointing from a comparative perspective. *Journal of Comparative Psychology* 113:417–425.

Leavens, D. A., W. D. Hopkins, and R. K. Thomas. 2004. Referential communication by chimpanzees *(Pan troglodytes)*. *Journal of Comparative Psychology* 118 (1):48–57.

Lock, A. 1980. *The Guided Reinvention of Language.* London: Academic Press.

Lyons, M. J., R. Campbell, A. Plante, M. Coleman, M. Kamachi, and S. Akamatsu. 2000. The Noh mask effect: vertical viewpoint dependence of facial expression perception. *Proceedings of the Royal Society of London B* 267:2239–2245.

Maestripieri, D., and J. Call. 1996. Mother-infant communication in primates. *Advances in the Study of Behavior* 25:613–642.

Maestripieri, D., S. K. Ross, and N. L. Megna. 2002. Mother-infant interactions in western lowland gorillas *(Gorilla gorilla gorilla)*: spatial relationships, communication, and opportunities for social learning. *Journal of Comparative Psychology* 116:219–227.

Marks, J. 2002. *What It Means to Be 98% Chimpanzee: Apes, People and their Genes.* Berkeley: University of California Press.

McGrew, W. C. 1992. *Chimpanzee Material Culture: Implications for Human Evolution.* Cambridge: Cambridge University Press.

———2001. The nature of culture: prospects and pitfalls of cultural primatology. In *Tree of Origins: What Primate Behavior Can Tell Us about Human Social Evolution,* ed. F. de Waal, pp. 231–254.

McGrew. W. C., and C. E. G. Tutin. 1978. Evidence for a social custom in wild chimpanzees? *Man* 13:234–251.

McNeill, D. 1992. *Hand and Mind: What Gestures Reveal about Thought.* Chicago: University of Chicago Press.

Melson, G. F. 2001. *Why the Wild Things Are.* Cambridge: Harvard University Press.

Menzel, C. R. 1999. Unprompted recall and reporting of hidden objects by a chimpanzee *(Pan troglodytes)* after extended delays. *Journal of Comparative Psychology* 113:426–434.

———In press. Progress in the study of chimpanzee recall and episodic memory. In *The Missing Link in Cognition: The Origins of Self-knowing Consciousness,* ed. H. Terrace and J. Metcalfe. New York: Oxford University Press.

Menzel, E. W. 1979. Communication of object-locations in a group of young chimpanzees. In *The Great Apes,* ed. D. A. Hamburg and E. R. McCown, pp. 359–371. Menlo Park, CA: Benjamin Cummings.

Mitani, J. C., and J. Gros-Louis. 1998. Chorusing and call convergence in chimpanzees: test of three hypotheses. *Behaviour* 135:1041–1064.

Mitani, J. C., and T. Nishida. 1993. Contexts and social correlates of long-distance calling by chimpanzees. *Animal Behaviour* 45:735–746.

Mitani, J. C., D. P. Watts, and M. N Muller. 2002. Recent developments in the study of wild chimpanzee behavior. *Evolutionary Anthropology* 11:9–25.

Mitchell, R. W. 1997. Anthropomorphic anecdotalism as method. In *Anthropomorphism, Anecdotes, and Animals,* ed. R. W. Mitchell, N. S. Thompson, and H. L. Miles, pp. 151–169. Albany: State University of New York Press.

———1999. Scientific and popular conceptions of the psychology of the great apes from the 1790s to the 1970s: déjà vu all over again. *Primate Report* 53:1–118.

Mitchell, R. W., N. S. Thompson, and H. L. Miles. 1997. *Anthropomorphism, Anecdotes, and Animals.* Albany: State University of New York Press.

Morgan, D., and C. Sanz. 2003. Naïve encounters with chimpanzees in the Goualougo Triangle, Republic of Congo. *International Journal of Primatology* 24 (2):369–381.

Muller, M. N. 2002. Agonistic relations among Kanyawara chimpanzees. In *Behavioural Diversity in Chimpanzees and Bonobos,* ed. C. Boesch, G. Hohmann, and L. F. Marchant, pp. 112–124. Cambridge: Cambridge University Press.

Nakamura, M. 2002. Grooming-hand-clasp in Mahale M group chimpanzees: implication for culture in social behavior. In *Behavioral Diversity in Chimpanzees and Bonobos*, ed. C. Boesch, G. Hohmann, and L. F. Marchant, pp. 71–83. Cambridge: Cambridge University Press.

Newton-Fisher, N. E. 2002. Relationships of male chimpanzees in the Budongo Forest, Uganda. In *Behavioural Diversity in Chimpanzees and Bonobos*, ed. C. Boesch, G. Hohmann, and L. F. Marchant, pp. 125–137. Cambridge: Cambridge University Press.

Nishida, T. 1980. The leaf-clipping display: a newly-discovered expressive gesture in wild chimpanzees. *Journal of Human Evolution* 9:117–128.

Nyland, B. 2001. A study of infants in the child care context. *Post-Script* 2:115–126.

Ottoni, E. B., and M. Mannu. 2001. Semi-free ranging capuchin monkeys *(Cebus apella)* spontaneously use tools to crack open nuts. *International Journal of Primatology* 22 (3):347–358.

Owings, D. H., and E. S. Morton. 1998. *Animal Vocal Communication*. Cambridge: Cambridge University Press.

Owren, M. J., and D. Rendall. 1998. An affect-conditioning model of nonhuman primate vocal signaling. In *Perspectives in Ethology*, vol. 12: *Communication*, ed. D. H. Owings, M. D. Beecher, and N. S. Thompson, pp. 299–346. New York: Plenum Press.

Papousek, M. 1995. Origins of reciprocity and mutuality in prelinguistic parent-infant "dialogues." In *Mutualities in Dialogue*, ed. I. Markova, C. Graumann, and K. Foppa, pp. 58–98. Cambridge: Cambridge University Press

Parker, S. T. 1995. A social-technological model for the evolution of language. *Current Anthropology* 26 (5):617–639.

————1996. Apprenticeship in tool-mediated extractive foraging: the origins of imitation, teaching, and self-awareness in great apes. In *Reaching into Thought: The Mind of the Great Apes*, ed. A. E. Russon, K. A. Bard, and S. T. Parker, pp. 348–370. Cambridge: Cambridge University Press.

————1999. The life history and development of great apes in comparative perspective. In *The Mentalities of Gorillas and Orangutans*, ed. S. T. Parker, R. W. Mitchell, and H. L. Miles, pp. 43–69. Cambridge: Cambridge University Press.

————2000. *Homo erectus* infancy and childhood: the turning point in the evolution of behavioral development in hominids. In *Biology, Brains, and Behavior: The Evolution of Human Development*, ed. S. T. Parker, J.

Langer, and M. L. McKinney, pp. 279–318. Santa Fe: School of American Research Press.

Parker, S. T., and K. R. Gibson. 1979. A developmental model for the evolution of language and intelligence in early hominids. *Behavioral and Brain Sciences* 2:367–408.

Parnell, R. J. 2002. Group size and structure in western lowland gorillas *(Gorilla gorilla gorilla)* at Mbeli Bai, Republic of Congo. *American Journal of Primatology* 56:193–206.

Parnell, R. J., and H. M. Buchanan-Smith. 2001. An unusual social display by gorillas. *Nature* 412:294.

Parr, L. A., W. D. Hopkins, and F. B. M. de Waal. 1998. The perception of facial expressions by chimpanzees, *Pan troglodytes. Evolution of Communication* 2:1–23.

Pika, S., K. Liebal, and M. Tomasello. 2003. Gestural communication in young gorillas *(Gorilla gorilla):* gestural repertoire, learning, and use. *American Journal of Primatology* 60:95–111.

Pinker, S. 1994. *The Language Instinct: How the Mind Creates Language.* New York: William Morrow.

Pinker, S., and P. Bloom. 1990. Natural language and natural selection. *Behavioral and Brain Sciences* 13 (4):707–784.

Plooij, F. X. 1978. Some basic traits of language in wild chimpanzees? In *Actions, Gesture and Symbol: The Emergence of Language,* ed. A. Lock, pp. 111–131. London: Academic Press.

Plooij, F. X. 1984. *The Behavioral Development of Free-living Chimpanzee Babies and Infants.* Norwood, NJ: Ablex.

Premack, D. 1971. Language in a chimpanzee? *Science* 172:808–822.

Proust, M. 1981. *Swann's Way.* Trans. C. K. Scott Moncrieff. New York: Vintage International.

Quammen, D. 2003. New hope in Goualougo, Congo. *National Geographic* April:90–103.

Rapaport, L. G., and C. R. Ruiz-Miranda. 2002. Tutoring in wild golden lion tamarins. *International Journal of Primatology* 23:1063–1070.

Reader, S. M., and K. N. Laland. 2002. Social intelligence, innovation, and enhanced brain size in primates. *Proceedings of the National Academy of Science* 99:4436–4441.

Reddy, M. J. 1993. The conduit metaphor: a case of frame conflict in our language about language. In *Metaphor and Thought,* ed. A. Ortony, pp. 164–201. Cambridge: Cambridge University Press.

Rendell, D., and P. Vasey. 2002. Metaphor muddles in communication theory. Comment on Shanker and King. *Behavioral and Brain Sciences* 25 (5):637.

Reynolds, V., and F. Reynolds. 1965. Chimpanzees of the Budongo Forest. In *Primate Behavior: Field Studies of Monkeys and Apes*, ed. I. DeVore, pp. 368–424. New York: Holt, Rinehart & Winston.

Robbins, M. M. 1995. A demographic analysis of male life history and social structure of mountain gorillas. *Behaviour* 132:21–47.

———2001. Variation in the social system of mountain gorillas: the male perspective. In *Mountain Gorillas: Three Decades of Research at Karisoke*, ed. M. M. Robbins, P. Sicotte, and K. J. Stewart, pp. 30–58. Cambridge: Cambridge University Press.

Robbins, M. M., P. Sicotte, and K. J. Stewart. 2001. *Mountain Gorillas: Three Decades of Research at Karisoke*. Cambridge: Cambridge University Press.

Rumbaugh, D. M., and D. A. Washburn. 2003. *Intelligence of Apes and Other Rational Beings*. New Haven: Yale University Press.

Savage-Rumbaugh, E. S. 1986. *Ape Language*. New York: Columbia University Press.

———1999. Ape language: between a rock and a hard place. In *The Origins of Language: What Nonhuman Primates Can Tell Us*, ed. B. J. King, pp. 115–188. Santa Fe: School of American Research Press.

Savage-Rumbaugh, E. S., and R. Lewin. 1994. *Kanzi: The Ape at the Brink of the Human Mind*. New York: John Wiley and Sons.

Savage-Rumbaugh, E. S., S. G. Shanker, and T. J. Taylor. 1998. *Apes, Language, and the Human Mind*. New York: Oxford University Press.

Savage-Rumbaugh, E. S., B. J. Wilkerson, and R. Bakeman. 1977. Spontaneous gestural communication among conspecifics in the pygmy chimpanzee *(Pan paniscus)*. In *Progress in Ape Research*, ed. G. H. Bourne, pp. 91-116. New York: Academic Press.

Schaller, G. B. 1963. *The Mountain Gorilla: Ecology and Behavior*. Chicago: University of Chicago Press.

———1964. *The Year of the Gorilla*. Chicago: University of Chicago Press.

———1965a. The behavior of the mountain gorilla. In *Primate Behavior: Field Studies of Monkeys and Apes*, ed. I. DeVore, pp. 324–367. New York: Holt, Rinehart & Winston.

———1965b. Behavioral comparisons of the apes. In *Primate Behavior: Field Studies of Monkeys and Apes*, ed. I. DeVore, pp. 474–485. New York: Holt, Rinehart and Winston.

Schmidt, K. L., and J. F. Cohn. 2001. Human facial expressions as adaptations: evolutionary questions in facial expression research. *Yearbook of Physical Anthropology* 44:3–24.

Shanker, S. G., and B. J. King. 2002. The emergence of a new paradigm in ape language research. *Behavioral and Brain Sciences* 25 (5):605–656.

Sheets-Johnstone, M. 1999. Sensory-kinetic understanding of language: an inquiry into origins. *Evolution of Communication* 3 (2):149–183.

Shostak, M. 2000. *Nisa: The Life and Words of a !Kung Woman*. Reprint edition. Cambridge: Harvard University Press.

————2000. *Return to Nisa*. Cambridge: Harvard University Press.

Sicotte, P. 2001. Female mate choice in mountain gorillas. In *Mountain Gorillas: Three Decades of Research at Karisoke*, ed. M. M. Robbins, P. Sicotte, and K. J. Stewart, pp. 59–87. Cambridge: Cambridge University Press.

Silverman, S. 2002. *The Beast on the Table: Conferencing with Anthropologists*. Walnut Creek, CA: AltaMira Press.

Slavoff, G. 1997. Interactional synchrony between capuchin monkeys *(Cebus apella)*. Paper presented at American Society of Primatologists, San Diego, June.

Small, M. 1998. *Our Babies, Ourselves: How Biology and Culture Shape the Way We Parent*. New York: Anchor Books.

————2001. Long live the !Kung. *Natural History*, February.

Smuts, B. 2001. Encounters with animal minds. *Journal of Consciousness Studies* 8:293–309.

Steklis, H. D. 1985. Primate communication, comparative neurology, and the origins of language re-examined. *Journal of Human Evolution* 14:157–173.

Strier, K. B. 1999. *Primate Behavioral Ecology*. Boston: Allyn and Bacon.

Strum, S. C. 2000. Science encounters. In *Primate Encounters: Models of Science, Gender, and Society*, ed. S. C. Strum and L. M. Fedigan, pp. 475–497. Chicago: University of Chicago Press.

Strum, S. C., and L. M. Fedigan. 2000. Changing views of primate society: a situated North American view. In *Primate Encounters: Models of Science, Gender, and Society*, ed. S. C. Strum and L. M. Fedigan, pp. 3–49. Chicago: University of Chicago Press.

Suzuki, A. 1973. Comment on article by Hewes. *Current Anthropology* 14:17–18.

Tanner, J. 1998. Gestural communication in a group of zoo-living lowland gorillas. Ph.D. diss., University of St. Andrews, Scotland.

Tanner, J., and R. W. Byrne. 1999. The development of spontaneous gestural communication in a group of zoo-living lowland gorillas. In *The
Mentalities of Gorillas and Orangutans,* ed. S. T. Parker, R. W. Mitchell,
and H. L. Miles, pp. 211–239. Cambridge: Cambridge University Press.

Taylor, T. J. 1997. *Theorizing Language.* Amsterdam: Pergamon.

Teleki, G. 2001. Sanctuaries for ape refugees. In *Great Apes and Humans:
The Ethics of Coexistence,* ed. B. B. Beck, T. S. Stoinski, M. Hutchins,
T. L. Maple, B. Norton, A. Rowan, E. F. Stevens, and A. Arluke, pp.
133–149. Washington, D.C.: Smithsonian Institution Press.

Thelen, E., G. Schoner, C. Scheier, and L. B. Smith. 2001. The dynamics of
embodiment: a field theory of infant perseverative reaching. *Behavioral
and Brain Sciences* 24:1–86.

Tomasello, M. 1999. *The Cultural Origins of Human Cognition.* Cambridge:
Harvard University Press.

Tomasello, M., and J. Call. 1977. *Primate Cognition.* New York: Oxford University Press.

Tomasello, M., J. Call, J. Warren, G. T. Frost, M. Carpenter, and K. Nagell.
1997. The ontogeny of chimpanzee gestural signals: a comparison
across groups and generations. *Evolution of Communication* 1 (2):223–
259.

Tomasello, M., and L. Camaioni. 1997. A comparison of the gestural communication of apes and human infants. *Human Development* 40:7–24.

Trevarthen, C. 1999. Musicality and the intrinsic motive pulse: evidence
from human psychobiology and infant communication. *Musicae
Scientiae* Special Issue 1999–2000:155–215.

Turner, J. H. 2000. *On the Origins of Human Emotions: A Sociological Inquiry
into the Evolution of Human Affect.* Stanford: Stanford University Press.

Tutin, C. E. G. 1996. Ranging and social structure of lowland gorillas in the
Lope Reserve, Gabon. In *Great Ape Societies,* ed. W. C. McGrew, L. F.
Marchant, and T. Nishida, pp. 58–70. Cambridge: Cambridge Univer-
sity Press.

Tutin, C. E. G., and M. Fernandez. 1985. Foods consumed by sympatric
populations of *Gorilla g. gorilla* and *Pan troglodytes* in Gabon: some preliminary data. *International Journal of Primatology* 30:195–211.

Van de Ritj-Plooij, H. H. C., and F. X. Plooij. 1987. Growing independence,
conflict, and learning in mother-infant relations in free-ranging chimpanzees. *Behaviour* 101:1–86.

Van Schaik, C. P. 1999. The socioecology of fission-fusion sociality in
orangutans. *Primates* 40:69–86.

Vea, J. J., and J. Sabater-Pi. 1998. Spontaneous pointing behaviour in the wild pygmy chimpanzee *(Pan paniscus)*. *Folia primatologica* 69:289–290.

Vygotsky, L. 1986 [1934]. *Thought and Language*. Cambridge: Harvard University Press.

Waldrop, M. M. 1992. *Complexity: The Emerging Science at the Edge of Order and Chaos*. New York: Touchstone.

Wallman, J. 1992. *Aping Language*. Cambridge: Cambridge University Press.

Washburn, S. L. 1973. Comment on article by Hewes. *Current Anthropology* 14:18.

Watts, D. P. 1994. Agonistic relationships of female mountain gorillas. *Behavioral Ecology and Sociobiology* 34:347–358.

———1995. Post-conflict social events in wild mountain gorillas (Mammalia, Hominoidea). I. Social interactions between opponents. *Ethology* 100:158–174.

———2001. Social relationships of female mountain gorillas. In *Mountain Gorillas: Three Decades of Research at Karisoke,* ed. M. M. Robbins, P. Sicotte, and K. J. Stewart, pp. 215–240. Cambridge: Cambridge University Press.

Weber, B., and A. Vedder. 2001. *In the Kingdom of Gorillas*. New York: Simon and Schuster.

White, F. J. 1996. Comparative socio-ecology of *Pan paniscus*. In *Great Ape Societies,* ed. W. C. McGrew, L. F. Marchant, and T. Nishida, pp. 29–41. Cambridge: Cambridge University Press.

Whiten, A., J. Goodall, W. C. McGrew, T. Nishida, V. Reynolds, Y. Sugiyama, C. E. G. Tutin, R. W. Wrangham, and C. Boesch. 1999. Cultures in chimpanzees. *Nature* 399:682–685.

Wootton, A. J. 1997. *Interaction and the Development of Mind*. Cambridge: Cambridge University Press.

Wrangham, R. W. 1980. An ecological model of female-bonded primate groups. *Behaviour* 74:262–299.

———2000. Making a baby. In *The Smile of a Dolphin,* ed. M. Bekoff, pp. 34–35. New York: Discovery Books.

Yamagiwa, J., and J. Kahekwa. 2001. Dispersal patterns, group structure, and reproductive parameters of eastern lowland gorillas at Kahuzi in the absence of infanticide. In *Mountain Gorillas: Three Decades of Research at Karisoke,* ed. M. M. Robbins, P. Sicotte, and K. J. Stewart, pp. 90-122. Cambridge: Cambridge University Press.

Yerkes, R., and M. I. Tomilin. 1935. Mother-infant relations in chimpanzees. *Journal of Comparative Psychology* 20:321–348.

# Acknowledgments

I‍n this book about how certain primates create meaning in their groups or families, I can begin only with my own family. To Charlie and Sarah, and the animals with whom we live, my gratitude for co-constructing happiness in our house, day in and day out. (And for enduring my tendency to analyze their every gesture, and to assess all manner of family events in detailed dynamic systems terms.)

For 10 years of sharing ideas, and sharing so much more as we work and write together, I thank Stuart Shanker. His influence on my thinking can be found in every chapter. Year by year, I have come to appreciate more deeply not only Stuart's insights but also his generosity.

I owe thanks to many people for making possible my research on African great ape gesture. At the National Zoological Park, I thank Lisa Stevens and the dedicated staff at the Great Ape House, especially Melanie Bond, Ann Hunter, Doug Donald, and Nicole Meese. William and Mary undergraduates Elizabeth Groneweg, Christy Hoffman, Margie Robinson, Rebecca Simmons, and Kendra Weber brought dedication and great skills of observation to the gorilla project.

At the Language Research Center (LRC) of Georgia State University, Duane Rumbaugh and Sue Savage-Rumbaugh provided access to the bonobos, intellectual guidance, and funding. I thank them, and Dan Rice of the LRC for excellent research assistance. William and Mary students Erin Selner and Heather Bond (now Heather Bond Poje), through summer internships at the LRC, ensured the project's success with countless hours of observations and data analysis. Charles Hogg has provided years of technical support in working with video cameras, video software, and computers.

My great ape research has been funded by the Wenner-Gren Foundation for Anthropological Research; the Templeton Foundation; the College of William and Mary; and, via the Language Research Center, the National Institutes of Health. For enabling a year of pure uninterrupted writing, resulting in this book, I am grateful to the Guggenheim Foundation.

Many scholars improved the content and clarity of this book. Sherman Wilcox and Joanne Tanner read the entire first draft and made invaluable comments. No author could ask for better constructive criticism and help than what they offered. Willow Powers's help with Chapter 2 (especially methodology in anthropology) was of enormous value. For reading sections of the manuscript, providing unpublished work, and/or answering my requests for information, I thank David Armstrong, Tecumseh Fitch, Carol Fowler, Ellen Ingmanson, David Leavens, Tetsuro Matsuzawa, Charles Menzel, Richard Parnell, and Janette Wallis. For sharing beautiful photographs of African great apes, I am grateful to Lucinda Baker, Ellen Ingmanson, and Frans de Waal.

For encouragement in "the early years" (when I was new to dynamic systems theory), I thank Grey Gundaker, Tim Ingold, Christine Johnson, Kathy Kerr, Michael Kerr, Sue Savage-Rumbaugh, and Talbot Taylor. Each of you made a bigger difference than you may realize.

Working with Harvard University Press has been a pleasure. I am grateful for Michael Fisher's keen understanding of my perspective on great ape communication, and for his skilled guidance in turning the book from an idea into a reality. Nancy Clemente enhanced the clarity and readability of the text, and Sara Davis capably assisted with numerous matters, including photo permissions.

# Index

thropology and, 179; mouth-gesture hypothesis and, 182; natural selection and, 199; *Ramapithecus* and, 179; Zihlman and, 196–201
*Evolution of Communication* (Hauser), 138
Extinction, 233–239

Facial expressions, 56, 138–139; chimpanzees and, 59; coordination and, 60, 60–61; distributed cognition and, 60; gender and, 57–58; gorillas and, 59; human, 57–59; intentionality and, 60–61; mental conditions and, 85; smiles, 57–58
Falk, D., 200
Falstaff (chimpanzee), 17–19, 164
Fay, Michael, 224
Fedigan, L. M., 67–68
Fernald, A., 6
Fifi (chimpanzee), 26
Figan (chimpanzee), 137
Fish, J. M., 66
Fitch, W. T., 48–50
Fivaz-Depeursinge, A., 11, 213–216, 231
Flint (chimpanzee), 137
Flo (chimpanzee), 26, 137
Fogel, Alan, 2, 9, 11, 66, 78
Food-begging, 169–171, 174, 217–218
Foraging, 25
Fossey, D., 156
Fouts, R., 206–207
Fowler, C. A., 55
Frustrative behavior, 150
Fruth, Barbara, 31

Gabon, 34, 224
Gardner, R. A., 183–184
Garner, R. L., 24
Gender: agonism and, 154–163; alpha males and, 151, 159–162; bipedal swagger and, 147; bonding and, 35–36; chestbeating and, 155–157; copulation initiation and, 152; courtship and, 146–154; facial expression and, 57–58; female transfer, 26–27, 35, 37; gregari-

ousness and, 27–28; rocking and, 140–146. *See also* Sexual behavior
Genito-genital rubbing, 30–31, 152–153
Gestalt effect, 2–3
*Gesture and the Nature of Language* (Armstrong, Stokoe, and Wilcox), 190–192
Gestures, 176–178, 221–222; age and, 100; alarm, 50–51; ape-human communication and, 202–209; audible, 95 (*see also* Vocalizations); beckoning, 148; bipedal swagger, 147–148; bonobos and, 31, 33, 104–115; categorization issues and, 59–61; chestbeating, 14, 95, 155–157; children and, 195–202; clapping, 136–137; cognition and, 60, 210–212; context and, 55, 139–140; courtship, 146–154; criteria for, 53–63; cross-body, 93; dynamic systems theory and, 42–83 (*see also* Dynamic systems theory); evolutionary theories on, 179–192; eye contact and, 94–95, 97–98; facial expression and, 56–60, 138–139; gestural protolanguage and, 195–196; glaring, 148; greeting, 146–154; grooming and, 163–168; hand extension, 84–85; human, 7–8, 55, 100, 209–218; iconic, 63, 91–104; information and, 84; interpretation of, 229–233; knock fists, 98; lies-down-on-back, 172–174; lip pursing, 153–154; mechanical effectiveness and, 54; Menzel studies and, 92–93; mother-infant behavior and, 7–11 (*see also* Mother-infant behavior); mouth-gesture hypothesis and, 182; mutual meaning and, 175–176; mutual shaping and, 91–104; ontogenetic, 100–134 (*see also* Ontogenetic ritualization [OR]); open-mouth threat, 14–15; patting, 15; play face, 56; qualitative research and, 87–91 (*see also* Qualitative research); reach interpretation and, 61–62; referential pointing and, 8–9; ritualization and, 99–100; rocking, 140–146, 164, 188–189; Savage-